HOUSING FOR NICHE MARKETS

HOUSING FOR NICHE MARKETS

CAPITALIZING ON CHANGING DEMOGRAPHICS

URBAN LAND INSTITUTE

ULI–the Urban Land Institute
1025 Thomas Jefferson Street, N.W.
Suite 500 West
Washington, D.C. 20007-5201

LIBRARY OF CONGRESS CATALOGING-IN-PUBLICATION DATA

Housing for niche markets: capitalizing on changing demographics / Urban Land Institute.

      p. cm.
Includes bibliographical references.
ISBN 978-0-87420-942-6 (alk. paper)
1. Housing—United States. 2. Housing—United States—Case studies. 3. United States—Population. I. Urban Land Institute.
HD7293.H586 2005
333.33'80973–dc22   2005028468

10 9 8 7 6 5 4 3 2 1
PRINTED IN THE UNITED STATES OF AMERICA

DESIGN AND COMPOSITION
Marc Alain Meadows, Meadows Design Office Inc.,
Washington, D.C. www.mdomedia.com

ULI–THE URBAN LAND INSTITUTE is a nonprofit education and research institute that is supported by its members. Its mission is to provide responsible leadership in the use of land in order to enhance the total environment.

ULI sponsors education programs and forums to encourage an open international exchange of ideas and sharing of experiences; initiates research that anticipates emerging land use trends and issues and proposes creative solutions based on that research; provides advisory services; and publishes a wide variety of materials to disseminate information on land use and development. Established in 1936, the Institute today has more than 27,000 members from 80 countries, representing the entire spectrum of the land use and development disciplines. The Institute is recognized internationally as one of the industry's most respected and widely quoted sources of objective information on urban planning, growth, and development.

PROJECT STAFF

Rachelle L. Levitt
Executive Vice President, Policy and Practice
Publisher

Gayle Berens
Vice President, Real Estate Development Practice

Jo Allen Gause
Senior Director, Residential Development
Project Director

Nancy H. Stewart, Director, Book Program

Lori Hatcher, Director, Publications Marketing

Libby Howland, Manuscript Editor

David James Rose, Assistant Editor

Betsy VanBuskirk, Art Director

Craig Chapman, Director, Publishing Operations

Karrie Underwood, Digital Images Assistant

EDITOR

Jo Allen Gause
Urban Land Institute
Washington, D.C.

AUTHORS: OVERVIEW CHAPTER

Deborah L. Brett
Deborah L. Brett & Associates
Plainsboro, New Jersey

Brooke H. Warrick
American LIVES Inc.
Carmel Valley, California

AUTHORS: CASE STUDIES

FRONT STREET AT LADERA RANCH,
GREENWOOD AVENUE COTTAGES
Steve Bergsman
SMB Comm Inc.
Mesa, Arizona

CAMPUS AT ALBUQUERQUE HIGH
Rebecca Bryant
Freelance Writer
Fayetteville, Arkansas

FALL CREEK PLACE
Deborah L. Myerson
Deborah L. Myerson LLC
Bloomington, Indiana

FRUITVALE VILLAGE
Jason Scully
Urban Land Institute
Washington, D.C.

HEARTHSTONE, LASELL VILLAGE, VICKERY
Stella Tarnay
Tarnay & Associates
Washington, D.C.

AMELIA PARK, THE EDGE LOFTS,
JEFFERSON COMMONS AT MINNESOTA,
SANTANA ROW, SOLIVITA, SPRING ISLAND
Dorothy J. Verdon
Freelance Writer
Hollywood, Florida

ACKNOWLEDGMENTS

Many professionals contributed time and talent to this book, for which I am grateful. I would like to thank particularly the principal authors of the overview chapter—Deborah Brett, who wrote about demographic trends, and Brooke Warrick, who wrote about market segmentation. The case study authors—Steve Bergsman, Rebecca Bryant, Deborah Myerson, Jason Scully, Stella Tarnay, and Dorothy Verdon—also deserve special thanks and recognition for their research and writing. Others who contributed to the manuscript include Alexa Bach, Mike Baker, and John Rodrigues.

I would also like to thank the many developers, architects, and planners who added immeasurably to this publication by working with the authors of the case studies and providing data, written materials, illustrations, and photographs.

Much appreciation goes to Libby Howland for her editing of the manuscript to make the presentation clear and useful to our audience. And a very special thank you to Marc Meadows of Meadows Design Office for his beautiful design and layout of the book and its cover.

Finally, I would like to thank a number of individual Urban Land Institute staff members for the skill and dedication they contributed to the manuscript development and book publication processes: Rachelle Levitt and Gayle Berens for their support and direction throughout the process; Nancy Stewart for taking care of every detail in her management of the editing process; David James Rose for proofreading assistance; Betsy VanBuskirk for her management of the design and layout process; Lori Hatcher for working to ensure that *Housing for Niche Markets* reaches a wide audience; Craig Chapman for coordinating the publication process; and Karrie Underwood for technical assistance with the hundreds of photographs submitted for consideration.

Jo Allen Gause
Editor

Contents

Overview

A one-size-fits-all approach to homebuilding is becoming less and less suitable for America's diversifying housing market. Aiming for a mass market with a limited number of tried-and-true housing products—the products that were once the profit-producing staples of most developers—is no longer a viable development strategy. This is because the market has become too fragmented, too diverse.

Consider the changing composition of American households. In the half century following World War II, married couples with children made up the largest share of households—40 percent as recently as 1970. And developers could predict with some certainty that the great majority of these households would want to live in a single-family house in the suburbs. Today, however, married couples with children constitute less than one-quarter of housing demand and by 2025 their share will fall to only one-fifth. Married couples without children are now the largest household segment (28 percent), followed by people living alone (26 percent).

Developers need to build housing that appeals to many different types of nontraditional households—people living alone, childless couples, single parents with full-time or part-time children, unmarried couples, same-sex couples, empty nesters, and multigenerational families. Add to this rich blend the additional filters of age, income, and the special nuances of ethnic or cultural communities, and the household mix diversifies exponentially.

Housing demand can be thought of as a pie. Even though the pie is getting larger—during the 1990s the United States added nearly 33 million people and 13 million new households and the population is expected to grow by nearly 2.7 million a year through 2020—it is being cut into more pieces, so the individual slices are getting smaller. These more numerous, smaller pieces of pie represent the most interesting and promising development opportunities in today's housing market.

Market segmentation and product customization will be the watchwords for successful projects. To compete, developers will have to define or segment their customers by income, race, family composition, and lifestyle choices. These are the primary factors that shape household decisions on where to live, whether to rent or buy, how much to pay, and which design features to seek. Over the coming decades, tailoring residential development to meet the needs of specific, well-researched target markets will be the key to success for residential developers, builders, and investors.

To illustrate the opportunities and dynamics of demographically tailored residential development, this book provides 14 case studies of housing designed for niche

Dōma lofts and townhouses in downtown San Diego's Little Italy district appeal to buyers in a wide range of ages seeking the convenience of living in a city.

BOOMERS LOOK BEYOND: DON'T CALL IT RETIREMENT

The first wave of America's largest age group, the baby boom generation, is about to enter its 60s. Boomers, however, do not see themselves as old, and they may not want to retire conventionally.

They do not seem poised to become the new leisure class in their retirement years. They will, in the words of a Yankelovich Group survey, "retread," not retire. It is hard for the boomers themselves to predict how they will live in the future. The fact that many boomers had their children relatively late in life is one of several reasons they will stay in the workforce longer. That they have not saved as much for their retirement as preceding generations is another.

The Del Webb model of age-restricted retirement communities and other active adult developments targeted healthy, financially secure Eisenhower generation retirees aged 55 to 75 seeking a resort setting—without children. That model has evolved, partly in response to the boomer market. Del Webb's Anthem master-planned communities, which have been marketed since 1998, include separate sections for active adults, families, and empty nesters. The neighborhoods targeting different segments of the market are separate, but they share some amenities. This remains a viable strategy, but it is not the only type of community likely to capture the imagination and investment dollars of retirement-age boomers.

The boomer's second home may evolve into his retirement home. Second homes are often in a resort area—that may not be explicitly marketed to older people—within a couple of hours of the primary residence. Up to 70 percent of second-home buyers in many markets are of retirement age or getting close.

Or the boomer—who has moved many times in her lifetime and no longer has to worry about the quality of schools—may make a transition back to the city to be closer to urban amenities. New retirement communities in urban settings are still relatively rare, but interest seems to be growing. Retirees attracted to an age-restricted environment have always been in the minority. Boomers seem less inclined than other generations to move away from their children upon retirement.

Much has been made of the empty-nester market for condos close to city theaters, restaurants, and museums. However, older households are less willing than young households to risk moving to urban neighborhoods, and the back-to-the-city market has so far been dominated by young first-time homebuyers. However, empty nesters are likely to make up a larger share of this market. High-rise condominiums, which have always been a niche product, will appeal to many retiring boomers seeking a maintenance-free lifestyle, but by no means a sedentary one.

What kinds of housing will boomers prefer? In keeping with their desire to remain active and even to continue working far into their "retirement" years, home offices will be essential. The many boomers who will transition from employee to independent consultant will demand state-of-the-art technology. Sunrooms, "flex" spaces accommodating a variety of activities, gourmet kitchens, and mother-in-law suites will be popular features. For the particularly well heeled, including childless couples (never-nesters), condos that provide hotel services will be increasingly attractive. In master-planned communities, clubhouses and other social spaces, fitness facilities, walking trails, swimming pools, and parks and open space will be popular amenities.

The first Del Webb communities communicated a brilliant, convincing message to Eisenhower generation retirees: "This is where you belong." They helped define a new stage of life for a generation that was wondering "what next?" as the boomers were pushing them out of the workforce.

Now that the boomers themselves are reaching a new stage of their lives, they will want it to be designed expressly for them. Eisenhower generation retirees sought to make up for years of deferred gratification. Boomers, by contrast, will seek a meaningful retirement in which they can continue their quest for self-improvement as well as continue to contribute to society. How developers go about translating boomer retirement goals into the features and amenities package of master-planned communities remains to be seen. Insofar as it is possible to generalize about aging boomers, we can expect them to be attracted to multiple options—from vacation-home retreats to urban condominiums. One size will not fit all, and that will keep it interesting.

Source: Adapted from Gregg T. Logan, "Boomers Look Beyond: Don't Call It Retirement," *The Advisory* (Robert Charles Lesser & Co. LLC), January 2005; reprinted with permission.

markets. These case studies involve the application of market-segmentation concepts to the programming and design of projects that meet the needs of a diverse housing market. They represent a wide range of project types and sizes, housing mixes, and densities. Each project was designed to capture a distinct and well-defined segment of the housing market. The case studies explore the developers' vision for the project, its target market, how it was designed and marketed to appeal to its defined market, and how well it succeeded in capturing its market segment.

The remainder of this introductory section of *Housing for Niche Markets* provides an overview of the demographics of the new housing demand profile and a discussion of market segmentation tools that can help developers identify and design for market niches.

The Changing Demographics of Housing Demand

America's demographic mosaic creates challenges and opportunities for homebuilders and developers. More nontraditional households, growing ethnic diversity, an aging population, an undersupply of affordable housing, and changing location preferences all suggest opportunities for niche products suited to large- and small-scale entrepreneurs alike.

Five fundamental demographic trends will significantly affect housing demand over the upcoming decades:

■ the aging of the baby boomers;
■ an explosion in the number of young households;
■ the changing composition of households;
■ a continuing high level of immigration; and
■ growing ethnic diversity.

The Aging of the Baby Boomers

The demographic profile of the U.S. population will change more dramatically over the next 20 years than at any time since the 1970s. After having been dominated by young families for a number of decades, U.S. society is evolving to where every five-year age group younger than 75 will be of roughly equal size

Top: Thea's Landing— an apartment and condominium development located in a formerly derelict waterfront industrial and red-light district in downtown Tacoma, Washington—initially targeted high-income young professionals, but has also attracted a siz- able number of empty nesters and retirees.

Bottom: Live/work units like these in downtown Atlanta can accommodate a variety of household sizes and lifestyles and can be adapted to residents' changing needs over time.

FIGURE 1:
POPULATION DISTRIBUTION BY AGE COHORT,
1970–2030
(PERCENT OF TOTAL POPULATION)

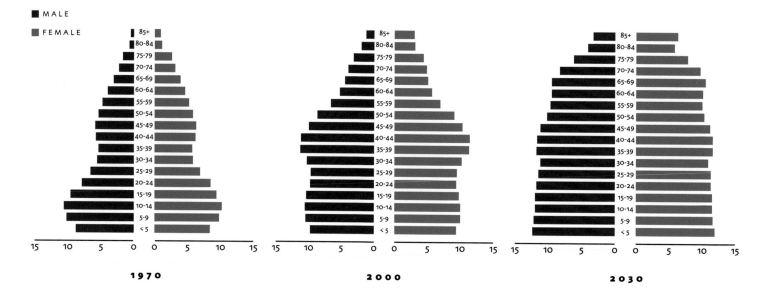

Sources: 1970 Census; and U.S. Census Bureau, *Interim Projections by Age, Sex, Race, and Hispanic Origin,* detail file released March 2004 (www.census.gov/ipc/www/usinterimproj/).

FIGURE 2:
POPULATION
AGED 55 TO 64,
1970–2020
(MILLIONS)

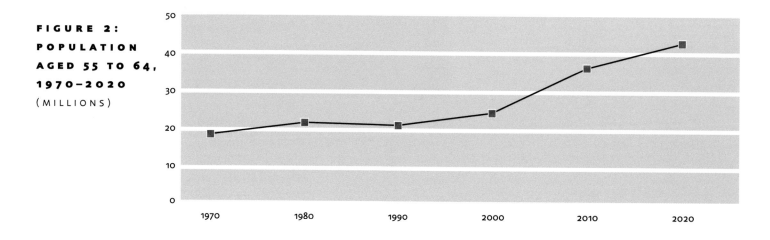

Sources: 1970 Census; and U.S. Census Bureau, *Interim Projections by Age, Sex, Race, and Hispanic Origin,* detail file released March 2004 (www.census.gov/ipc/www/usinterimproj/).

(see figure 1, which illustrates the progressive flattening of the population profile from a pyramid shape in 1970 to a cube shape in 2030). In 2000, for the first time in the nation's history, more than half of U.S. residents were at least 35 years old.

The reason for these changes is the aging of the baby boomers. Born between 1946 and 1964, the baby boomers represent the largest single generation in U.S. history. They have been defining and reshaping major aspects of the economy for half a century. The boomers have been driving residential development for more than 30 years. The country saw more housing construction in the decade when they came of age—the 1970s—than ever before or since, as well as an unprecedented market share for multifamily housing. Now the passage of the 80 million boomers into their retirement years will have an equally profound effect on housing demand.[1]

The increase in the number of empty-nest, preretirement households represented by people in the age 55 to 64 group will prove to be one of the most significant market factors for residential developers over the next 20 years. People in this age group numbered 24 million in 2000; in 2010 they will number 36 million and in 2020 nearly 43 million (see figure 2).

Homeownership among baby boomer households exceeds 70 percent. As boomers move into their preretirement years, some will trade up to larger residences, others will use their tax-free equity gains to purchase smaller (but more luxurious) primary residences, and others will invest in a second home or a time-share unit. Still others, wishing to reduce their ownership responsibilities, will rent housing on a permanent basis or on a temporary basis until they make a decision on where to retire. Many, however, will opt to stay in their current homes.

Most Americans have tended not to move as they age unless compelled to by failing health or finances. Historically, most active seniors have elected to not change residence upon retirement—and only a few who did chose to move to a new city or state. Sunbelt retirement communities became popular in the 1970s, but even then they attracted less than 10 percent of all retirees.

Baby boomers are unlikely to pick up and move to other parts of the country at greater rates than earlier generations of retirees; however, they may be more likely to opt for a change in residence within their community after their children leave home or after they reach retirement age. Rather than changing residence based on health concerns, boomers are more likely to make a move based on lifestyle choices, leisure-time interests, friendships, and family relationships.

Average life expectancy is on the increase: In 1950 it was 68 and in 2000 it was 77. People turning 65 are expected to live, on average, another 18 years.[2] The number of households headed by a person aged 65 and older will grow by 2.9 million between 2000 and 2010 (see figure 3). After the first baby boomers reach age 65 in 2011, an explosion in the number of elderly households will occur.

With an increase of 8.7 million senior households taking place in the 2010s, the share of all households that are headed by a person aged 65 or above will exceed 26 percent in 2020, compared with 21 percent in 2000. The 65 to 74 age group—often called "active seniors"—will account for most of the increase in elderly households. Although not all individuals in this age group are in good health, most are looking forward to their early retirement years as a time for enjoying outdoor pursuits, hobbies, and travel.

Housing that has been specifically designed for the seniors market runs the gamut from modest rental projects offering few or no recreational amenities or supportive services to upscale communities offering independent living arrangements as well as a continuum of personal care and skilled nursing services. Housing developers targeting the seniors market must take into account a diversity of housing preferences, among which a number of niches can be identified, including:

- amenity-rich retirement communities with rental or for-sale units catering to active and relatively affluent households;
- affordable rental communities offering limited supportive services;
- fully equipped apartments offering congregate meal plans, activities, and services catering to seniors who are able to live independently;

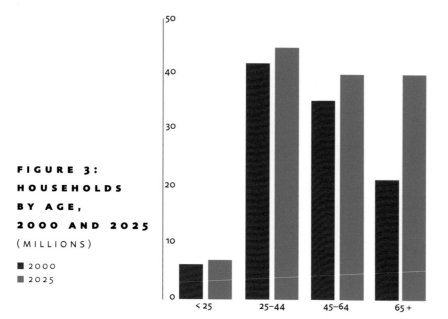

FIGURE 3:
HOUSEHOLDS
BY AGE,
2000 AND 2025
(MILLIONS)

■ 2000
■ 2025

Sources: Martha Farnsworth Riche, "How Changes in the Nation's Age and Household Structure Will Reshape Housing Demand in the 21st Century," *Issue Papers on Demographic Trends Important to Housing*, commissioned by the U.S. Department of Housing and Urban Development, February 2003, pp. 125–147; projections based on 2000 Census data.

- assisted-living facilities catering to frailer elderly persons who do not stand in need of skilled nursing services; and
- facilities offering skilled nursing services.

Nearly 64 percent of Americans aged 65 to 74 are married and living with their spouses.[3] Retirees who can afford upscale retirement living often decide to remain in their long-time home and community, choosing to spend their money on travel, vacation homes, hobbies, or charity or to leave larger inheritances for their children and grandchildren. Healthy older retirees ready to give up the responsibilities of owning a large single-family house are more likely to consider buying a non-age-restricted condominium than moving into a seniors housing development. Locations close to shopping, entertainment, and public transportation are popular choices among retirees who are motivated to move by a desire to reduce their need to drive for everyday needs.

The demographic profile of the population over 75 changes dramatically. Less than half of Americans aged 75 to 84 are living with a husband or wife—about 40 percent of people in this age group are widowed. These older households tend to have lower cash incomes and have already used up at least a portion of the assets they

held immediately after they left the workforce. The ability of older retirees to pay for market-rate rentals or congregate housing is generally limited. Thus, the housing choices of the nation's oldest seniors are often determined by financial limitations and health problems rather than by lifestyle preferences.[4]

Developers can count on one given when marketing to baby boom retirees—they will redefine retirement just as they have redefined culture and society at every other stage in their lives. Rest assured that boomers are not going to define themselves as "old." This means that developers would be well advised to avoid using descriptives like "for active adults" or "for seniors" when marketing housing geared to the 55-plus market.

Explosion of Young Households

Throughout the first decade of the 21st century, much of the demand for family housing will come from Generation X, the cohort born between 1965 and 1976. Although a smaller group than the preceding baby boom or the succeeding Generation Y, the GenX-ers number 47 million (2000) and are well into the process of starting families and buying homes. For families with school-age children, the quality of public schools and recreation opportunities will continue to strongly influence location decisions.

But even though proximity to jobs is not a paramount location consideration for families with children, the persistence of traffic congestion and the prospect of ever-longer commutes that cut deeply into family time are helping to propel a niche market for transit-oriented residential development in both urban and suburban areas.

Nonfamily GenX households tend to be more footloose than their parents, basing their housing decisions on a location's lifestyle amenities and convenience. These households will seek housing with the latest technology options and space configurations that allow them to work from home.

The formidable Generation Y—Americans born between 1977 and 1994 (and thus being in the 11 to 28 age group in 2005)—numbered 73 million (26 percent of the population) in 2000. Because many immigrants are between the ages of 20 and 34 years, Generation Y is pro-

Top left: The demand for second homes like those at Kicking Horse Lodges, a golf and ski resort community in Silver Creek, Colorado, is being fueled by baby boomers in their peak earning years.

Top right: Suburbanites downsizing to an urban location typically seek spacious units (by urban standards) sited close to convenience retail and services. The Louisa, a high-rise townhouse and apartment development in downtown Portland's Pearl District, meets these criteria.

Bottom: The demand for urban housing for seniors—like the Jefferson in Arlington, Virginia—is being driven by the desire of a growing number of retirees to be close to adult children and friends and to take advantage of the convenience of urban living.

jected to increase to 82 million by 2030 (see figure 4).

GenY-ers are different in almost every way from their baby boomer parents. They are more diverse—one in three is not Caucasian, one in four lives in a single-parent household, three in four have working mothers—as well as more inclusive and more environmentally conscious. For the next two decades, young adult GenY-ers will be leaving home, entering the labor force, starting families, renting apartments, and buying their first homes. Over this time period, this generation will represent distinctly good news for the housing industry—in particular, for the multifamily housing industry.

Between 2004 and 2010, more than 4 million Americans will turn 18 each year. Not since the baby boomers in the 1970s have so many people entered adulthood annually. The number of young adults aged 20 to 29 will increase from 38 million in 2000 to 43 million in 2010 to a peak of 44 million in 2015 (see figure 5).

Young adults tend to start living on their own once they find full-time work, and some rent apartments while they are still in school. According to the Census Bureau, 43 percent of men and 53 percent of women aged 18 to 24 do not live with their parents (not including unmarried college students living in dormitories, who are counted as living with their parents).[5]

The market for housing for single young adults is strengthened by the trend to delay marriage. (Note that a declining number of Americans ever marry at any time in their lives.) Demand from single young adults is limited only by what they can afford. Households under 30—whether composed of a single person, roommates, or couples—have always been the most important source of new tenants for rental apartments. During the economic boom years of the 1990s and the subsequent period of historically low interest rates, they also became homeowners in record numbers (see figure 6).

Nevertheless, young households will continue to mostly rent. Many cannot raise the cash needed for a down payment and closing costs. And young people are mobile; renting is simply more practical than owning while the likelihood of moving is still high, even for those who have the wherewithal to buy. In contrast to low- or moderate-income young households for whom affordability is the paramount housing issue, higher-income renters (renters by choice) focus on housing amenities

Highland Lake in Flat Rock, North Carolina, a new community that has attracted a multigenerational mix of residents—young people just starting out, families, and retirees—exemplifies the appeal of well-executed traditional neighborhood design to all demographic groups.

BOOMER HAVENS AND YOUNG ADULT MAGNETS

Baby boomers' economic clout is reaching its peak, yet boomers are no longer the only game in town. The smaller post-boomer young adult cohort, defined here as those born between 1966 and 1980, is beginning to flex its economic muscles, start families or companies, and amass disposable income. Moreover, this MTV generation has adopted a somewhat different demographic personality from the boomer culture it grew up in—more independent and entrepreneurial, and a bit rebellious in career and family choices. Census 2000 data show a spatial generation gap as well, with boomers and young adults literally choosing to live in different parts of the country.

Boomer Havens

Currently in their 40s to late 50s, boomers are in the nesting stage of their lives. Only 1.9 percent of leading-edge boomers made a residential move across state lines between 1999 and 2000. Rather than relocating to any of today's "hot spots," boomers are choosing to stay in or return to more "mature" (and often more pricey) regions of the country.

Boomer nesting grounds are most prevalent in New England and the easter seaboard, the upper Midwest, the upper Rocky Mountain West, and the Pacific Northwest (see map). States with the largest share of baby boomers include Alaska, New Hampshire, Vermont, and Maine (more than 32 percent of each state's total population is made up of boomers), followed closely by Colorado, Connecticut, Maryland, and Virginia. Minnesota, Wisconsin, and Michigan have retained a good share of the boomer population. Many boomers live in suburban areas where housing prices have escalated out of

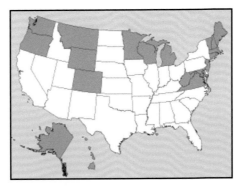

BOOMER HAVENS

the reach of most young adults.

The metropolitan areas with the largest share of boomers include Falls Church, Virginia, in suburban Washington, D.C.; Marin County, California, in suburban San Francisco; and Putnam County, New York, in suburban New York City. A number of jurisdictions within metropolitan areas with the largest boomer shares are known for having attracted "yuppie" baby boomers in the 1970s and 1980s—including some in Seattle, San Francisco, Atlanta, and Washington, D.C. The cultural attractions and amenities in many of these places have matured along with their boomer residents, and housing prices have generally escalated along with boomer incomes.

Boomers represent a large market segment in most parts of the country, including the fast-growing areas that are attracting young adults—that is, young adult country. However, in their nesting grounds, boomers still tend to dominate in terms of market share, political clout, and the general cultural scene. Their influence is likely to persist in these locales, since most boomers are likely to continue living in them in their retirement years.

Young Adult Magnets

The states with the greatest share of young adults show little overlap with the states having the largest share of boomers (see map).

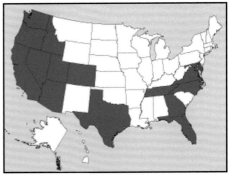

POST-BOOMER / YOUNG ADULT MAGNETS

Boomer nesting grounds are often too expensive for young adults, or they lack attractive job prospects. Only six of the 20 metros with the largest share of young adults are also on the list of metros with the largest share of boomers. The regions that are magnets for young adults are heavily concentrated in the South and the West.

Prominent among young adult-dominated areas are fast-growing Sunbelt metros—such as Raleigh/Durham, North Carolina; Salt Lake City; Austin; and Dallas/Fort Worth—as well as metros with a large number of recent immigrants—such as Salinas, California, and Los Angeles. Also prominent on the list of places that attract young adults are metros that have large universities, including such Midwest locations as Madison, Wisconsin; Lansing/East Lansing, Michigan; and Columbus, Ohio.

The attraction of young adults—singles, families with children, and new immigrants—to all parts of the growing "new" Sunbelt is bound to shape emerging regional distinctions between the now "aging" boomers and a generation that is much more multicultural, entrepreneurial, and Web-savvy than their elders.

Source: Adapted from William H. Frey, "Boomer Havens and Young Adult Magnets," *American Demographics*, September 2001; reprinted by permission of PRIMEDIA Business Magazines and Media Inc., copyright 2001, all rights reserved.

TODAY'S GENERATIONS

	Millennials	Generation Y	Generation X	Baby Boomers	Great Depression/ WWII Generation	Silent Generation
Born	1995+	1977–1994	1965–1976	1946–1964	1930–1945	Before 1930
Age in 2005	0–10	11–28	29–40	41–59	60–75	76+
Number in 2000 (millions)	19.2	73.1	47.2	80.2	37.0	25.5

FIGURE 4: SIZING UP THE GENERATIONS, 2000–2030

PERCENT OF POPULATION

- NEXT GENERATION
- MILLENIALS
- GENERATION Y
- GENERATION X
- BABY BOOMERS
- GREAT DEPRESSION/ WWII GENERATION
- SILENT GENERATION

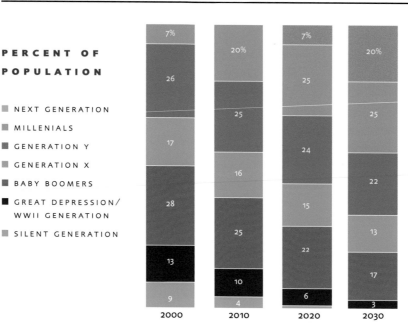

Sources: Generational definitions from *American Demographics* magazine; population data from U.S. Census Bureau, *Interim Projections by Age, Sex, Race, and Hispanic Origin*, detail file released March 2004 (www.census.gov/ipc/www/us interimproj/).

FIGURE 5: GROWTH OF YOUNG ADULT POPULATION, 2000–2020

(MILLIONS)

- 20–24-YEAR-OLDS
- 25–29-YEAR-OLDS

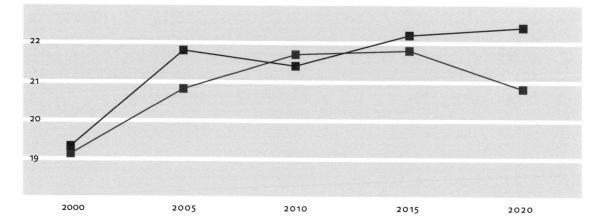

Source: U.S. Census Bureau, *Interim Projections by Age, Sex, Race, and Hispanic Origin*, detail file released March 2004 (www.census.gov/ipc/www/usinterimproj/).

and location. They look for recreation facilities, covered parking, high-speed Internet access, concierge services, and security; and they pay premiums to live close to restaurants and entertainment. Young professionals who want an urban lifestyle are often willing to trade off space for location and amenities.

The Changing American Household

A combination of factors—especially people living longer, declining birth rates, later and fewer marriages, and higher divorce rates—have dramatically altered the size and composition of America's households, which are smaller and more diverse than ever before.

In 1970, 40 percent of all households—the biggest slice of the pie—were married couples with one or more children; by 2000, this share had plummeted to 24 percent; and by 2025, only 20 percent of households will be married couples with children (see figure 7).

Married couples without children are now the most common type of household in the nation. They constitute 28 percent of all households, and this share is expected to grow to 31 percent by 2025.

The second largest household type is people living alone. Singles represented 26 percent of all households in 2000 (up from 17 percent in 1970), and are expected to account for 28 percent by 2025.

Married couples with children is the third most common household type, followed by other families with children. Other families with children include single parents—mostly single mothers—with children under 18.

One of the fastest-growing types of households is other nonfamilies, which includes unmarried partners and roommates. Though still relatively small in number, nonfamilies containing two or more people grew from just under 2 percent of households in 1970 to 6 percent in 2000.

Immigration

Immigration will continue to be an important driver of housing demand in the years ahead. Immigrants accounted for more than one-third of population and household growth in the 1990s; households headed by a person born outside the United States made up 12 percent of households in 2003. Although the number of

Gateway Lofts in Charlotte, North Carolina, targets first-time homebuyers in their 20s and 30s who are willing to trade off square footage for industrial design and downtown living. The units feature stained concrete floors, exposed brick, steel fixtures, and expanses of glass.

Top: As Generation Y comes of age over the next decade, the young adult population will grow at a rate not seen since the baby boom effect in the 1970s, and demand for student housing—like Nordheim Court, an off-campus housing complex located near the University of Washington's Seattle campus—will rise.

Bottom: Pierce Elevated, a 15-story loft apartment building, taps into an unfilled market for downtown living in Houston.

PERCENT OF HOUSEHOLDS OWNING THEIR HOME

	1996	1997	1998	1999	2000	2001	2002	2003
Married Couples								
Under 25	29.8%	31.4%	33.1%	33.5%	35.1%	36.1%	35.0%	32.8%
25–29	53.0	51.7	54.0	54.6	55.9	56.8	56.9	57.9
Male Householders [1]								
Under 25	15.5	15.1	16.5	18.4	20.0	21.9	22.2	23.3
25–29	23.5	25.3	25.9	25.5	27.2	27.3	27.8	30.4
Female Householders [2]								
Under 25	11.9	11.5	10.6	13.1	15.3	15.7	17.2	17.6
25–29	15.8	17.6	18.5	19.4	21.1	23.1	23.2	23.5

1. *Includes one-person households, families headed by single males, and other 2+ person households.*
2. *Includes one-person households, families headed by single females, and other 2+ person households.*

**FIGURE 6:
HOMEOWNERSHIP
RATES FOR
HOUSEHOLDS
UNDER 30,
1996–2003**

Source: U.S. Census Bureau, *Housing Vacancies and Homeownership, Annual Statistics: 2003.*

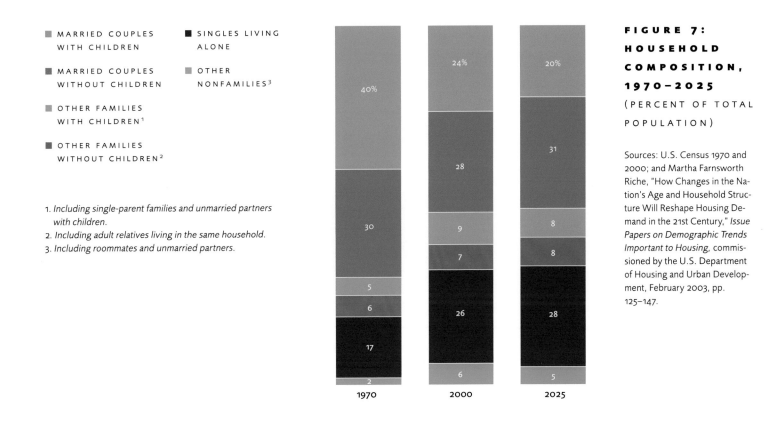

- ■ MARRIED COUPLES WITH CHILDREN
- ■ MARRIED COUPLES WITHOUT CHILDREN
- ■ OTHER FAMILIES WITH CHILDREN[1]
- ■ OTHER FAMILIES WITHOUT CHILDREN[2]
- ■ SINGLES LIVING ALONE
- ■ OTHER NONFAMILIES[3]

1. *Including single-parent families and unmarried partners with children.*
2. *Including adult relatives living in the same household.*
3. *Including roommates and unmarried partners.*

**FIGURE 7:
HOUSEHOLD
COMPOSITION,
1970–2025**
(PERCENT OF TOTAL POPULATION)

Sources: U.S. Census 1970 and 2000; and Martha Farnsworth Riche, "How Changes in the Nation's Age and Household Structure Will Reshape Housing Demand in the 21st Century," *Issue Papers on Demographic Trends Important to Housing,* commissioned by the U.S. Department of Housing and Urban Development, February 2003, pp. 125–147.

RAINBOWVISION: A GAY RETIREMENT COMMUNITY

The National Gay and Lesbian Task Force estimates there are almost 3 million gay and lesbian Americans over age 65. This number is growing. By 2030, one in five Americans will be 65 or older, and 4 million of them will be gay. But traditional retirement communities have made it difficult for gay couples to live together. This emerging niche market is exploring alternative options. A handful of communities targeted to gay seniors can be found in traditional retirement havens in Florida, California, and the Southwest, another five or so projects are under construction, and about a dozen are in the planning stages.

Developer Joy Silver was not happy with traditional retirement communities and instead decided to create her own. She found a 12.7-acre site in Santa Fe, New Mexico, a city second only to San Francisco in the percentage of households with same-sex couples, according to the 2000 Census, and set to work.

RainbowVision, Silver's dream project, is the first gay resort retirement community in the United States. It focuses on holistic wellness through health, fitness, and an active lifestyle. When completed in 2005, the community will offer 120 apartments and condominiums for independent living and 26 assisted-living residences, in 20 residential buildings that are arranged around a 22,224-square-foot community building called El Centro. El Centro houses a full-service spa/salon, a fitness center, medical facilities, a cabaret, a club café, a rooftop lounge, art studio space, and multiuse banquet rooms. Round-the-clock, on-site medical (traditional and alternative) and home health care services are available. Other amenities in the $34 million project include

Left: Exterior.
Bottom: Dining room.

cooking classes, a concierge, fitness classes, outdoor hot tubs, an organic garden, walking and biking trails, and panoramic views of the Sangre de Cristo, Sandia, Jemez, and Ortiz mountains.

Located just south of downtown Santa Fe, RainbowVision is within two miles of St. Vincent's Hospital and within a mile of Santa Fe Community College, the College of Santa Fe, and two shopping malls. Condominium sale prices start at $200,000 (plus annual club fees and monthly maintenance fees) and

rental units range from $2,600 to $4,100 per month. Rent for independent living includes utilities, property maintenance, weekly cleaning, two meals per day, social activities, health club membership, and à la carte health care services. Assisted-living renters receive on-site medication management, help with daily living activities, and three meals per day. All residents are members of the RainbowVision Club, which provides access to the El Centro facilities, guest accommodations, and postal and banking services.

immigrants arriving over the next decade may be smaller than in the last decade due to legal restrictions and more stringent security in the wake of September 11, 2001, foreigners will continue to be admitted as students, temporary workers, and permanent residents.

Demographers expect that immigration, including illegal aliens who remain permanently in the country, will top 1 million people per year on average through 2020.[6] Overall, more than one in ten households are headed by a person born outside the United States. Among younger households, the proportion headed by an immigrant is even higher.

Foreign-born residents are highly concentrated in ten metropolitan markets: Miami, Los Angeles, New York, San Francisco, Houston, Chicago, Washington, Boston, Dallas, and Atlanta. While more than half of all immigrants live in these so-called "gateway" cities, an increasing number of immigrants are moving to smaller towns in rural areas in the South and the Midwest, according to the 2000 Census. Recent immigrants to the United States tend to be of working age. About 43 percent of the immigrants who entered the country in the 1990s were between 20 and 34 years of age in 2003, whereas only 19 percent of the native-born population falls within this age group.

Compared with native-born households, average immigrant households differ dramatically in composition and size. Immigrant families are larger. Multiple generations often live under one roof, as do adult siblings—even after a decade or more of residence in the United States. The reasons are both cultural and financial. In many traditions, unmarried children are expected to remain with their parents and middle-aged adults must care for aging grandparents. And although immigrant family incomes rise over time, they are often too low to allow young adults or elderly parents to live independently.[7] Immigrant families with multiple wage earners often can move to better neighborhoods, afford more spacious apartments, or save enough money for a down payment on a house.

Homeownership rates among immigrants fall short compared with those for native-born households in the same age group, but they rise dramatically the longer immigrants have been in the country. Immigrants who have been here more than 30 years have above-average homeownership rates.[8] The combination of a growing number of immigrant families, their larger households, and their changing residency patterns suggest a number of housing market opportunities, as follows:

■ Although they may initially settle in small apartments or bungalows in older neighborhoods, immigrants will be attracted to more spacious apartments and houses and will move to the suburbs if and when they can afford to.

■ Members of immigrant families may pool their resources to buy small, multiunit buildings—occupying one or more units and renting out the others—in order to build equity.

■ Whether located in cities or suburbs, housing targeting immigrant households should provide ample space for family gatherings and food preparation as well as private, quiet spaces for older family members. Accessory apartments, where permitted, are one solution for elderly relatives who want to remain with their families but still have space to call their own.

Ethnically Diverse Population

America is becoming an increasingly diverse nation racially and ethnically. Non-Hispanic whites accounted for 76 percent of the U.S. population in 1990, but will account for only 68 percent by 2010. The fastest-growing minority population is Hispanics—a by no means homogeneous group.

In large metropolitan areas, neighborhoods tend to become established along specific ethnic lines—Puerto Rican, Mexican, Central American, or Dominican neighborhoods; Chinese, Korean, Vietnamese, Indian, or Pakistani neighborhoods. Ethnic households are drawn to these neighborhoods by the availability of stores and services that cater to newcomers' distinct tastes and languages. For the most part, ethnic neighborhoods have attracted little infill housing development, but new housing can be very marketable in these locations. It can easily capture the attention of current residents of the neighborhood as well as former residents who tend to make frequent trips back to eat at familiar restaurants and buy ethnic groceries and clothing.

The housing goals of majority (non-Hispanic white)

Left: The developer of Birkdale Village, located outside of Charlotte, North Carolina, targeted "lifestyle renters"—defined generally as households (usually without children) seeking an urban style live/work/ play environment in a suburban setting.

Right: Metro Hollywood Apartments in Los Angeles is one of the first of southern California's transit villages to target low-income households.

and minority households are not dissimilar, but their age profiles, household characteristics, income, and assets clearly differ. Minority households are, on average, younger and larger than white households. Families make up a relatively larger share of Asian and Hispanic households and many more Asian and Hispanic family households consist of five or more people. Asian and white median household incomes are higher than those for African American and Hispanic households, making it possible for them to qualify for larger mortgages and purchase larger or more expensive housing.

Minority households are expected to play a major role in shaping housing product and creating demand for housing—new and existing—over the coming decades. Harvard University's Joint Center for Housing Studies projects that minorities will account for just under two-thirds of household growth between 2005 and 2015.[9]

Because they represent a growing share of all households, minority households are receiving more attention from developers and homebuilders. At the same time, government agencies, lenders, and secondary mortgage market agencies (Fannie Mae, Freddie Mac) are developing programs to increase home-ownership opportunities in minority neighborhoods by lowering down-payment requirements, easing access to credit, and providing homeownership counseling.

Market Segmentation: Defining Niche Markets

Not so long ago, it was commonly assumed that the market for housing could be defined fairly accurately by age and income brackets—that all households within a particular bracket were attracted to the same kinds of products and locations. Young adults almost always rented small, inexpensive apartments. Then they started families. These families (married couples with children) almost always bought or aspired to buy houses with a yard in the suburbs. Retirees moved to Sunbelt golf communities.

Of course, these stereotypes were never completely—or even largely—true, but today they are ludicrous. Today's demographic mosaic is so complex that developers cannot begin to fully understand a site's potential for housing without first defining the target market. Furthermore, housing consumers are increasingly sophisticated and demanding; they will not settle for a unit or a location that they do not want. In today's competitive environment, a nuanced understanding of local consumers and a finely drawn marketing program that targets specific segments can help set a project apart from its competition.

The process of identifying submarkets or segments of a larger market and targeting projects to those seg-

ments is called market segmentation. Market segmentation is a search for important socioeconomic and behavioral distinctions among potential customers. It uses demographic variables such as age, sex, race, income, occupation, education, household status, and geographic location; as well as psychographic variables such as lifestyle, activities, interests, values, and opinions. The most sophisticated market segmentation combines demographic and psychographic variables to identify target-market segments that consist of a distinctive combination of people, lifestyles, purchasing power, and place.

Why segment markets? The main benefits of market segmentation for developers are that it helps them

- design housing products that speak to what consumers value most,
- identify niche markets,
- position projects more accurately in the marketplace, and
- create more effective sales and marketing strategies.

It has been argued that slicing the market into narrow segments inherently ignores potential customers for a development, particularly for a project such as a master-planned community that will offer a wide mix of products. But experience has shown the opposite to be true. Projects designed to appeal to broadly defined target markets have a hard time speaking to the particular needs of potential housing customers and the market-

Left: Belle Creek in Denver offers a range of housing types, including affordable housing for first-time buyers.

Right: Seattle's Uwajimaya Village, five floors of market-rate and affordable apartments located over a Japanese grocery store, targets the predominantly Asian population of its International District neighborhood.

RACE/ORIGIN OF POPULATION (PERCENT)

	2000	2010	2020
White	81.0%	79.3%	77.6%
Black	12.7	13.1	13.5
Asian	3.8	4.6	5.4
Other[1]	2.5	3.0	3.5
Total	100.0	100.0	100.0
Hispanic[2]	12.6	15.5	17.8

1. *Other races includes American Indian and Alaska Native alone; Native Hawaiian and Other Pacific Islander alone; and two or more races.*
2. *Hispanic of any race. Individuals can identify as white Hispanic, black Hispanic, or other Hispanic.*

Source: U.S. Census Bureau, *Interim Projections by Age, Sex, Race, and Hispanic Origin,* detail file released March 2004 (www.census .gov/ipc/www/usinterimproj/).

ing messages tend to miss the real hot buttons. Buyers and renters are brought to the door by the developer's ability to identify hot buttons and articulate them to the proper market segments.

Demographic Segmentation

The first step in almost any housing market study is to detail and analyze the demographics of the trade area—including, at a minimum, Census data and reliable current estimates from local government or economic development agencies pertaining to various population and household characteristics. Beyond basic age, household, and income characteristics, demographic analysis can provide insight into the lifestyle choices, ethnicity, educational attainment, and occupation and employment patterns of people in the trade area. Projections of demographic change are also important, especially for larger projects that will be built and marketed over a period of years.

Traditional demographic analysis is an extremely important market-segmentation tool, but it does not give a complete picture of the potential buyers for a prospective development. Household age and income data, no matter how detailed, do not provide enough information on which to base the development program and project design. Developers who look at only traditional demographic factors can seriously miss the market.

For example, an investor considering developing an active adult community in the Sunbelt who defines potential demand as all income-qualified households in the trade area with one member older than 55 years of age will overestimate demand for housing in the planned development—and will be no wiser about the preferences of the potential buyer pool. Age and income are not sufficient identifiers of the potential customers of an active adult community because, as numerous studies and surveys have shown, only a small percentage of households over 55 would consider living in one. To more precisely segment the potential market, the developer could survey households in the required age and income brackets using

- an attitudinal measure, such as the respondents' reactions to the statement: "I would consider living in an active adult community,"
- a geographic variable, such as the respondents' reactions to the statement: "I'd move to a Sunbelt location," or
- a psychographic variable, such as the respondents' reactions to the statement: "It's important to me to belong to a community."

Life-Cycle Segmentation

Life-cycle segmentation combines such demographic variables as age, income, and household composition in different ways to examine the stage-of-life distribution of the potential market. It provides a good measure of when households are in the housing market. The following typical life-cycle segments exemplify ways in which a potential market can be more precisely defined:

- first-time buyers;
- move-up buyers (typically with children living at home);
- empty nesters and never-nesters;
- active seniors;
- moderately active seniors; and
- seniors with limited mobility.

Life-cycle segmentation is a tool that can help developers identify their specific target market, position their project within the overall marketplace, and market their project more effectively. However, segmenting the market based on life cycle does not provide all the information that is needed. Once a target-market seg-

Concern over high energy costs and indoor air quality is spurring the market for green building. The Henry's luxury condominium units in Portland's Pearl District incorporate energy-efficient features and environmentally friendly materials.

The pocket-size Cottages at Poulsbo Place in Poulsbo, Washington, are designed to appeal to singles and couples without children seeking moderately priced, well-crafted houses within commuting distance of Seattle.

ment, such as empty nesters or move-up buyers, is defined, the developer has to be careful not to over-generalize about the segment's housing needs. The actual market represented by broad life-cycle segments can be quite diverse. Not all first-time buyers want single-family houses with yards. Not all households moving up the income ladder are looking for more square footage. Not all empty nesters are looking to downsize.

To reach potential customers, housing developers must understand the preferences of the households within the life-cycle segment(s) being targeted. Various techniques for learning about household preferences are available, including focus groups, surveys of households residing in the trade area, and surveys of people currently shopping for housing within the trade area.

Generational Segmentation

Generational segmentation is based on the idea that the attitudes and values of age cohorts—the people born within a particular period of time—are shaped by the historical era during which they came of age. That is, each generation is shaped by the events of its time. While people's needs change with age, the attitudes and values that they formed early in life tend to stay with them. This tendency produces generational cohorts with distinctive tastes and preferences.

There is no standard definition of the various generations. For example, some analysts define Generation X

SECOND HOMES

Second homes represent one of the fastest-growing sectors in the U.S. real estate industry and one set to rise dramatically over the next decade due to the confluence of a number of powerful demographic, socioeconomic, and cultural trends. Baby boomers have reached, or soon will reach, the stage in their life at which they have the time, financial means, and lifestyle orientation to buy second homes. In addition, the increasing viability of long-distance employment and the promising investment potential of second homes support this housing niche.

Even though many popular second-home locations are running into environmental, regulatory, and land supply issues that create significant challenges for development, experts project that the number of U.S. households owning second homes will rise to 10 million by the end of the decade, a 56 percent increase.

The primary market for current second-home purchases consists of older baby boomers (those in their 50s), many of whom are experiencing a rise in disposable income as they reach their peak earning years, pay down or pay off mortgages, downsize their primary residence, and reduce childraising and education expenses. Most also have more free time as their children are grown and they are less focused on career building. They are also beginning to enter the time of life at which savings, nonsalary income (such as income from investments and the sale of businesses and partnerships), and inheritance income typically peak, adding to their financial ability to acquire second homes.

Younger baby boomers typically have up to a decade to go before they become free from college tuition and mortgage commitments on their primary residences. At the

In recognition that resort homes are increasingly being used as off-site workplaces, Old Greenwood at Tahoe Mountain Resorts will include townhouses (left) and cabins (right) with high-speed Internet connections, satellite television, and other advanced telecommunication capabilities.

present time, they represent a target market for lower-end second homes, timeshares, fractionals, and vacation rentals—the starter market for second homes. In a decade, today's younger boomers will emerge as the primary market for higher-end second homes.

Ownership of second homes fits well with the baby boom culture, which stresses spending money to enjoy life and adopts the philosophy that "families that play together stay together."

Increasing work flexibility may be the most important element in the rising demand for second homes. Expanding electronic connectivity and changes in the culture of workplaces make short-term telecommuting a viable work alternative for many office employees and long-term telecommuting an alternative for a small but increasing number of others as well as for consultants and other self-employed individuals. This is key, because many boomers are not disposed to just work until a set retirement date and then play golf. Before fully retiring, a large number of boomers will con-

tinue to work past age 60 or 65—perhaps part time and perhaps in new positions.

While most people buy second homes for their own use and enjoyment, demand is also shaped by expected investment value. For a significant minority of buyers and owners, investment potential—for oneself or one's children and grandchildren—is the principal motivation to buy.

According to the National Association of Realtors (NAR), 15 percent of second-home owners lease their properties at least part of the year. The growing strength of the vacation market enhances owners' rental prospects and pricing power. Equity appreciation—from 1999 to 2003, second-home prices rose on average 13 percent per year—also remains a powerful motivation for buying a second home.

The geography of demand for second homes is characterized by four themes:

Proximity. The majority of second homes are located within a two- or three-hour drive of the owner's primary residence, shortening vacation times and making their use for long weekends feasible.

Recreational Opportunities. The 2002 NAR study found that 76 percent of second-home owners want to be near water and 38 percent want to be close to mountains or other natural attractions. (Note, however, that many households opting to convert their second home into a primary residence before retirement still want to maintain a second-home urban pied-à-terre for cultural or business purposes.)

Favorable Weather. Locations with warm weather in the winter are most popular, while locations with cooler weather in the summer are rising in popularity.

Familiarity. Many people buy second homes in areas where they have vacationed or where they already own a second home.

Over the balance of this decade and into the next, the second-home market will experience a dramatic growth in demand, and the ownership of second homes will significantly increase, even in the face of supply limitations. This should create opportunities for industry participants for many years to come.

Source: Adapted from Jeanette I. Rice, "Second Homes," *Urban Land*, February 2005.

Developed by a public/
private partnership, the
Village at Overlake Station
in Redmond, Washington,
provides apartments for
lower-income working
households and a daycare
center above a bus transit
facility.

The Epicenter loft apart-
ment project in Seattle's
Arts District appeals to its
target market with a design
incorporating commis-
sioned art outside and inside the building.

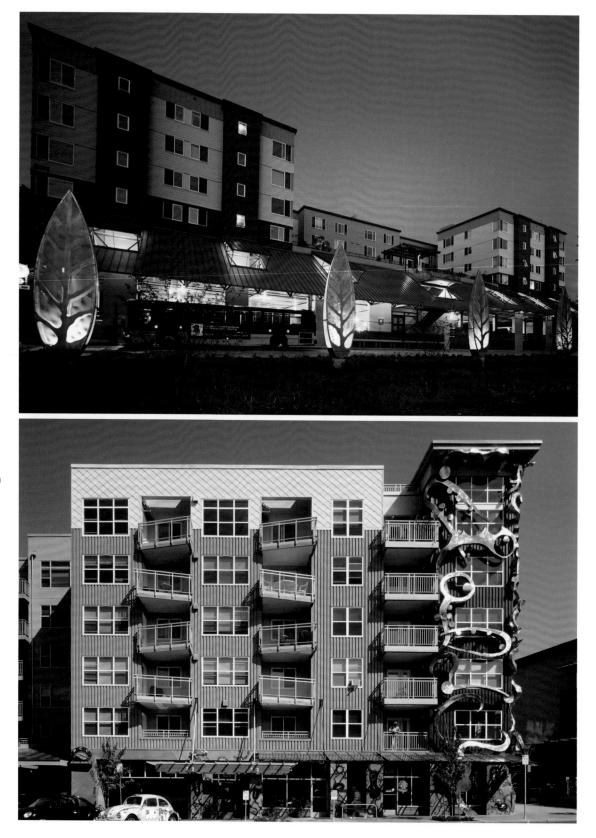

as including people born between 1965 and 1976 and others define it as people born between 1965 and 1980. The specific names given to the generations vary as well. However, for developers trying to segment markets the precise age range of a generation is less important than the characteristics that seem to define that generation. In this book, the following generational categories are used to characterize the U.S. population under the age of 75 (see figure 4):

■ the Great Depression and World War II generation (born between 1930 and 1945)—affected in its formative years by the Depression, World War II, the beginning of the Cold War, and the Korean War;

■ the baby boom (born between 1946 and 1964)—shaped by the optimism of an expanding postwar economy, high rates of employment, plentiful suburban housing, TV, its own enormous purchasing power, flower power, and rock-and-roll culture; followed by America's loss of innocence with the assassination of President Kennedy, civil rights violence, and the Vietnam War;

■ Generation X (born between 1965 and 1976)—shaped by the rise of a knowledge-based economy; the computer revolution; the ascendancy of yuppiedom and Madison Avenue; and the end of the Cold War;

■ Generation Y (born between 1977 and 1994, a.k.a. echo boomers)—shaped by a media-saturated, computer-savvy, brand-conscious culture; and an explosion of social and cultural diversity; and

■ millennials (born after 1995)—as the first generation to come of age in the 21st century, (to be) shaped, no doubt, by 9/11 and the increased threat of terrorism.

Generational segmentation begins to put a face on consumers, but just as stereotyping life-cycle segments can reduce the accuracy of market analysis, assuming that an entire generation shares the same attitudes and values would be a mistake. Within generations that are shaped by common experiences and that seemingly share some generational values, a great diversity of values and attitudes still persists.

Geodemographic Segmentation

When Census data were first made readily available for market research in the early 1970s, analysts started using a statistical technique called cluster analysis to de-

lineate demographically similar geographic areas, or geodemographic segments, that could be used by marketers to locate and reach target markets. The theory is that similar people in terms of income, education, race, and family composition tend to live near each other—that birds of a feather flock together.

Geodemographic data providers use information from a variety of sources—television and radio rating services, newspaper and magazine circulation bureaus, retailers' frequent-buyer programs, and so on—to characterize the socioeconomic lifestyles of households within a trade area. They tend to give colorful names to the lifestyle clusters that they identify. Claritas, for example, a national marketing information resources company, assigns households to one of 62 clusters among which are "shotguns and pickups," "blue-blood estates," "pools and patios," and "bohemian mix." Geodemographic cluster analysis will generally identify at least two lifestyle clusters in small trade areas; whereas large trade areas generally contain many lifestyle clusters.

Retail analysts use lifestyle cluster analysis to determine the types of stores that would be best suited for new shopping centers, and retail chains use it to determine how closely the trade area surrounding a proposed location fits the profile of their existing customer base.

But can geodemographic segmentation help residential developers identify their target markets or better understand the preferences of those markets? For the most part, no. Lifestyle clusters often do not match the small trade area from which a particular housing project will draw. For residential developers performing regional market analyses, the technique can have some validity. If a developer wanted to compare major U.S. metropolitan markets, for example, geodemographic segmentation can help paint a picture of the differences among cities.

Psychographic Segmentation

Motivational factors—such as lifestyle, world view, beliefs, recreational pursuits, and community involvement—greatly influence housing preferences. But standard demographic data do not measure such factors. Some residential developers have turned to psychographics—the study of attitudinal and behavior distinctions—to gain a better understanding of the

So much of the marketing builders do is grounded in demographics: age, income, and life stage. But builders who delve deeper into consumer behavior find that targeting traditional demographic segments can be strengthened considerably by understanding personal values and the way people think.

This is called psychographics. And perhaps nobody is better at creating and executing detailed marketing programs directed to distinct like-minded groups than Rancho Mission Viejo LLC in southern California. A case in point is the underlying marketing for the ongoing buildout of the Ladera Ranch master-planned community in Orange County. In fall 2003, the company rolled out a 1,260-unit neighborhood called Terramor designed entirely around the wants and needs of "cultural creatives" (see accompanying matrix).

One of four principal values-oriented groupings, cultural creatives tend to be well educated, interested in environmental issues, and centered around quality of life. They also tend to have the highest incomes among the psychographic groups. Cultural creatives have been a problem for homebuilders because they seek ways to reuse and remodel rather than buy a new home. For these reasons, the group is a tough but potentially lucrative nut for Rancho Mission Viejo to crack.

The developer believed it could attract cultural creatives by making Terramor as green as it could be. It might be the greenest large-scale residential development in the United States today. Runoff areas are designed to cleanse water naturally before it gets to the ocean. The 15 builders who have signed up to build at Terramor must meet

Solar panels (shown above) and photovoltaic roof tiles contribute to the green orientation of Ladera Ranch's Terramor neighborhood.

rigorous green building criteria in model homes with both standard and optional features. These include photovoltaic roof tiles that send electricity back to the utility during the day when usage is low. Small neighborhood electric vehicles will be displayed in the garage of each model home. And a massive construction-waste recycling program will be put in place, among many other green features.

But knowing that cultural creatives desire authenticity in their lives above just about everything else, the developer and its

consultants were careful not to label the community green. They took a subtler approach so authenticity-minded buyers would not be turned off by the heavy message. Instead they will market Terramor under the slogan "360-Degree Living."

Adapted from "Focus on Psychographic Targets," *Professional Builder,* May 2003; reprinted by permission.

| ATTRIBUTES OF CULTURAL CREATIVES | | TERRAMOR COMPONENTS | | |
Frame of Mind	Personal Values and Preferences	Village	Neighborhoods	Housing Units
Green Orientation Support use of recycled materials and ecological best practices in building techniques and physical siting; opt for renewable energy sources	Sustainability Recycling Reduced toxicity Renewability Energy conservation Elimination of waste	Stormwater biofiltration system Climate sensitivity Computerized irrigation Interpretive environmental education features	Low-flow stormwater management system Strategic use of plants and trees for shading in summer and sun penetration in winter	High-rated insulation Reduced solar loading Recycled materials Nontoxic materials Renewable materials Prewiring for electric car Subsidized solar panel
Preference for Authenticity Brought authenticity to the marketplace; led the consumer rebellion against plastic, fake, imitation, clichéd, throwaway, poorly made, or high-fashion goods; have penetrating perception; are not status-oriented.	Honesty Clarity Craftsmanship Simplicity Actions that match beliefs	Clear, straightforward marketing	Clear, straightforward marketing	Authentic expression of architectural style
Focus on Nest Making Want their homes to be a nest; prefer interesting nooks and niches in living spaces	Privacy—visual and acoustic Aesthetic charm Personal scale Nooks and crannies Personal spaces Warm colors and textures	Nestled valley setting Village-scale gathering places Diversity of neighborhood types	Neighborhood-scale gathering places Landscaping for privacy Staggered setbacks Variety of housing styles and character	Internal courtyards Landscape screens on front patios Aesthetically pleasing massing and elevations Second-story setbacks
Focus on Place Making Connected to their community and neighborhood; interact with neighbors on a daily basis; participate in organized events, clubs, and groups.	Connectivity Gathering places Chance encounters Sense of belonging Engaged action Participation Process Volunteerism	Village commons Shared recreational amenities Central trail system Village gathering places Reduced auto/street presence	Reduced auto/street presence Open spaces used as gathering places Neighborhood trail system	Front porches, stoops, and patios Rear-loaded garages Pedestrian-friendly streets
Love of Nature Live in harmony with nature, which is seen as sacred; see nature as a whole system; and feel environmentally responsible to future generations.	Preservation of natural legacy Holistic protection of ecosystems Natural surroundings Sense of harmony Sense of well-being Reduced pollution Environmental activism	Native and naturalized plant material Mix of rustic and manicured landscaping Preservation of adjacent natural open space	Neighborhoods oriented to open space Ample open space Mix of rustic and manicured landscaping	Units oriented to open space Mix of rustic and manicured landscaping
Support for Arts and Culture Attuned to sensory stimulation in music, art, and architecture; get involved in arts and culture; attend meetings and workshops involving creative endeavors; are literate, discriminating, and experiential; read books and magazines; listen to NPR and watch little TV.	Engaged learning Creation of a better society	Village arts and crafts shows Farmers' market Soft infrastructure programs		

Sources: EDAW; and American LIVES Inc.

housing preferences of their potential customers. Psychographic segmentation groups people by their values and attitudes rather than their demographic characteristics.

Psychographics helps housing developers understand why consumers act as they do. The more developers know about what motivates their target market(s), the better they can design products and neighborhoods that respond to the market's needs—and the more effectively they can market those products.

Psychographic market research for a proposed residential development typically begins with a values-oriented survey of recent homebuyers or renters in the area or of people who have expressed interest in the project. Cluster analysis is used to group the survey responses into psychographic categories. Typically, the analyst will use the following categories, although the names may vary:

■ *Traditionalists*. They want to fit in, not stand out. They are family-oriented and tend to be politically and socially conservative. They are not attracted to housing that makes a personal statement and they typically will not pay for high style design. They prefer traditional architectural styles, predictable floor plans, big back yards, and privacy.

■ *Winners*. They are achievement-oriented and seek status and material possessions. They want housing that lets the world know what they have achieved in life.

■ *Cultural Creatives*. They are well educated, socially aware, and environmentally sensitive. They are interested in knowing themselves and in expanding their horizons. They tend to be successful, but are not motivated by the trappings of success. They seek authenticity in their lives, their housing, and their neighborhoods.

NOTES

1. Al Ehrbar, *The Housing Boom: Another 20 Years of Growth*, report prepared for NAHB International Builders' Show (Washington, D.C., National Association of Home Builders, 2003).

2. National Center for Health Statistics, *Health, United States, 2002*, table 28.

3. U.S. Bureau of the Census, *The Older Population in the United States: March 2002* (April 2003), table 2.

4. According to the 2000 Census, 20 percent of the noninstitutional population aged 65 and older reported difficulty going outside their homes. Self-care was a problem for just 9.5 percent.

5. U.S. Bureau of the Census, *America's Families and Living Arrangements: March 2000*, Current Population Reports P20-537 (June 2001).

6. See Barry R. Chiswick and Paul W. Miller, "Issue Paper on the Impact of Immigration on Housing," in *Issue Papers on Demographic Trends Important to Housing* (U.S. Department of Housing and Urban Development, Office of Policy Development and Research, February 2003).

7. In 2002, the median income of immigrant families whose householder came to the United States after 1990 was $36,911, compared with $53,909 for native-born family households.

8. Among immigrant householders who came to the United States prior to 1970, 83 percent of families and 58 percent of nonfamilies were homeowners in 2002. The homeownership rate in 2002 for native-born families was 79 percent and for native-born nonfamilies it was 55 percent.

9. Joint Center for Housing Studies of Harvard University, *State of the Nation's Housing: 2004* (Cambridge, Massachusetts: Joint Center for Housing Studies), table W-1.

The Solaire building in Battery Park City in Lower Manhattan was the nation's first green residential high rise. The apartment building's marketing tagline—"Live healthy, live green"—trumpets the health benefits of cleaner indoor air.

Case Studies

PROJECT	LOCATION	COMPONENTS AT BUILDOUT	UNIT TYPES	RESIDENT PROFILE
Amelia Park	Fernandina Beach, Florida	453 dwelling units Retail, office, and civic uses	SF detached SF attached (townhouses, duplexes) Condominium apartments Accessory dwelling units Live/work units	Age diversity Mostly singles and couples without children
Campus at Albuquerque High	Albuquerque, New Mexico	304 dwelling units Retail and office uses Adaptive use and new construction	Condominium apartments Rental apartments	Mostly in 20s and 30s Mostly singles
The Edge Lofts	Portland, Oregon	123 dwelling units Retail uses	Condominium apartments	Age diversity; mostly younger than 40 Mostly singles and couples without children
Fall Creek Place	Indianapolis, Indiana	427 dwelling units (including 58 rehabilitated SF houses) Retail and office uses	SF detached Townhouses Live/work units Includes affordable units	Mostly first-time buyers Mostly singles and couples without children
Front Street at Ladera Ranch	Orange County, California	22 dwelling units	SF detached All live/work units	Mostly couples with children Home-based business operators
Fruitvale Village	Oakland, California	47 dwelling units Retail and office uses	Rental apartments Includes affordable units	Age diversity Ethnic diversity Low- and middle-income households Mostly singles and couples without children

PROJECT	LOCATION	COMPONENTS AT BUILDOUT	UNIT TYPES	RESIDENT PROFILE
Greenwood Avenue Cottages	Shoreline, Washington	8 dwelling units	Small SF detached	Mostly single women and empty-nester couples
Hearthstone	Denver, Colorado	33 dwelling units	Townhouses	Age diversity Half singles, half couples Two-fifths of households include children
Jefferson Commons at Minnesota	Minneapolis, Minnesota	164 dwelling units	Apartments (individual bedrooms are the rental unit)	Undergraduate students
Lasell Village	Newton, Massachusetts	171 independent living units Educational facilities 38-bed skilled nursing facility	Apartments secured by a 90% refundable entry fee and monthly fee for services	Retirees Average age 83
Santana Row	San Jose, California	1,201 dwelling units Retail and hotel uses	Rental apartments Rental townhouses Rental villas	Mostly in 20s and 30s Mostly singles
Solivita	Poinciana, Florida	6,500 dwelling units Retail uses Extensive recreational uses	SF detached SF attached (duplexes)	Mostly active adults aged 55 to 64
Spring Island	Beaufort, South Carolina	407 homesites Recreational facilities Extensive open space	Cottage lots (.25 to .5 acre) Estate lots (2 to 5 acres)	Active adults and retirees High-income households
Vickery	Cumming, Georgia	564 dwelling units Retail and office uses	SF detached Townhouses Live/work units	Age diversity Mostly couples and families with children

Amelia Park

SIGNIFICANT FEATURES

- Programmed to attract a diverse range of households

- Optional accessory dwelling units

- PUD zoning allowing home-based businesses

- Mixed-use town center

Amelia Park is a new urbanist community on a 118-acre greenfield site in the historic oceanside town of Fernandina Beach. Its development partners drew inspiration from well-known and successful new urbanist developments elsewhere in Florida, like Seaside and Celebration. Their intention when they set out in the mid-1990s to develop the site was to provide a mix of housing, commercial land uses, recreational opportunities, and infrastructure that would attract a multigenerational market and allow households to age in place comfortably and affordably.

At buildout in 2008, Amelia Park will consist of 453 dwelling units; a mixed-use town center; civic buildings; and open space. The housing mix will be 301 single-family detached houses and 152 attached townhouses, condominiums, and live/work units. In addition, the zoning code permits 308 accessory dwelling units (ADUs)—often called "granny flats"—which are offered to homebuyers as an optional upgrade.

Site and Surroundings

The site is located at the center of Amelia Island in Nassau County, one mile from Atlantic Ocean beaches and approximately 30 minutes northeast of Jacksonville International Airport. It is surrounded by primarily nonresidential commercial and institutional development—retail land uses, schools, and medical facilities. Amelia Park introduced residential uses to its immediate neighborhood.

The site is bounded on the west by South 14th Street—a major thoroughfare that intersects Route A1A—and on the east by Citrona Drive. Its neighbors are, to the north, Baptist Medical Center-Nassau and, to the south, Island Walk Shopping Center, which features a Kmart and Publix grocery store along with smaller shops.

Development Process and Financing

Joel Embry is a local broker and developer who had developed six small-scale residential and commercial developments in the area between 1982 and 1992, when he became interested in a three-acre parcel. An adjacent parcel happened to be in foreclosure. Finding "the deal too good to resist," Embry formed a partnership with several other investors to purchase the entire 109 acres. Eventually Embry bought out his partners, acquired nine additional acres, and formed Amelia Park Development LLC with Mike Antonopoulos as partner.

The site was zoned for medium-density residential use, which would have allowed 800 townhouses. The developer's initial planned unit development (PUD)

Master plan.

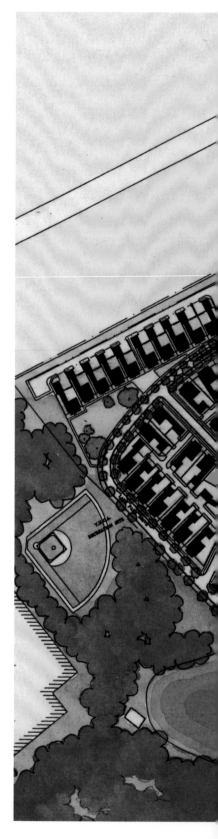

Accessory dwelling units (ADUs) can be used as a home office, as lodging for teenage children or elderly family members, or as a rental property. Amelia Park offers an optional ADU for both single-family and attached houses, with most being connected to the main house by a breeze-way, as shown.

The community contains a mix of land uses and housing types designed to attract a multigenerational market. The developer sought to provide a range of housing options that would allow residents to age in place comfortably and affordably.

application was approved for 415 residential units, a 105,000-square-foot mixed-use town center, and various civic uses.

A series of master-planning charrettes was put together. About 250 people attended, including city officials who became part of the process. Approvals and permits were facilitated through this collaborative approach. Amelia Park obtained 23 exemptions to the city's land development regulations and Fernandina Beach adopted a proprietary zoning ordinance— Amelia Park Plans and Codes—for the PUD.

No local financial institutions had financed a traditional neighborhood design (TND) project before, and they were cautious about Amelia Park. To secure bank financing, Embry sought a builder that could make a significant financial commitment in addition to the developer's equity investment. Brylen Homes, a production homebuilder from Jacksonville with a custom-home division, was brought onto the team. Although Brylen Homes invested no capital in the project, it committed to a substantial deposit on lots, built seven speculative houses, and contracted to buy the entire first phase on a take-down schedule of three lot purchases per month whether or not they had been sold. This was the kind of proof of market demand that the bank wanted, and construction financing was granted.

Planning and Design

Before it began the master-planning and site-design process, the development team drew up several specific goals for Amelia Park. The development had to

- allow for aging in place;
- facilitate a live/work/play lifestyle;
- be affordable; and
- represent a model for new development in the region.

The goal of allowing households to continue living at Amelia Park as they age would require building in walkability and accessible services, providing a range of housing at a range of prices, and facilitating connections among neighborhood and civic destinations.

The goal of facilitating a multidimensional lifestyle would require permitting home-based businesses, pro-viding an advanced communications infrastructure, incorporating neighborhood office uses and recreational and shopping opportunities within the development, and designing a pedestrian-oriented community that provides opportunities to hobnob with neighbors and fosters a strong sense of place.

The goal of affordability is met most notably by the inclusion of accessory dwelling units (ADUs), which are basically studio apartments that provide affordable rental options.

Fulfilling the first three goals makes Amelia Park a model for growth in this part of Florida and thus contributes to the fourth planning goal. The development's architecture, color palette, landscaping, and associated design components are drawn from a variety of sources to create a diverse community that by design promotes friendship and neighborliness and discourages competitiveness and isolationism.

To implement his vision of Amelia Park as a compact, walkable community, Embry brought in Duany Plater-Zyberk & Company (DPZ), a Miami-based pioneer in new urbanist planning, to provide the master plan and formulate design standards.

DPZ led a weeklong charrette, which was attended by the members of the development and building team, local architects, prospective residents, media representatives, and other interested parties. This participatory process—itself a principle of new urbanist development—helped the plan to coalesce.

A key assumption of the plan was that Amelia Park should be a coherent, cohesive neighborhood rather than a collection of discrete pods. The developer's intention was to promote urban style diversity and shared equity among neighbors through a fine-grained mix of housing within blocks—for example, by putting a $250,000 house next to a $450,000 house or by siting townhouses facing single-family houses.

The master plan is logical and simple. A mixed-use town center on the western edge gives way to a one-block open green space known as the town square. Residential blocks radiate outward from the town square. Civic uses are placed at the eastern border.

Buildings in the town center are limited to three stories, counting the ground floor. The town center goes along Park Avenue, the development's main thorough-fare, starting at South 14th Street. Taking advantage of the high levels of traffic along South 14th Street, the tenant mix in the western block of the town center will be oriented to community rather than only neighborhood uses. The portions of Park Avenue nearer the town square will be developed—in the town center's final development phase—with a more neighborhood-oriented blend of retail and commercial uses and residential units above the retail.

Tree-lined residential streets and boulevards radiate north, south, and east from the town square. Houses along these streets have large front porches and are set back a maximum of eight feet from the sidewalk. Yards are small. Garages are in the rear, accessed by service alleys. Blocks are small, which promotes walking.

Amelia Park's streets and walkways form an efficient circulation network that integrates the community with its environs. An extensive greenway made up of pedestrian paths and interconnected parks—including an eight-acre lake surrounded by jogging trails, playing fields, and a fishing dock—highlights the site's natural beauty. The "garden walk," a seven-block landscaped path, forms the centerpiece of the pedestrian network. Both sides of the garden walk are lined with houses that face it, creating Amelia Park's "garden district."

Unit Design

The guiding idea for architectural design has been a bungalow neighborhood in a southern port town vernacular style. Think Bermuda, Key West, Beaufort (South Carolina). "We like to leave some things on the houses that are prone to flutter in the breeze in true Fernandina style," says Embry.

Four housing types were offered in Phase 1:

Courtyard homes—three styles; one or two stories; detached garages; from 2,010 to 2,865 square feet; and from $311,700 to $414,400.

Houses built along the garden walk—nine styles, the most popular of which is a cottage with a garden beyond the front porch; one or two stories; detached garages in the rear accessible from a service alley;

from 1,535 to 2,913 square feet; and from $276,500 to $427,000.

Townhouses—15 styles; two stories; two-car garages; from 1,554 to 2,427 square feet; and from $227,900 to $295,900.

Granny flats (accessory dwelling units)—four options; from 400 square feet (above a two-car garage) to 600 square feet (above a three-car garage); and from $54,445 to $76,445.

ADUs are considered part of the main house—not a separate dwelling unit that is included in housing density calculations. Among the first 136 homebuyers, 33 opted for ADUs. Twenty-one ADUs are associated with single-family dwellings (12 above a two-car garage and nine above a three-car garage) and 12 are associated with townhouses. The ADUs are basically a single room with a bathroom. A kitchenette is optional. Most are connected to the main house by a breezeway.

The ownership of ADUs at Amelia Park must be the same as the ownership of the principal residence. ADUs require an additional off-street parking space, which is created by the builder adjacent to the garage or, in some cases, inside the garage. The cost of the added parking space is built into the price of the ADU option.

Most of the homebuyers choosing the ADU option want a rental unit or a guest room. But many plan to use their ADU for a home-based business or for telecommuting. Before Amelia Park was developed, home-based businesses in Fernandina Beach required a special exception. In anticipation of buyer preferences, the developer was able to obtain a PUD provision for home-based businesses with two stipulations: no on-site customers and no signage.

ADUs at Amelia Park provide important community benefits. With people living in the garage apartments, the alleyways become more active and safer. Also, the garage apartments are affordable for people in lower-income brackets. A survey conducted in late 2004 revealed that the ADUs are being used as

- rental units occupied by persons not in the family (33 percent);
- home offices (24 percent);

- rental units occupied by family members (22 percent);
- additional bedroom or living space (15 percent); or
- weekend and vacation residence for preretirement homeowners who rent out the main house for income (6 percent).

Monthly rents on ADUs are generally between $650 and $750, depending on unit size and amenities.

Target Market and Resident Profile

The sales office opened in April 1999 when housing construction began. An aggressive sales goal was set, but because traditional neighborhood design was a new concept locally, sales in the initial two years barely met expectations. Now, however, absorption targets are being exceeded with sales of more than 60 units annually.

In terms of price and positioning, Amelia Park aims at the market area's middle range—below the better-known resort communities at the south end of Amelia Island and above the tract subdivisions on the island. Being extremely competitive within its geographic market and being competitive within the established TND market in other locales were two key marketing goals. Since opening, Amelia Park has captured approximately 30 percent of the Fernandina Beach new-home sales market and 15 percent of the Amelia Island market. Another indication of the strong market acceptance for the new urbanist community is that sale prices have increased about 60 percent since the project opened.

As expected, the project got off to a slow start because it is not a typical subdivision with large lots, wide streets, cul-de-sac streets, and garages accessible from the front. According to Embry: "TND must be built first to educate the market to its advantages. You cannot sell it with words or pictures alone. Buyers have to see, touch, and feel." After two streets with around 40 houses had been finished, market acceptance of Amelia Park grew exponentially. It can be argued that the implementation of the TND concept succeeded in creating its own market.

In hopes of attracting a range of ages, lifestyles, and income levels, a mixed bag of households was targeted, including active retirees, young families, singles, and semi-retirees. In fact, buyers match this broad target

market fairly well. About 40 percent of Amelia Park's residents are between 35 and 55 years of age, and about 40 percent are over 55. Married-couple households account for more than 70 percent of households. About 15 percent of current households have children living at home. Single-person households are mostly women, and the majority of them buy townhouses or cottages.

Marketing

The developer and the builder put together a coordinated marketing plan that assured consistency of message and materials. Amelia Park Development concentrated on marketing the community as a whole by means of press releases distributed to trade publications and national media outlets, a brochure, and a DVD. Brylen Homes focused on promoting the housing. It used an independent marketing consultant, an advertising agency, and an interior design firm to help launch its marketing campaign, which included model homes; public relations and promotions activities; image creation activities;

To better enable residents to continue living at Amelia Park as they age, the design emphasizes walkability through features such as this "garden walk," a landscaped path—lined on both sides with houses—that meanders through the entire community.

local print advertising; mass mailings; interior merchandising; and a strong broker incentive program.

Experience Gained

■ Amelia Park has been a learning experience for the development partners. Some things worked and some things surprised the developer. Experience has led to the modification of a number of project elements, and each modification has paved the way to a more thoroughly considered outcome.

■ Although sales quotas have been met and buyer satisfaction is high, marketing and sales will be brought in-house for the final release of Phase 2 units. This is being done in order to exercise greater control over the sales and marketing process, representation of the brand, product development, and overall management.

■ In order to accommodate unexpected market responses for a development that is untested in the market, flexibility should be built into the physical and business plans. At Amelia Park, for example, downstairs master bedrooms proved popular and so many one-story units were sold that maintaining architectural variety became a challenge. The developer has thus stepped up efforts to design and sell two-story units featuring a master suite on the first floor. Also unexpected was the popularity of townhouse units, more of which were added in Phases 1 and 2.

■ Inclusion of the garden district was a radical and successful departure from the original plan, revealing a strong market demand for an untested product type. Many garden district houses face a garden and not a street, which saves 70 percent of the cost of road infrastructure for each house. Furthermore, the builder achieved a 20 percent premium on the price of garden district lots.

■ Sales of accessory dwelling units (ADUs)—a new urbanist option on which Embry's associates were less keen than he was—have not been nearly as successful as Embry had hoped. Most homebuyers have found it hard to justify another $54,000 to $76,000 for a spare room, while others have been put off by the fact that the ADUs were reachable only by stairs. Also, many homebuyers are not interested in becoming a landlord. However, now that the development of Amelia Park is well underway and prospective buyers can see how it is evolving, more of an effort is being made to market ADUs as a lifestyle option with a potential return on investment.

■ Homebuyers may relish exteriors that contribute to an old-time neighborhood ambience, but they expect modern interior features—high ceilings, natural light, designer appliances, high-end surfaces and finishes, energy-efficiency, high-tech wiring, and the ability to customize through an array of options. Incorporating such features in a shell that resembles a traditional bungalow or cottage proved to be one of the toughest design challenges of this project.

■ A location near community amenities is important for a middle-market project that lacks the financing to construct amenities before houses are built. The Amelia Park Y—a 45,000-square-foot YMCA that was constructed just east of the site at the same time that Amelia Park's first model homes went up—was a big boon to marketing the project.

■ The development team felt confident in its knowledge of and experience with residential development, but felt it needed support on the town center component, which was for it an unfamiliar program element. The developer brought in the Gibbs Planning Group to provide market research and make recommendations on the land use mix.

■ Embry would have liked to achieve a readily identifiable architectural style, but he has concluded that Amelia Park's hybrid architecture—a mélange of components borrowed from a historic and regional American lexicon—serves a higher purpose in that it gives a sense of comfort to people who have moved from other parts of the country.

Top left: Setting houses no more than ten feet apart and within at least eight feet of the sidewalk promotes walking and neighborliness. Garages are accessed by rear alleys

Top right: An eight-acre lake surrounded by open space, trails, and ball fields is a popular amenity.

Bottom left: Townhouses face the town square, a one-block open space at the center of the community.

Bottom right: The town center features two-story office condominiums for small professional service businesses. Residential units above neighborhood-oriented retail space will be added in future development phases.

PROJECT WEB SITE

www.ameliapark.com

DEVELOPERS

Amelia Park Development LLP

P.O. Box 401

Fernandina Beach, Florida 32035

904-261-8300

www.ameliapark.com

HomeTown Neighborhoods Inc.

1405 Park Avenue, Suite 101

Fernandina Beach, Florida 32034

904-261-8300

ARCHITECTS/PLANNERS

Duany Plater-Zyberk & Company (Town Planner)

1023 Southwest 25th Avenue

Miami, Florida 33135

305-644-1023

www.dpz.com

Starr Sanford Design Associates
(Town Center Architect)

902 Ladies Street

Fernandina Beach, Florida 32034

904-277-0850

Gibbs Planning Group (Town Center Consultant)

330 East Maple, Suite 310

Birmingham, Michigan 48009

248-642-4800

www.gibbsplanning.com

ENGINEERS

Michael Antonopoulos & Associates

2021 Art Museum Drive, Suite 200

Jacksonville, Florida 32207

904-396-5583

**AMELIA PARK
PROJECT
INFORMATION**

DEVELOPMENT SCHEDULE

Site Purchased:	June 1992
Planning Started:	July 1992
Construction Started:	1998
Project Completion:	
Phase 1	2004
Phase 2	2007
Town Center	2008
Buildout	2008

LAND USE INFORMATION

Site Area:	118 acres
Dwelling Units:	
single family	301
attached	152
Residential Density:	3.8 units per gross acre
Parking Ratio:	2 spaces per housing unit

LAND USE PLAN

	ACRES	PERCENT OF SITE
Residential	59	50 %
Commercial	12	10
Civic Uses	13	11
Roads/Parking	19	17
Open Space	15	12

ACCESSORY DWELLING UNIT INFORMATION

Number of ADUs:	
Allowed	308
Built [1]	33
Average Size:	440 square feet
Cost:	
Without Kitchen	$54,500
With Kitchen	$77,500
Average Rental Income:	$700 per month
Parking:	1 additional space required
Average Impact Fee: [2]	$4,000
Use by Owner:	
Rented Out	60%
Home Office	24%
Primary Living Space	15%

1. *As of December 30, 2004.*

2. *Fee in addition to average $5,200 impact fee per single-family unit.*

RESIDENTIAL UNIT INFORMATION

| UNIT TYPE | LOT SIZE[1] | UNIT SIZE[1] | NUMBER OF UNITS | | SALE PRICE RANGE |
			PLANNED	BUILT	
Single Family	5,500	2,300	301	176	$176,000 – $325,000
Attached[2]	2,640	1,500	104	66	134,000 – 200,000
Condominium	TBD[3]	1,746	48	0	250,000 – 325,000

1. *in square feet.*
2. *Live/work units, duplexes, and townhouses.*
3. *To be determined.*

DEMOGRAPHIC PROFILE

	PERCENT OF ALL RESIDENTS OR HOUSEHOLDS
AGE RANGE	
<18	8 %
18–24	2
25–34	10
35–44	20
45–54	20
55–64	25
65+	15
HOUSEHOLD TYPE	
Singles with Children	2
Singles without Children	25
Couples with Children	13
Couples without Children	60
GENDER (SINGLE-PERSON HOUSEHOLDS)	
Male	40
Female	60

DEVELOPMENT COST INFORMATION

Site Acquisition	$ 2,970,000
Site Preparation and Infrastructure	8,000,000
Amenities and Civic Uses	1,000,000
Soft Costs	2,600,000
TOTAL DEVELOPMENT COST	$ 14,570,000

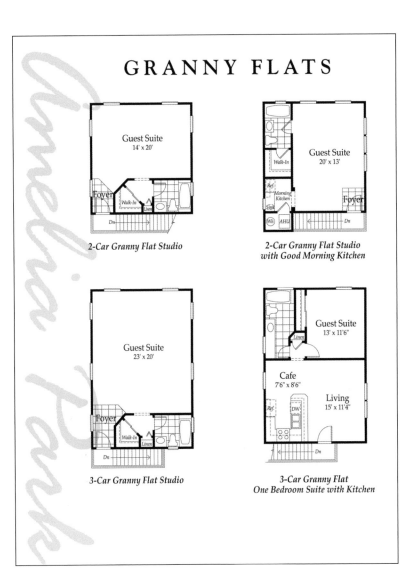

GRANNY FLATS

2-Car Granny Flat Studio

2-Car Granny Flat Studio with Good Morning Kitchen

3-Car Granny Flat Studio

3-Car Granny Flat One Bedroom Suite with Kitchen

Alternative floor plans for accessory dwelling units.

Campus at Albuquerque High

ALBUQUERQUE, NEW MEXICO

In 1974, the 7.26-acre campus of the centrally located Albuquerque High School was vacated, the latest symptom in the decline of the city's core, which had started with the construction of interstate highways through downtown in the 1950s and continued with the failure of urban renewal schemes in the 1960s. Subsequently, many efforts were made to redevelop the school's grand Jacobean revival buildings dating to 1914, but they all failed. In the late 1990s, the city of Albuquerque finally mounted a concerted effort to preserve its beloved landmark.

A competitive proposal process resulted in a partnership between the city and Paradigm & Company to develop the Campus at Albuquerque High, a mixed-use infill project that initially targeted "urban pioneers," defined as people with a higher-than-average tolerance for the risks associated with marginal or transitional neighborhoods.

The project entails the restoration of five historic buildings and the construction of a public parking garage and five additional buildings. At buildout (and after the 70 Phase 1 rental units have been converted to condominiums), the Campus will contain 124 rental apartments, 180 condominiums, 16,000 square feet of retail and restaurant space, and 18,200 square feet of office space.

Located in the east downtown (EDO) neighborhood, the Campus serves as a model of profitable new urbanist development. It is the first infill project in Albuquerque designed to accommodate a full array of new urbanist principles and it has inspired the adoption of a 20-year area master plan that aims to reestablish the kinds of lively neighborhoods and streets that characterized the EDO area before the advent of the auto.

Site and Surroundings

The Campus at Albuquerque High is on the eastern edge of downtown, one mile from the University of New Mexico and near several major hospitals. Two major street corridors—Central Avenue (the old Route 66) on the south and Broadway Boulevard on the west—together with two smaller streets—Arno on the east and Tijeras on the north—circumscribe a central quadrangle that is dominated by five historic, three- and four-story, red-brick buildings known as Old Main, the Classroom, the Gym, the Library, and Manual Arts. At buildout, the development will

SIGNIFICANT FEATURES

- Historic high-school campus

- Combines adaptive use and new construction

- Mixed-use development

- Anchor for neighborhood redevelopment master plan

- LEED certification for gym conversion to housing

- Public/private development

- New urbanist design

Historic buildings on the landmark high-school campus, which is being redeveloped as an infill urban village.

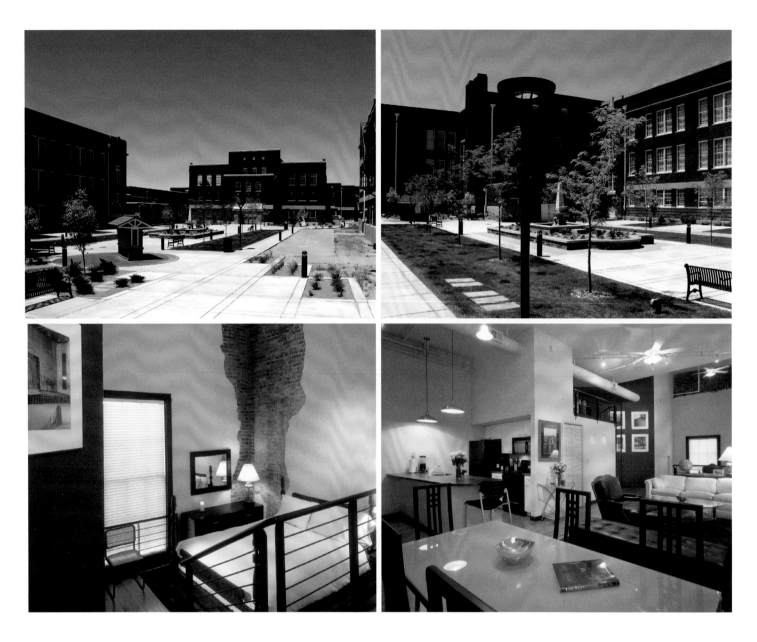

Top: The Classroom (left) and Old Main (right) buildings, the first of five historic buildings to be redeveloped, have been converted to loft apartments targeted to young urban pioneers willing to risk living in an untested downtown location. The average tenant in the historic buildings is 31 years old and single and makes $40,000 per year.

Bottom: Urban pioneers tend to care more about cubic footage than square footage. Most of the lofts in the Old Main building are less than 900 square feet and they feature open floor plans, high ceilings, exposed mechanical systems, brick walls, and plenty of glass.

include five new residential buildings as well.

The Campus is the heart of the surrounding east downtown (EDO) neighborhood, a 45-acre, L-shaped area adjacent to Broadway Boulevard and Central Avenue that is characterized by a potpourri of building styles, including Queen Anne, Pueblo revival, Mediterranean revival, and Southwest vernacular. The EDO master plan, which was put together in response to the opportunity provided by the redevelopment of the high-school campus, envisions the addition of 1,500 housing units and 500,000 square feet of ground-level commercial space within the EDO area.

Development Process

After the closing of the high school in 1974, title to the property followed a complicated path from a private out-of-state owner to a bank, to the FDIC, to the California-based Parking Company of America. The prospect of the demolition of the school buildings caused a public outcry that impelled city leaders to action. In 1996, the city acquired all of the campus except the manual arts building through condemnation and issued a request for proposals (RFP).

At the time, Paradigm was based in Austin—a one-person company that bought, upgraded, and resold $3 million to $10 million apartment and office complexes across the United States. Its owner, Robert Dickson, had been monitoring the Albuquerque high-school campus since 1989. Viewing the RFP as an opportunity to further several goals—make money, shift Paradigm's focus from real estate asset management to development, promote new urbanism, and contribute to the redevelopment of downtown Albuquerque—he teamed up with three local firms—Dekker/Perich/Sabatini (land use planning and design), R. Davis Companies (development), and Richardson & Richardson (general contracting)—to draft a proposal.

The decision process was highly competitive. Paradigm's offer was accepted by the city in 1997 and negotiating a development agreement took another year. Under the agreement, the city retains ownership of the site's common areas, which include everything outside the building footprints and an interior courtyard and a plaza on Central Avenue. These common areas are

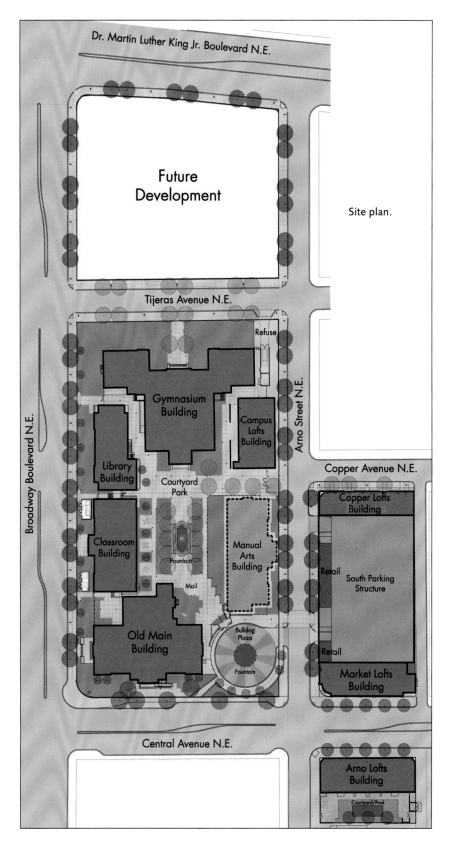

Site plan.

maintained by the Albuquerque High Historic Campus Association.

Under the development agreement, Paradigm, now based in Albuquerque, is developing all of the campus, except for the library building, which R. Davis Companies is converting into 10,000 square feet of office space to be marketed for a single corporate tenant on a long-term lease, and the manual arts building, which belongs to a third party and is currently planned for a restaurant and for-sale apartments.

Phase 1, which concluded in December 2002, entailed the reconfiguration of Old Main and Classroom into 70 loft style apartments renting for $485 to $1,265 a month, common area improvements, and the construction of a 261-space, city-owned parking garage incorporating a small amount of office space.

Phase 2, completed in June 2004, involved the construction of 56 for-sale units in four new buildings—Arno Lofts, located on an outlot across Central Avenue; Campus Lofts, which fills a void at the northeast edge of the quad; Copper Lofts, which wraps the north side of the garage; and City Market, which wraps the south side of the garage and contains ground-level retail space that is designated for, but not yet leased as, a neighborhood grocery store.

Phase 3, which is scheduled for completion in spring 2005, involves the conversion of the Gym into 54 loft condominiums. Paradigm expects that the Gym will receive certification under the Leadership in Energy and Environmental Design (LEED) program of the U.S. Green Building Council—the first residential building in New Mexico to obtain the LEED certification, which is based on a point system that addresses site development, water savings, energy efficiency, materials selection, and indoor air quality.

The final phase of the project, scheduled for completion in 2006, will be a new building located across Tijeras Street on a vacant block that was used for athletic fields. It will contain 124 rental units over ground-level commercial space.

The old manual arts building, which was not acquired by the city in its 1996 condemnation procedure, is a wild card in the Campus development project. The building is not part of the development agreement, but

its development must adhere to the city's historic preservation regulations. In the spring of 2004, the owner proposed converting it into a 372-seat restaurant. Paradigm joined area residents and businesses in opposing a restaurant of that size, and the planning commission limited it to 200 seats. The owner envisions two floors of rental units above the restaurant.

The EDO redevelopment master plan is an integral part of the Campus development. Dickson had made it clear from the beginning of his involvement that the Campus development should not be an island in a sea of unplanned, ad hoc redevelopment. At his behest, a clause was included in the development agreement committing the city to sponsor a master-planning process for the EDO area. Because the first attempt, which was made in 2001, proved inadequate, neighborhood businesses and residents led by Paradigm formed the Broadway + Central Corridors Partnership.

This partnership sponsored a five-day charrette in September 2003 that was coordinated by Moule & Polyzoides Architects and Urbanists. Hundreds of residents were involved. From this effort there emerged a 20-year master plan for the EDO that aims to make Central Avenue between I-25 and downtown the best main street shopping district in New Mexico. The plan identifies needs for street improvements, buildings, and public spaces in the neighborhood; establishes design guidelines for buildings and public improvements; and outlines financing mechanisms. If approved by all necessary boards and commissions, it will become, in essence, a traditional neighborhood overlay zoning ordinance.

Financing

Construction financing for the conversion of the old main and classroom buildings came from bank loans ($2.4 million) and city gap funds ($3.9 million) earmarked for the historic buildings. Permanent financing came from developer equity based on syndication of the historic tax credits ($1.2 million), permanent bank loans ($3.2 million), and city gap funds structured as a cash flow second mortgage ($1.9 million). The city and developer split the residual cash flow on a 50/50 basis. The historic tax credits require that the Phase 1 apartments be leased for at least five years. Beginning in 2008, these units will be

sold as condominiums, and the proceeds will repay the city's gap fund balance. The developer anticipates making about $3 million on its $1.2 million investment.

Per the development agreement, the city agreed to finance up to $2 million in Phase 1 streetscape, plaza, and courtyard improvements, $1 million of which came from a U.S. Department of Commerce grant. The city also financed the $3.35 million public parking structure constructed in Phase 1.

Financing for the $8.9 million Phase 2 housing and retail space was completely private. The developer provided $2.2 million through a private equity investor and a bank loan provided the balance based on 50 percent presales. The project should generate a 30 percent internal rate of return (IRR) for the equity investor.

Financing for the $7 million Phase 3 conversion of the old gym building into 54 condominium units will include $1.4 million of city gap funds, a developer investment of $.45 million, and a $5.2 million construction loan based on 50 percent presales. The project should generate a 35 percent IRR on equity.

Construction of the mixed-use residential building in Phase 4, which is estimated to cost $10 million including 150 podium parking spaces, will be financed by developer equity (25 percent) and a construction/permanent loan (75 percent). The conversion of the old library building to office space, a project expected to cost $1.6 million, will be financed with $1.3 million of private equity and debt and $.3 million of city gap funds.

Project Design and Target Market

Because the layout of the historic old main, classroom, gym, and manual arts buildings suggested their conversion to residential space and the market for office space was poor, the development of a residential neighborhood seemed the best approach for the Campus site. In order to take advantage of historic tax credits, apartments developed in Old Main and Classroom would have to be rental units for at least five years. Also, at the time that planning started on this site, the east downtown neighborhood was perceived by many metropolitan residents as somewhat unsafe and unsavory.

Left: A city-owned parking garage incorporating ground-floor commercial space is flanked by two new condominium buildings, one of which will contain a 6,000-square-foot grocery store.

Right: The classroom building. To take advantage of historic-preservation tax credits, the redeveloped Old Main and Classroom buildings must be kept as rental units for at least five years.

The names of Albuquerque High School alumni who contributed to the effort to preserve the school's buildings are inscribed on bricks paving the courtyard.

The Copper Lofts condominiums as seen from the courtyard of the historic buildings across the street.

All these factors—the adaptive use of historic buildings, rental apartments, and an untested downtown location—dovetailed to define the ideal demographic for this project: urban pioneers, people willing to test the waters of downtown living as renters. According to the project's leasing manager, urban pioneers are risk-tolerant and in search of the experience of an urbane city; they want to live near lively streets filled with a diversity of people and to be able to walk from their residences to daily entertainment, dining, and other destinations.

According to the project's architect, pioneers care more about cubic footage than square footage. They want large, open, airy, trendy spaces with plenty of glass. To maximize a sense of authenticity and uniqueness, the tall ceilings, wood floors, chalkboards, and tall double-hung windows of the historic buildings were retained. Where possible, brick walls and mechanical sys-

tems were left exposed. High-tech and high-touch finishes were used.

To deal with concerns about security, the architect chose to subtly enclose spaces between buildings instead of building a wall around the complex that would have cut off the Campus visually and psychologically from its neighborhood. The design of the project's four new residential buildings echoes the three- and four-story scale of the historic buildings and their red-brick facades, while also adding such modern elements as French doors and balconies, in order to create a graceful transition into existing neighborhoods.

For the Phase 1 conversion of Old Main and Classroom, a range of unit sizes was programmed in order to capture as much of the pioneer rental market as possible: 17 units in the 500- to 600-square-foot range, 14 in the 600- to 700-square-foot range, 18 in the 700- to 800-square-foot range, ten in the 800- to 900-square-foot range, and 11 units larger than 900 square feet. These units rent for approximately $1 per square foot.

As the perceived riskiness of the location has decreased, the market appeal of the Campus has widened to include homebuyers. Furthermore, the EDO master plan assures buyers that they are investing in more than a single unit. Many buyers of Campus apartments have been strongly motivated by the opportunity to help create a vital urban neighborhood. Because of the new urbanist cachet of this project, when Phase 2 condominiums went on the market in January 2003, the presale prices of loft apartments ($100,000 to $350,000) showed a 20 percent premium over comparably sized houses on small lots in outlying suburbs.

The 124 rental units planned for Phase 4 will include families in the target market. The street-facing units will be accessible through a private interior courtyard. They will offer up to three sleeping areas, ample storage, on-site parking, and safe play areas for children.

Resident Profile

The 70 Phase 1 rental units were quickly snapped up and have been fully occupied ever since. The average age of tenants is 31 years (with a range of 20 to 83 years) and their average household income is $40,400 (with a range of $9,600 to $200,000). They are predominantly white, but Hispanics and Native Americans are represented in substantial numbers. White-collar professionals dominate the occupational mix, but there are many blue-collar workers as well as a few students and retired people. They tend to be well educated. Renter households are almost exclusively single persons or couples without children.

As of late 2004, more than 200 applicants were waitlisted for the first 54 for-sale units. This was accomplished with very little marketing, involving ads only in business and art journals, theater programs, and alternative weeklies. According to the broker, the Campus buyers are

- young professionals;
- single women entering the housing market for the first time;
- gays and lesbians seeking a diverse, interesting environment;
- 35- to 40-year-olds who are divorcing or returning to school or whose children are leaving home;
- downsizing baby boomers;
- seniors seeking accessibility to medical facilities and other amenities; and
- households relocating from other urban areas.

Experience Gained

- Creation of a new urbanist, form-based development code for the broader EDO neighborhood earlier in the Campus's development process would have greatly helped the implementation of the project. Having such a plan in place would have avoided the repeated need to seek rezoning relief from a suburban style development code. Also, it would have accelerated other redevelopment initiatives along the Broadway and Central corridors.
- Public officials come and go during the course of a multiphase project like the Campus, and the political winds can shift. Therefore, when entering public/private partnerships, developers should seek contract provisions that limit the discretion of public officials to make decisions related to the project.
- Authentically open and collaborative planning and approval processes are needed to gain public support for an infill development. But expect some neighbor-

hood resistance even then.

- According to the designer, the up-front creation of an owner/architect/contractor team was a major factor in the project's success because it allowed for continuous feedback regarding design, pricing, and economic constraints. Also critical was the early production of a good set of as-built drawings that indicated what was economically feasible at every stage of the process. These drawings became the foundation for a comprehensive set of construction documents, which led to a fixed-price contract between the owner and the contractor.
- The success of the Campus at Albuquerque High illustrates an important rule: Catalytic main street projects require leadership on the part of the developer and collaboration on the part of the public sector, as well as a clear vision but a flexible attitude on how to get there. Participants in the development process must have patience, endurance, and thick skins.
- Infill urban village development is residentially driven. Developers can find a strong base of market support and many possible locations. Robert Dickson believes that one-third to one-half of American households at various stages of life would consider an urban village environment. He also thinks that the project's development approach—new urbanist design, mixed land uses, and strong support for the master-planned redevelopment of the surrounding neighborhood—will work for a large number of the country's functionally and economically obsolete commercial corridors that have the potential of becoming great main streets.
- By attending to the revitalization of the corridors and neighborhoods surrounding their sites, developers can increase the value and absorption rate of their own projects.
- Urban pioneers want, above all, a truly urban diversity in their neighborhoods. A predominantly residential project can include some nonresidential urban amenities, such as the 6,000-square-foot neighborhood grocery planned for the ground floor of the City Market building. However, in most cases a collaborative effort among property owners in urban neighborhoods will be needed to create or resurrect a lively urban village. The EDO neighborhood's master plan catalyzed by the Campus development is a giant step in that direction.

CONTACT INFORMATION

PROJECT WEB SITE
www.abqhigh.com

DEVELOPER
Paradigm & Company
302 Central Avenue SE
Albuquerque, New Mexico 87102
505-243-0132

ARCHITECT
Dekker/Perich/Sabatini
6801 Jefferson NE, Suite 100
Albuquerque, New Mexico 87109
505-761-9700
www.dpsabq.com

GENERAL CONTRACTOR
Richardson & Richardson
4100 Menaul NE, Suite D-2
Albuquerque, New Mexico 87110
505-881-2268
www.richardsonrichardson.com

RESIDENTIAL SALES
Thresholds Realty
312 Central Avenue SE
Albuquerque, New Mexico 87012
505-243-5638
www.thresholdsrealty.com

RESIDENTIAL LEASING/MANAGEMENT
Monarch Properties
301 Central Avenue NE, Suite 400
Albuquerque, New Mexico 87012
505-489-5638

DEVELOPMENT SCHEDULE

Development Agreement Signed:	October 27, 1999
Planning Started:	October 27, 1999
Construction Started:	April 2001
Sales/Leasing Started:	January 2002
Project Completion:	
Phase 1[1]	December 2002
Phase 2[2]	June 2004
Phase 3[3]	March 2005
Phase 4[4]	2006

1. *Includes 70 rental housing units in two historic buildings and a city-owned parking garage that includes 8,200 square feet of office space.*
2. *Includes 56 for-sale housing units in four new buildings and 6,000 square feet of shell space for a grocery store.*
3. *Includes 54 for-sale housing units.*
4. *Includes 124 rental housing units in a new building and 10,000 square feet of office space.*

LAND USE INFORMATION

Buildings:	10 plus parking garage
Site Area:	7.6 acres[1]
Dwelling Units:	304
Residential Density:	40 units per gross acre
Parking:	
Spaces	261 (garage) plus 126 (street)
Parking Ratio	1.3 spaces per housing unit

1. *Includes an outlot; the area of the original high-school campus was 7.26 acres.*

LAND USE PLAN

	ACRES	PERCENT OF SITE
Residential	4.14	52%
Office	.15	2
Roads and Parking	1.75	24
Open Space	1.56	22

RESIDENTIAL AND COMMERCIAL USES

	BUILDING SQUARE FOOTAGE	
	GROSS	NET
RESIDENTIAL	246,904	195,784
Old Main	50,000	34,500
Classroom	25,000	17,000
Gym	68,000	48,700
Manual Arts	30,000	24,000
Arno Lofts	21,300	21,300
Copper Lofts	10,872	10,872
Campus Lofts	21,284	21,284
City Market	20,448	18,128
OFFICE	18,200	18,200
RETAIL/RESTAURANT	16,000[1]	16,000[1]
TOTAL	281,104	229,984

1. *Grocery (6,000 square feet) and restaurant (10,000 square feet) uses located within residential buildings.*

DEMOGRAPHIC PROFILE

	PERCENT OF ALL HOUSEHOLDS	
	PHASE 1 RENTERS	PHASE 2 BUYERS
AGE RANGE		
18–24	30 %	—
25–34	55	—
35–44	2	—
45–54	7	—
55–64	3	—
65+	3	—
HOUSEHOLD SIZE		
1 Person	70	50 %
2 Persons	30	50
GENDER (SINGLE-PERSON HOUSEHOLDS)		
Male	65	45
Female	35	55

RESIDENTIAL UNIT INFORMATION

	SIZE RANGE (SQUARE FEET)	NUMBER OF UNITS		INITIAL MONTHLY RENT RANGE	INITIAL SALE PRICE RANGE
		PLANNED	BUILT[1]		
PHASE 1 RENTALS					
1 Bath	485– 1,100	67	67	$500–$1,110	—
1½ Baths	1,150–1,329	3	3	1,150– 1,300	—
PHASES 2 AND 3 CONDOMINIUMS					
1 Bath	600– 1,100	71	24	—	$88,700–$176,000
2 Baths	1,163–1,895	39	16	—	164,000– 341,000

1. *As of mid-2004. All planned units in Phases 2 and 3 expected to be built as of spring 2005.*

DEVELOPMENT COST INFORMATION

PHASE 1	
Construction Cost	$4,945,820
Soft Costs	1,398,160
TOTAL	6,343,980

PHASE 2	
Land Acquisition	844,000
Construction Cost	6,750,000
Soft Costs	1,267,670
TOTAL	8,861,670

OTHER COSTS	
Phase 3 Development[1]	7,035,500
Phase 4 Development[1]	10,000,000
Library Building Development	1,600,000
TOTAL DEVELOPMENT COST	$33,841,150

1. *Estimated costs.*

The Edge Lofts

PORTLAND, OREGON

SIGNIFICANT FEATURES

■ "Edgy" location adjacent to freeway

■ New construction on an infill, brownfield site

■ Major retail anchor tenant

■ Residential floors clad in distinctive steel-and-glass curtain wall

The Edge Lofts is an 11-story building with residential condominiums on the top seven stories, four levels of parking, a vertical anchor retail tenant and other ground-floor retail space. It is located on the northwestern edge of the Pearl District in downtown Portland, a 260-acre district containing a mix of residential, commercial, retail, industrial, and institutional land uses.

John Carroll, the developer, purchased the property in December 2000 with the idea of developing an office building, but he soon shelved that idea because the high-tech office market had begun to nosedive. Carroll Aspen LLC, the property owner, was in a position to hold onto the property until the market changed or another opportunity presented itself. In 2002, Carroll heard that Recreational Equipment Inc. (REI), a specialty outdoor gear and clothing retailer, was searching for a location in downtown Portland for one of its first vertical retail models. REI was drawn to the Pearl District by its resident population and daytime employee population and its access to public transportation. Specifically, the strategic location of the Edge site could offer REI adjacent structured parking and freeway exposure for signage.

The developer's willingness to accommodate REI's program and accelerated schedule and to switch from commercial uses to residential uses for the floors above the retail space clinched the deal. REI signed a 15-year lease and moved into its 35,500-square-foot store a mere 16 months after groundbreaking.

The residential component was completed in June 2004; the last unit sold in October 2004. The 123 units range from 842 to 2,454 square feet. Sale prices ranged from $184,000 for the smallest apartments to $920,000 for the most desirable terrace penthouse.

Site and Surroundings

High-end design and fringe location have attracted young professionals to The Edge's one- and two-bedroom lofts, which were developed above a four-story REI outdoor gear and clothing store.

The Edge Lofts building is located between Northwest 14th and 15th Avenues and Kearney and Johnson Streets and, except for sidewalks, street trees, and parking-lot driveways, it occupies the entire city block, which is just shy of an acre. At the time of purchase, a surface-parking lot and an inactive Pacific Galvanizing plant occupied the site. The industrial use had created minimal site pollution, which was quickly mitigated during site preparation.

Just beyond 15th Avenue to the west lies the I-405 freeway. Before the Edge was developed, a 24-hour towing operation and a sizable homeless population shared the street below the freeway. This side of the block has been transformed into a well-

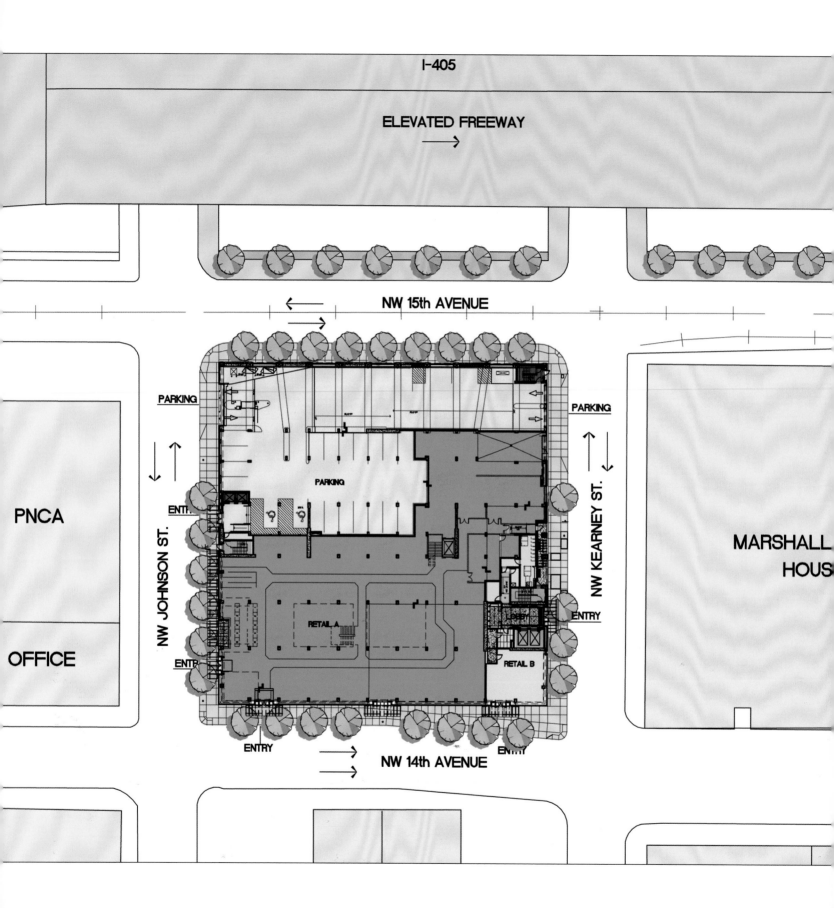

I-405

ELEVATED FREEWAY
→

NW 15th AVENUE
←

PARKING

PARKING

PNCA

NW JOHNSON ST.

PARKING

NW KEARNEY ST.

MARSHALL

HOUS

OFFICE

ENTRY

RETAIL A

ENTRY

RETAIL B

ENTRY

ENTRY

ENTRY

ENTRY

NW 14th AVENUE
→
→

lighted, fenced, and safe border, due in large part to Carroll's efforts to relocate the towing operation, which moved several blocks north, and to assist the homeless in relocating to shelters or finding alternative outdoor accommodations.

The Marshall-Wells Lofts, a seven-story former warehouse converted to residences, occupies a full city block across Kearney Street to the north. Across 14th Avenue to the east are several low-rise cinder-block industrial and warehouse buildings. A self-storage facility, the Pacific Northwest College of Art, and the certified historic American Chicle Building line the south side of Johnson Street across from the Edge.

The north and south routes of the new Portland streetcar system run on 10th and 11th Avenues three blocks from the Edge. The Pearl District is designated a no-fare zone for streetcar riders traveling to or from downtown.

Among the many urban amenities located within three blocks of the Edge are a 24-hour fitness facility; Jamison Square, a public park featuring interactive fountains; a number of art galleries; and a number of restaurants and retail shops, including convenience stores. Currently, the closest major supermarket—Whole Foods—is eight blocks away on the streetcar route, but the development of a supermarket has been proposed for the neighborhood.

Development Process and Financing

When this project was being planned, Carroll had already developed more residential loft units in the Pearl than had any other developer, including:

Chown Pella Lofts—renovation of a historic six-story building; 68 residential units; six commercial/retail spaces; 1996 completion.

McKenzie Lofts—new six-story building; 68 residential units; seven commercial/retail spaces; 1997 completion.

The Gregory—new 12-story building; 133 residential units; four stories of commercial/retail space and parking; 2001 completion.

The Elizabeth—new 16-story building; 182 residential units; 8,000-square-foot public plaza; 10,000-plus

square feet of retail and parking; scheduled May 2005 completion.

The Edge Lofts, however, differs from these earlier projects in several ways. These differences include its less desirable "edge of the Pearl" location adjacent to the freeway; the REI deal, which accelerated the project's design and construction schedule considerably; its use of a curtain wall system to project a sleek, modern, and decidedly nonresidential appearance; and subtle variations in the marketing approach.

REI wanted early occupancy. Planning on the project commenced in February and design work in May 2002. The building broke ground in September and the developer's sales and leasing program was underway by December 2002. Phase 1 construction, including REI's space, was completed in February 2004 and the entire project was ready for occupancy by June of that year.

Financing for the construction loan was provided through Bank One. The balance of the project's financing came from the Aspen Group, a consortium of six private investors with whom Carroll had partnered in the past. REI's ambitious schedule had put the project on a fast track. In the developer's view, fast-tracking necessitated timely decision making, which would be easier with private investors than with an institutional lender.

Planning and Design

The primary factors that determined the project's orientation on the site and the placement of program elements within the building were view potentials, proximity to the freeway, vehicular and pedestrian circulation, existing uses on bordering streets, and the need for dedicated parking for various uses. The residential component is designed to minimize freeway noise and maximize views of the scenic western hills and Forest Park beyond. The retail and parking components are designed to facilitate vehicular circulation and take advantage of heavy foot traffic at the southeast corner of 14th and Johnson. In effect, the design divides the building into two sections—floors 1 to 4 comprising the retail and parking components and floors 5 through 11 comprising the residential component.

Covering the entire block, the four-story base is faced with cast-in-place concrete embellished with

Site plan.

stainless-steel mesh and subtle sculptural elements, except for the walls enclosing the REI space and retail space next to the residential entrance on Kearney, which are windowed. A two-story wall of glass marks REI's entrance at the high-foot-traffic southeast corner, through which is clearly visible a 20-foot-high climbing wall that makes the store hard to miss.

A below-grade level includes 132 parking stalls dedicated for resident use—one stall per typical unit and two stalls per terrace-level and larger corner unit. Residents enter and exit the garage through Kearney Street. A 124-stall parking area dedicated for REI use is located on the first through third levels and a 94-stall area on the fourth level handles daily and monthly commercial parking as well as occasional overflow REI parking needs. The nonresidential parking is accessed from Johnson Street. The total 350 stalls include ten spaces for handicapped parking as required by code.

The residential portion of the building steps back from the western perimeter of the base structure by nearly 80 feet, creating a physical and psychological distance from the noisy freeway. The layouts of floors 5 through 10 are identical, except for the addition of terraces on fifth-floor units facing west. Each of these floors contains 19 units, with one of the units on the fifth floor having been converted to a meeting space/party room, including a kitchen, for residents. On floor 11 there are ten premium "penthouse" units, all with terraces.

Most of the units are oriented to the east or west along the long sides of the residential portion of the building. Corner units enjoy ampler views. Only one noncorner unit faces fully south and no units face directly north, because the Marshall-Wells building blocks views in that direction.

Unit sizes were dictated by the size of the residential tower's column bays—approximately 18 feet wide by 27 to 30 feet deep. All typical noncorner units are 18 feet wide. Their depths vary depending on the side of the building on which they are located. Building core and circulation elements dictated irregular shapes for the corner units, which are 36 feet wide at their widest points. Terrace units are at least 36 feet wide by 54 feet deep, excluding the outside terrace.

The residential corridors, at roughly 160 feet, are long, but certain design elements—six-foot widths, 9.5-foot-wide alcoves at each unit's front door, decorative soffits to break up the ceiling, and creatively applied colors and creative signage and lighting—work to mitigate their potential resemblance to airplane aisles. Positive air pressure helps keep corridors odor-free.

The glass-and-steel curtain wall on the floors rising above the concrete, stainless-steel, and glass four-story base gives Edge Lofts a distinctive—yes, edgy—look. This look became one of the project's most compelling marketing devices. Although the building's exterior has received much favorable comment, the curtain wall was not devised solely to be admired from the exterior. Its more important function is to provide wall-to-wall and floor-to-ceiling glass that lets natural light into the long, narrow units and capitalizes on the extraordinary views to the west, east, and south.

The quality and modern European styling of the interior finishes also appeal to the market. The developer kept choices to a minimum in order to avoid the scheduling and budget problems involved in "customizing" production units. The customization philosophy was to provide buyers with a small but solid selection of good-value options, giving them the feeling that they have some autonomy in the process.

Birch hardwood floors were standard. The standard stainless-steel kitchen countertops could be upgraded to stone, with several granite options. Two wood kitchen cabinet options were available. The standard stone bathroom vanity could be upgraded to glass. Several types of bathroom flooring were available, as were several colors of window shades. Floor plan permitting, buyers could choose glass and wood partitioning for the bedroom and the design left ample opportunities for adding other room dividers and custom closets, especially in the laundry rooms. The inclusion of a liberal number of junction boxes in the ceilings allowed residents to customize their lighting solutions.

The small kitchens on floors 5 through 10 were designed for people who eat out more often than they eat in. They feature stainless-steel appliances, including a small two-foot by two-foot refrigerator above a small freezer, and only limited cabinet space.

Top left: Most of the residential units are oriented to the east and west to take advantage of the best views.

Top right: REI's entry points and access to dedicated retail parking are located on the south side of the building.

Bottom: The residential entrance (left) and lobby (right) are on the north, as is access to residential parking, which is located below grade.

By virtue of its location
adjacent to a freeway, the
project could afford to
offer higher-end finishes
and more space at com-
petitive prices.

Target Market and Resident Profile

The developer hired a market research firm to analyze Portland's housing market in relation to three current condominium projects—the Edge, the Elizabeth (also in the Pearl District), and Eliot Tower (a 223-unit high-rise building being planned for downtown Portland). The news was encouraging:

■ Portland's condominium market is strong, with new projects preselling 50 to 70 percent of their units.

■ Prices are more than three times higher than the regional average on a square-foot basis.

■ Property appreciation is 6 percent annually.

The market study confirmed the developer's belief that the most viable market segments for the Edge would be young single and married professionals, residents of earlier Carroll Aspen buildings (who tend to follow the developer from project to project), and, to a smaller degree, downsizing empty nesters. With a young target market in mind, the developer limited the number of larger units to 28 out of 123—18 two-bedroom units and ten large open-floor-plan penthouse units.

The developer and Debbie Thomas Real Estate, the firm that has exclusively marketed Carroll's last six residential projects in Portland, have evolved a process for identifying a market that is both instinctive and knowledge-based. Debbie Thomas explains: "When we look at a location, we talk to the people we think might be our target market, the general public, and other sales offices. From this we get a pretty good sense of current and projected trends. The next step is to take a careful look at what the competition is offering and who is buying from them."

The location of the Edge site, according to Thomas, "was somewhat pioneering, but Marshall-Wells Lofts had proven that residential development near the freeway was a safe enough bet. Not taking anything for granted, we questioned why and discovered that product and pricing trumped living next to a freeway. This insight gave us the information we needed to design the Edge to meet the target market's expectations in terms of aesthetics, functionality, and affordability."

The buyer profile at the Edge has proved to be fairly close to the developer's target market for the project, although more older buyers than expected purchased the one-bedroom units. Buyers are

■ predominantly younger than 40 (60 percent)—another 20 percent are between 40 and 50 and the remaining 20 percent are over 50;

■ almost exclusively single-person (59 percent) or two-person (39 percent) households;

■ fairly evenly divided as to the location of their previous residence—31 percent from the Portland suburbs, 15 percent from Portland's urban areas, 25 percent from elsewhere in the Pearl District, and 29 percent from out of state;

■ mostly upsizing (54 percent), but with a significant share (46 percent) downsizing; and

■ overwhelmingly former homeowners (85 percent)—almost evenly divided among owners of condominiums (42 percent) and owners of single-family houses (43 percent).

Marketing

Before the start of construction, the developer set up a sales office in the McKenzie Lofts building, which is five blocks away. Early prospects were able to view kitchen and bathroom mockups and sample boards containing finish materials. The interior design firm, Soderberg Laman, trained the sales staff to be conversant about the finishes being offered under the developer's customization program. A Soderberg Laman representative met with contracted buyers ready to make finish selections.

The sales process accelerated when the developer was able to make model units available for viewing in the Edge. In the first two months after the model apartments were opened, more than 20 units were sold—one-sixth of the total. The model units were a tremendous selling point for people with no prior experience with loft living. In fact, a number of buyers wanted to purchase fully furnished models. At least five model units were sold, causing the marketing team to scramble to furnish other units for use as models.

Unit pricing was a major marketing consideration. In this respect, the Edge Lofts had an edge over the competition because, by virtue of its fringe, freeway-impacted location, it could offer higher-end finishes and more space for slightly less money.

Going from the lowest to highest floor, identical units went up in price by approximately $5,000 to $8,000 per floor. Pricing priorities, going from the least expensive to the most expensive units, were as follows:

- #1—floor 5, noncorner units, east side;
- #2—floors 6 through 10, noncorner units, west side;
- #3—floors 6 through 10, noncorner units, east side;
- #4—floor 5, noncorner terrace units, west side;
- #5—floors 5 through 10, corner units; corner units were priced according to their orientation, with the southeast corner considered first in desirability followed by the southwest corner in second place, the northeast in third, and the northwest last; and
- #6—floor 11 penthouse terrace units.

Typical noncorner units on the east side ranging from 1,014 to 1,042 square feet were priced at $230,000 to $340,000. Smaller noncorner units facing west and ranging from 836 to 847 square feet started at $184,000 and went up to $256,000. Of the Edge's 123 total units, 42 are east-facing noncorner units and 41 are smaller, west-facing noncorner units.

Thomas explains the design and pricing strategy: "We love small, efficiently laid-out apartments where no one really looks at the price per square foot, because the units are priced under $250,000, which is the magic number with our target market. We typically do a full pricing exercise and then artificially reduce prices on certain units on lower floors to jump-start sales."

Sales have been brisk. The preconstruction sales office opened in December 2002, and within 90 days 35 percent of the units had signed sales contracts. A year later, 75 percent had been sold. At the end of June 2004, only ten units remained unsold—three of which were larger, more expensive corner units located on the northwest corner, which offers slightly compromised views. By October, all units had sold.

The marketing campaign included media advertisements—in *The Oregonian,* the daily newspaper; *Portland Monthly,* a lifestyle magazine; *Oregon Home; Just Out,* a publication aimed at the local gay population; the *Northwest Examiner;* and the in-flight magazine of Alaska Airlines—a flashy, interactive Web site (www. edgelofts. com) at which prospects could arrange selected furniture in any of the units, a direct-mail campaign, and signs on the building.

Experience Gained

- Developers need to understand who buys their products—in this case condominiums in downtown Portland—and what they want. And then they should diversify to meet demand, even if the changes they make are subtle. Carroll is programming and designing the Eliot Tower condominium project somewhat differently than the Edge to attract the different demographic that makes up the potential market for the newer project.
- Having a core team that has worked together for many years can be key to development success. The development of the Edge Lofts required an extraordinarily strong team effort because of the accelerated construction schedule. In this case, the two architectural firms were the new members of a team—developer, contractor, interior designer, and marketer—that had worked together on a number of similar projects.
- People attracted to loft style living may still prefer some division of their space. When the loft sales were being made from floor plans rather than models, the units with kitchens running parallel to the window wall and forming a natural divider were easier to sell than units with kitchens running perpendicular; and optional room dividers were popular. After the models were set up, buyers opted in equal measure for truly open layouts and layouts with more dividers.
- Although the standard small LG refrigerator/freezer model selected was thought to suit the target market for the Edge because they eat out more than in, it may be too small to be practical for residents who tend not to grocery-shop daily.
- Window treatments should be standardized in mid- or high-rise projects, because it gives them a uniform look. Left to their own devices, residents may choose incongruous window treatments.

The ten premium penthouse units feature terraces.

CONTACT INFORMATION

PROJECT WEB SITE

www.edgelofts.com

DEVELOPER

Carroll Investments, LLC

420 NW 11th Avenue, #1004

Portland, Oregon 97209

503-228-7276

ARCHITECTS

GBD Architects

1120 NW Couch Street, Suite 300

Portland, Oregon 97209

503-224-9656

www.gbdarchitects.com

Holst Architecture PC

537 SE Ash, Studio 42

Portland, Oregon 97214

503-233-9856

www.holstarc.com

GENERAL CONTRACTOR

Howard S. Wright Construction Company

425 NW 10th Avenue, Suite 200

Portland, Oregon 97209

503-220-0895

www.hswcc.com

INTERIOR DESIGNER

Soderberg Laman Designers

1100 NW Glisan, Suite 2C

Portland, Oregon 97209

503-227-2505

www.soderberglamen.com

SALES AND MARKETING

Debbie Thomas Real Estate

402 NW 13th Avenue

Portland, Oregon 97209

503-226-2141

www.debbiethomas.com

DEVELOPMENT SCHEDULE

Site Purchased:	December 2000
Planning Started:	February 2002
Construction Started:	September 2002
Sales Started:	December 2002
Initial Occupancy:	February 2004
Housing Units Completed:	June 2004

LAND USE INFORMATION

Site Area:	.9 acre
Dwelling Units:	123
Residential Density:	134 units per gross acre
Parking Ratio:	1.1 spaces per unit

LAND USE PLAN

	PERCENT OF SITE
Residential	44 %
Retail	12
Parking	44

DEMOGRAPHIC PROFILE

	PERCENT OF ALL HOUSEHOLDS
AGE RANGE	
20–30	24 %
30–40	36
40–50	20
50–60	16
60–70	4
HOUSEHOLD SIZE	
1 Person	59 %
2 Persons	39
4+ Persons	2
MOVED TO THE EDGE FROM . . .	
Pearl District	25 %
Portland Metro Urban Area	15
Portland Suburban Area	31
Out of State	29
REASON FOR BUYING	
Location of Neighborhood	40
Want More Space	13
Relocating to Oregon	20
To Own Residence	12
High Quality of Edge Lofts	5
Not Primary Residence	10

| UNIT TYPE | SIZE RANGE (SQUARE FEET) | NUMBER OF UNITS | | INITIAL SALE PRICE RANGE |
		BUILT	SOLD	
1 Bedroom/1 Bath	842–1,041	89	89	$184,000–$340,000
1 Bedroom/1 Bath (Corner)	1,120	6	6	270,000– 365,000
2 Bedrooms/2 Baths	1,430–1,700	18	18	382,000– 582,000
Penthouse	1,440–2,454	10	10	486,000– 920,000

DEVELOPMENT COST INFORMATION

SITE ACQUISITION	$3,065,000
SITE IMPROVEMENT COST	1,048,000

CONSTRUCTION COSTS

Superstructure	7,222,000
HVAC/ Elevators	1,838,000
Electrical	2,308,000
Plumbling/Sprinklers	1,568,000
Finishes	8,373,000
Interior Walls	2,305,000
Fees/General Conditions	2,803,000
Exterior Glass	3,126,000
TOTAL	29,543,000

SOFT COSTS

Architecture/Engineering	$2,008,000
Permits	687,000
Marketing	882,000
Legal/Accounting	246,000
Taxes/Insurance	324,000
Financing Costs	1,023,000
Other	1,255,000
TOTAL	6,425,000

TOTAL DEVELOPMENT COST	$40,081,000
Construction Cost per Square Foot	84

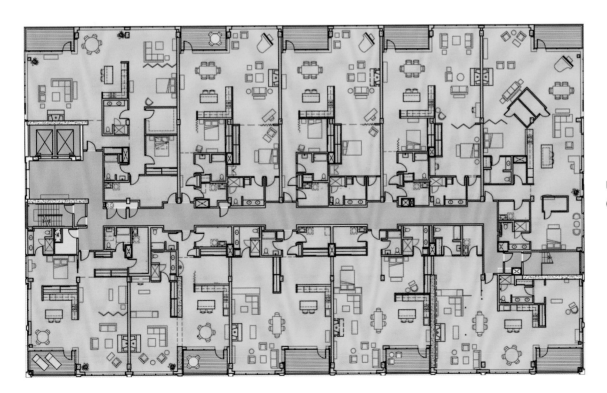

Floor plan for the 11th (penthouse) story.

Fall Creek Place

INDIANAPOLIS, INDIANA

SIGNIFICANT FEATURES

■ Public/private redevelopment of an inner-city neighborhood

■ 51/49 mix of affordable and market-rate housing

■ New housing interspersed with rehabilitated historic houses

■ Marketing focus on first-time homebuyers

An innovative public/private endeavor has transformed Fall Creek Place—once a crime-ridden, deteriorating inner-city neighborhood in Indianapolis with many vacant lots and a waning population—into an attractive, mixed-income residential neighborhood. The city of Indianapolis's use of a U.S. Department of Housing and Urban Development (HUD) grant for land assembly as well as other subsidies and incentives provided solid footing for Mansur Real Estate Services to build and market 369 new residences (307 detached houses, 53 townhouses, and nine live/work units) in the 26-block site and for nonprofit partners to stabilize or restore 58 historic houses.

As part of HUD's grant requirements for the project, 51 percent of the residences are reserved for low- and moderate-income households earning 80 percent or less of the area median income. The remaining housing units are being sold at market rates. In Indianapolis, the income threshold for low- to moderate-income households ranges from $35,900 for a one-person household to $51,300 for a four-person household.

Site and Surroundings

Located on the near north side of Indianapolis two miles from downtown, the Fall Creek neighborhood covers 26 blocks (160 acres). Before the current redevelopment effort, its history dating back to the 1950s was one of poverty and neglect. The neighborhood lost nearly 80 percent of its housing stock between 1956 and 1999. In 1999, only about 90 houses were owner-occupied. The Fall Creek Place site is bounded by Fall Creek Parkway on the north, Pennsylvania Street on the west, East 22nd Street on the south, and Park Avenue on the east.

The revitalization of the surrounding residential neighborhoods started in the 1980s with successful efforts to bring new life into downtown that subsequently spread to Herron Morton Place, a historic district just south of Fall Creek Place. In the mid-1990s, the redevelopment of this district took off with the widespread rehabilitation of its stock of large, historic houses. The other neighborhoods adjacent to Fall Creek Place face challenges similar to those faced by Fall Creek Place prior to its redevelopment and offer great potential for rehabilitation. These currently undervalued neighborhoods stand poised to benefit from the success of the Fall Creek Place development.

Fall Creek Place lies close to the Monon Greenway, a rails-to-trails preserve that stretches 10.5 miles through the city—and one of Indianapolis's newest civic treasures.

An aerial view of Fall Creek Place, a new urbanist, mixed-income neighborhood located less than two miles from downtown Indianapolis.

Master plan.

Opposite top: Aimed at first-time homebuyers, the marketing strategy included model homes (depicted here), as well as direct mailings to downtown renters, special events, a project Web page, and a welcome center.

Opposite bottom: A range of housing options and homebuyer financial assistance have attracted a diverse resident population, including many single professionals.

Building Legend

- Existing Business
- Multi-Family
- Existing Residential
- Existing Residential Rehabilitation
- Proposed Commercial/ Multi-Family
- Public
- Proposed Residential

A planned Fall Creek Trail will connect Fall Creek Place to the greenway.

Development Process

The redevelopment of the neighborhood was launched with the help of a $4 million homeownership zone (HOZ) grant from the U.S. Department of Housing and Urban Development that was awarded to the city of Indianapolis in 1998. The HOZ program is designed to support the construction of housing in blighted urban areas. The $4 million grant was made to help fund a redevelopment effort undertaken by a partnership between the city of Indianapolis and the King Park Area Development Corporation.

Upon the award of the grant, the city initiated a year-long master-planning and urban design effort, the goal of which was to reinvent the blighted Fall Creek neighborhood as a diverse, mixed-income community providing a range of housing choices. The city determined that its role would be to provide necessary infrastructure and offer incentives to lay the groundwork for the project. It hoped that its preparatory efforts to remove many of the barriers to the redevelopment of this area would suffice to attract builders and homebuyers in a range of incomes. The city would let the private sector assume many of the traditional development responsibilities for the project—including residential construction, construction financing, marketing, and sales.

The HUD grant was used primarily for property acquisition and the relocation of residents who had been living in substandard rental housing. Federal community development block grant funds and HUD home investment partnership program (HOME) funds were allocated by the city to provide income-qualified homebuyers with down-payment assistance.

The city also committed $10 million—funded with a bond approved by the city/county council in 2001—to finance infrastructure improvements, including new streets, curbs, sidewalks, alleys, street lighting, and landscaping. The city's infrastructure investment also included providing water and sewer connections for each lot, which helped to keep housing prices affordable. Committed to providing fully buildable homesites, the city also underwrote the cost of removing subsur-

Top left: Fifty-eight historic houses, such as this
19th-century Queen Anne
house, will be renovated
as part of the HOZ (home-
ownership zone) redevel-
opment.

Top right: Attached town-
houses make up about 15
percent of the new resi-
dences.

Bottom left: New infill
construction reflects the
character of existing
houses, while updated
curbs and sidewalks make
the neighborhood more
pedestrian friendly.

Bottom right: Market-rate
and affordable houses are
built side by side, and the
differences are generally
indistinguishable from the
street.

face debris from lots on which basements of formerly demolished housing units were found.

In 2000, the city selected Mansur Real Estate Services, a local company specializing in urban development, to be the project developer. As such, Mansur was responsible for overseeing the implementation of the Fall Creek Place master plan and coordinating the selection process for builders. Mansur worked with a project team that included the city and the King Park Area Development Corporation. Mansur structured the project management to resemble the management of a conventional subdivision development—including model homes, lot purchases, multiple builders, and multiple buying choices. But rather than merely selling lots to individual builders as many conventional subdivisions do, the developer focused the team's marketing efforts on attracting first-time homebuyers to the development.

The project also includes the stabilization or renovation of 58 historic houses in the Fall Creek neighborhood, which is being implemented by the King Park Area Development Corporation and the Historic Landmarks Foundation of Indiana.

Financing

Fall Creek Place involves financial assistance to both builders and buyers.

Eight builders were selected to construct housing on the site, a number that has since decreased to five. To provide equal opportunity to builders large and small, the project team gave each builder sufficient funding to construct one model home and worked with local banks to secure a line of credit for each builder.

Homebuyer financial assistance involves below-market-rate mortgages and down-payment assistance, as well as property tax abatements. A process was established under which six local banks offer below-market-rate mortgages (generally one percentage point below conventional loan rates). The lender provides interested applicants a preapproval letter that indicates the loan amount for which the buyer qualifies and states the total city down-payment grant amount the buyer may obtain based on household income. With a preapproval commitment, buyers are permitted to reserve a lot, choose a builder, and choose a house.

The city assists below-market-rate homebuyers with their down payment. Income-qualified households are eligible for up to $24,000 in down-payment assistance. In 2004, the income limits are as follows:

- $35,900 for a one-person household;
- $41,000 for a two-person household;
- $46,150 for a three-person household;
- $51,300 for a four-person household; and
- $55,400 for a five-person household.

The covenants on below-market-rate units state that buyers must use their house as their primary residence for at least five years. Buyers who receive down-payment assistance are further restricted. Down-payment assistance is financed as a soft second mortgage, which is paid back after five to ten years. Buyers who sell before year six must give back their entire down-payment grant; those who sell between years six and ten must give back some of their grant. Additionally, buyers who received grants and sell before year ten must sell to a qualified low- or moderate-income buyer.

At the start of the project, buyers of market-rate units were offered matching down-payment assistance of up to $10,000. Intended to stimulate interest in Fall Creek Place, this incentive was offered for only six months.

All homebuyers with building permits issued before December 31, 2002 are eligible for a five-year property tax abatement of 100 percent on the first $36,000 of assessed valuation—for an average annual savings of about $1,300 (in 2002).

The three homebuying incentives combined—lower-rate mortgages, down-payment assistance, and property tax abatement—enable a household that ordinarily would qualify for a $100,000 house to afford a $140,000 house. For income-qualified households, the choice of type of unit is limited only by what is affordable. Financial incentives have been highly successful in attracting low- and moderate-income households as well as market-rate buyers to Fall Creek Place.

Design and Architecture

Three high-priority goals influenced the project's design and architecture. The developer sought to

- respect the neighborhood's historic character;
- make the units allocated for low- and moderate-

All Fall Creek residents
live within four blocks of
a public park and only
steps from the Monon and
Fall Creek pedestrian
and bicycle trails that connect to the extensive Indy
Greenways.

income households indistinguishable from the market-rate units; and

■ construct a well-designed neighborhood that is affordable to homebuyers in a wide range of incomes.

Mansur, the Historic Landmarks Foundation of Indiana, and the city of Indianapolis worked together to formulate guidelines for the design and appearance of new houses in Fall Creek Place. These architectural guidelines emphasize scale, proportions, orientation, and elevation. The project's design rules are inspired by the styles of housing once characteristic of the neighborhood, but modified to fit into today's urban fabric.

Rottmann Architects, a local firm, worked with Mansur to design five model homes meeting the criteria. Builders may use a model-home design or their own designs as long as they respect the design guidelines. A design review committee that includes representatives from Mansur, the city, and the project's architect must approve each house plan before it can receive a building permit from the city.

Consistent with a new urbanist style, such features as a detached, rear-entry garage with access through an alley; double-hung windows; and deep front porches are typically required. The master plan preserves the original street grid in order to retain the neighborhood's urban character. The rehabilitation of many of the larger historic houses within the neighborhood has helped maintain its historic character. Lot sizes and setbacks for all new houses are uniform. New streetlights resembling antique lighting and brick crosswalks have been installed.

Affordable and market-rate houses are generally indistinguishable, differing only in size and interior detail. Nearly all affordable houses are built on crawlspaces, while nearly all market-rate houses are built on basements. The interiors of the affordable houses are fairly basic. The market-rate houses are characterized by higher-end cabinetry, flooring, tiling, and trim. Exterior vinyl trim is allowed in all the units to make them more affordable, but it has to be smooth and tucked behind the wood window trim.

Marketing and Resident Profile

The target market for an urban mixed-income housing project is broad and can be difficult to identify. The downtown Indianapolis housing market was strong, but offered very little affordable detached housing for sale. To attract first-time buyers and low- to moderate-income buyers, the developer knew Fall Creek place would have to offer a wide mix of housing types and price points, as well as financial incentives. Suspecting that most buyers would be downtown Indianapolis residents, Mansur direct-mailed marketing materials to local renters.

The project has attracted a diverse resident population much more quickly than had been anticipated. Market studies had estimated that 40 units would be absorbed in the first year. However, in the first 12 months more than 200 new houses were under contract. More than half of the buyers already lived downtown or near downtown and 60 percent are first-time homebuyers. Most buyers are single professionals (65 percent), followed by couples without children (20 percent), single parents (9 percent), and married couples with children (6 percent). Many buyers are gay. Fall Creek Place residents are racially diverse, with 75 percent of households being Caucasian and the remaining 25 percent being African American, Hispanic, Asian, or Native American.

The allocation of lots to low- and moderate-income buyers has been a challenge for the developer. Only one out of every ten low- or moderate-income prospects who are referred to participating banks for preapproval is likely to actually become a buyer. Six out of ten prospects do not get preapproved for financial/credit reasons, while three of the four who get approved do not like any of the remaining lots.

Fall Creek Place has had no problems with mixing affordable and market-rate housing. Side-by-side houses may differ in price by $100,000, but their designs are compatible and their occupants appear to get along well as neighbors.

The project's marketing program, which is managed by Mansur, received $250,000 in seed money from the city of Indianapolis. To help fund the project's umbrella marketing program, builders pay a 1.5 percent marketing fee on each house sale—which is included in closing costs—up to a maximum of $2,500.

The marketing program has included the distribution of brochures and flyers, a number of special events publicizing the development, and a project Web page.

The planned live/work lofts shown in this rendering will offer ground-floor storefronts and upstairs residences. Also planned is a neighborhood retail center.

A welcome center, funded in part by a $50,000 donation from Citizens Gas and Coke Utility, provides information on Fall Creek Place, available purchase incentives, available homesites, builders and their model homes, and the homebuying process.

Experience Gained

■ Although it is obvious that the market for homeownership in inner-city Indianapolis was strong, the city had to overcome the reluctance of private sector builders and developers to invest in an undervalued neighborhood. It succeeded in doing this by proposing a public/private partnership in which the city would be committed to standards of design, affordability, land assembly, and neighborhood safety that would reassure the target market, potential developers and builders, and lenders.

■ Community support was essential for the development of Fall Creek Place. The city worked hard to involve members of the community in the planning process and establish public support prior to the start of development. The strong support of the mayor's office played a significant role in establishing the project's credibility with the public.

■ A clearly defined partnership structure that set forth each partner's role contributed to the success of the project. The city provided the necessary public in-

centives to launch the development, find subsidies, and select a private developer. Mansur Real Estate Services managed the development process and oversaw the selected builders. The builders purchased lots and financed the construction of the houses.

■ Fall Creek Place demonstrates that large and small builders can be included in a single development team. The participating builders here include relatively large production homebuilders, relatively small custom-home builders, and several woman-owned and minority-owned companies.

■ The project's financial strategy and its design strategy are each a key element in Fall Creek Place's success as a stable mixed-income community. Below-market-rate mortgages, down-payment assistance, and property tax abatements helped to generate a strong effective demand among low- and moderate-income households. Careful design and planning to make the affordable units indistinguishable from the market-rate units helped avoid the kinds of market and community problems that can arise in developments intermixing market-rate and affordable housing.

CONTACT INFORMATION

PROJECT WEB SITE

www.fallcreekplace.com

DEVELOPERS

Mansur Real Estate Services
700 Market Tower
10 West Market Street
Indianapolis, Indiana 46204
317-464-8200
www.mansurrealestateservices.com

City of Indianapolis
Department of Metropolitan Development
200 East Washington Street
City County Building, Suite 2042
Indianapolis, Indiana 46204
317-327-5861
www.indygov.org/dmd

King Park Area Development Corporation
2430 North Delaware Street
Indianapolis, Indiana 46205
317-924-8116
www.kpadc.org

PLANNERS

Urban Design Associates
Gulf Tower, 31st Floor
707 Grant Street
Pittsburgh, Pennsylvania 15219
412-263-5200
www.urbandesignassociates.com

Schneider Corporation
Historic Fort Benjamin Harrison
8901 Otis Avenue
Indianapolis, Indiana 46216
317-826-7319
www.schneidercorp.com

ARCHITECTS

Rottmann Architects
1060 North Capitol Avenue, Suite C-360
Indianapolis, Indiana 46205
317-767-9807
www.rottmannarchitects.com

Historic Landmarks Foundation of Indiana
(Historic Rehab)
1028 North Delaware Street
Indianapolis, Indiana 46202
317-639-4534
www.historiclandmarks.com

LANDSCAPE ARCHITECT

Kevin K. Parsons and Associates
212 West Tenth Street, Suite A-290
Indianapolis, Indiana 46202
317-955-9155
www.landarkkt.com

SALES AND MARKETING

Hirons and Company
135 South Illinois Street
Indianapolis, Indiana 46225
317-977-2206
www.hirons.com

INFRASTRUCTURE ENGINEERING

Mid-States Engineering LLC
350 East New York Street, Suite 300
Indianapolis, Indiana 46204
317-634-6434
www.mid-stateseng.com

FINANCIAL PARTICIPANTS

U.S. Department of Housing and Urban Development
City of Indianapolis
Indianapolis Bond Bank
Indianapolis Neighborhood Housing Partnership
Fannie Mae
Citizens Gas
Local Initiative Support Corporation
Fund for Landmark Indianapolis Properties
Key Bank
Bank One
National City Bank
National Bank of Indianapolis
Fifth Third Bank
Huntington Bank

FALL CREEK PLACE PROJECT INFORMATION

DEVELOPMENT SCHEDULE

Property Acquisition Started:	fall 1998
Planning Started:	fall 1998
Master Plan Completed:	fall 2000
Financing Completed:	summer 2001
Sales and Marketing Started:	summer 2001
Infrastructure Started:	fall 2001
Housing Construction Started:	fall 2001
Phase 1 Sales Completed:	spring 2002
Phase 2 Sales/Construction Started:	summer 2002
Phases 1/2 Infrastructure Completed:	spring 2003
Phase 3 Infrastructure Started:	summer 2003
Phase 3 Sales/Construction Started:	summer 2003
Phase 1 Housing Completed:	fall 2003
Phase 2 Housing Completed:	winter 2003
Phase 3 Infrastructure Completed:	summer 2004
Estimated Project Completion:	2005

LAND USE INFORMATION

Site Area:	160 acres
Dwelling Units:	
New	369
Stabilized/Restored	58
Residential Density:	
Single Family	8 units per gross acre
Townhouses	13 units per gross acre
Average Lot Size:[1]	5,400 square feet

1. For single-family houses.

NONRESIDENTIAL LAND USES

	SQUARE FEET	
	EXISTING	AT BUILDOUT
Retail	10,000	35,000
Office	5,000	5,000
Live/Work Units	0	38,800
Parks	174,240	174,240

DEMOGRAPHIC PROFILE

	PERCENT OF ALL HOUSEHOLDS
HOUSEHOLD TYPE	
Single Professionals	65%
Couples without Children	20
Single Parents	9
Married Couples with Children	6
RACIAL MIX	
Caucasian	75
Non-Caucasian[1]	25
MOVED TO FALL CREEK FROM . . .	
Downtown or Near Downtown	>50
PRIOR RESIDENCE	
Rented	60
Owned	40

1. Non-Caucasian households include African Americans, Asians, and Native Americans.

DEVELOPMENT COST INFORMATION

SITE ACQUISITION[1]	$9,000,000
SITE IMPROVEMENT COSTS	
Subsurface Debris Removal	3,100,000
General Cleanup/Lot Maintenance	150,000
Earthwork	950,000
General Conditions[2]	1,300,000
Fall Creek Improvements	250,000
Drainage/Storm Improvements	400,000
Sanitary Taps	700,000
Water Laterals and Meter Pits	500,000
Streets and Streetscape[3]	4,750,000
Parks	600,000
Traffic Signal Upgrades/Bus Shelters	100,000
Construction Management Fees	700,000
TOTAL	13,500,000
CONSTRUCTION COSTS	
New Single-Family Houses	55–65 per square foot
Townhouses	52–57 per square foot
Rehabilitated Houses	80,000–165,000 each
Model Homes (for nine models)	1,100,000
On-Site Welcome Center	100,000
SOFT COSTS[4]	
Engineering/Staking/Inspections	1,200,000
Landscape Architect	100,000
Master Architect	95,000
Master Planning/Infrastructure Plan[5]	410,000
Developer Fees	1,600,000
Nonprofit Project Sponsor Fees	330,000
Legal/Accounting	150,000
Title Fees/Survey/Closing Costs	400,000
Marketing	500,000
Appraisals	200,000
TOTAL	4,985,000

1. Includes $5 million in relocation, demolition, and down-payment assistance costs.
2. Includes several design change orders added to the budget after the start of infrastructure construction.
3. Includes street paving, curbs, sidewalks, street lighting, street trees, and decorative pavers and monuments.
4. Costs for overall site development. Soft costs incurred by home-builders or for commercial construction are not included.
5. Includes $110,000 in environmental and geotechnical testing.

RESIDENTIAL UNIT INFORMATION

| UNIT TYPE | SIZE RANGE[1] (SQUARE FEET) | NUMBER OF UNITS | | INITIAL SALE PRICE RANGE[2] |
		BUILT	SOLD	
New Single Family	—	307	221	—
2 Bedrooms	1,265	—	—	$108,000–$162,000
3 Bedrooms	1,620–1,774	—	—	112,000– 240,000
4 Bedrooms	1,995–2,400	—	—	155,000– 260,000
Custom Homes	up to 3,000	—	—	175,000– 330,000
Rehabilitated Single Family	—	58	36	—
Townhouses	1,260–1,640	53	30	104,900– 156,000
Live/Work Units	—	9	0	—

1. Garages, porches, basements, and lofts not includes in square footage; many units have a finished loft and basement and some have finished space above the garage.

2. As of September 2004, 277 new units (not including rehabilitated units) had been sold.

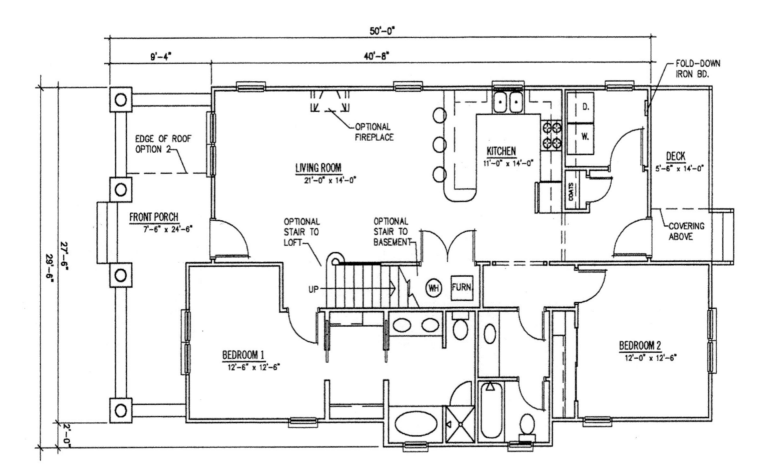

The Belmont single-family plan offers as options a loft, rear deck, basement, and fireplace, as well as full handicapped accessibility.

Front Street at Ladera Ranch

Front Street at Ladera Ranch is a suburban neighborhood in which each residence is designed (and permitted) to include a home office. It is essentially an enclave of home-based businesses—one of the first in the nation—that is more residential than commercial in character. The project's 22 single-family, detached live/work units are more than just houses with a den or second bedroom used as a home office. They are designed to incorporate 450 to 700 square feet of dedicated office space with separate entrances provided for the living and office areas.

Aware of the increasing trend of working from home, DMB Ladera LLC, the developer of Ladera Ranch, a 4,000-acre master-planned community, wanted to suburbanize the concept of live/work housing. Before this project, the only true live/work housing that was being developed in the United States was located in mixed-use, urban neighborhoods and in design it was typically townhouses with commercial space on the first level and living areas on the upper floors. Front Street at Ladera Ranch was an experiment in the development of hybrid houses in which residents could conduct a business in one part of the house and function as a family in the other part. It introduced the concept of live/work housing on a neighborhood scale in a suburban community.

The Front Street houses sold out quickly when they became available in March 2003. Based on this success, DMB Ladera and homebuilder Standard Pacific Homes went back to the drawing board to design a second live/work neighborhood, which is called Banister Street at Ladera Ranch and features hybrid townhouses.

Development Process and Financing

The guiding concept for the Ladera Ranch development is "neighborhood as amenity." Ladera Ranch comprises 8,100 dwelling units and associated land uses organized within a hierarchy of community, villages, and neighborhoods. Its initial phase opened in 1999.

Community is fostered by a computer network—an intranet—that links all residences. Six villages are planned, each with its own core of social and recreational facilities. Neighborhoods within villages are provided with their own complement of

SIGNIFICANT FEATURES

- Enclave of detached live/work houses in a suburban location

- Separate entrances for living and business areas

- Standards for allowable business uses set by homeowners association

- Planned as a land use that could help activate a master-planned community's village cores

Front Street's central park.

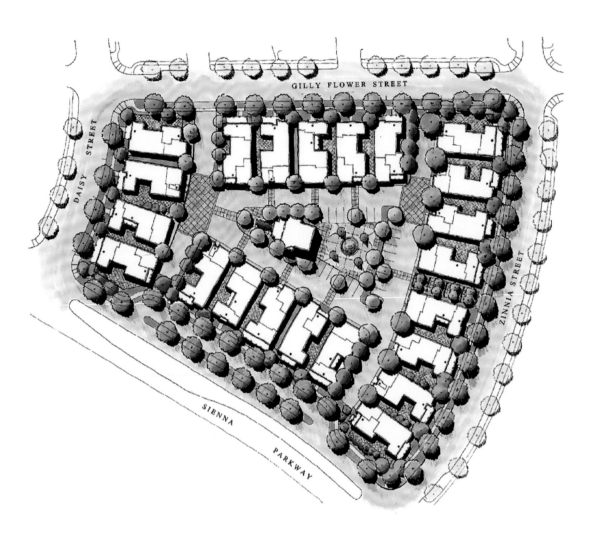

Site plan. Parking for business visitors and employees is located on the perimeter of a small wedge-shaped park at the center of the live/work neighborhood.

GILLY FLOWER STREET

DAISY STREET

ZINNIA STREET

SIENNA PARKWAY

open space and amenities. Pedestrian pathways link neighborhoods to the village core and the community's civic and commercial districts.

DMB Ladera is a joint venture formed in 1996 between Rancho Mission Viejo (owned by the O'Neill/ Moiso family and other individuals), the second biggest landowner in Orange County, and DMB Consolidated Holdings LLC, an Arizona-based developer. Its principals aimed to develop housing that met consumer demand better than the cookie-cutter, mass-produced subdivisions that are found throughout southern California. DMB Ladera succeeded in enlisting high-velocity production homebuilders to the cause of neighborhood building by specifying detailed design criteria. The builder of the Front Street live/work neighborhood is Standard Pacific Gallery Communities, a division of Standard Pacific Homes.

The idea for Front Street came into being as planners sought land uses that could activate village cores in locations where retail uses by themselves were inappropriate. The possibility of live/work space over ground-floor storefronts was discussed but deemed too risky. The planners developed the concept of a home-based business enclave that would be more residential than retail in character, and therefore less of a risk.

A new housing concept is certain to entail regulatory trial and tribulation. Front Street required a special zoning classification: home-based business enclave (HBBE). Although the Orange County building department was open to the idea of home-based business at Ladera, several thorny issues had to be worked through.

Would commercial or residential building codes apply? What types of business would be permitted? How many employees could a business have? Where would

Left: All of Front Street's 22 live/work units include separate entrances for the living and working areas.

Above: Subtle signs related to the business inside may be placed on the front of houses.

This unit plan offers a front entrance for the living area (top left) and a rear entrance for the business area (top right). The office space (bottom) includes a reception area.

employees and visitors park? The county already had a zoning designation that allowed certain businesses to operate in residences, but it drew the line at employees or signage. The HBBE designation addressed a number of these issues, including the following:

- Fire sprinklers are not required.
- Handicapped access is required. (Providing this access created somewhat convoluted sidewalk configurations.)
- Each unit is allowed to have two part-time employees.
- A small sign related to the business inside may be placed on the front of the house.

Believing that retail businesses would require more employees and more parking than appropriate in this suburban setting, the county wanted to ensure that only professional services would be allowed. The county chose not to ban specific types of businesses in the HBBE designation, but rather to rely on standards set by Ladera Ranch—first by the developer and ultimately by the homeowners association, the Ladera Ranch Master Maintenance Corporation (LARMAC). DMB Ladera's initial standards allow certain types of professional services (accountants and consultants, for example) and ban other types (tattoo parlors and escort services, for example).

Two HBBE requirements posed particular planning challenges. First, an additional parking space was required for each unit to accommodate a home-based business, which the builder provided in a small parking bay behind each unit. Second, the HBBE dwellings had to be clustered in a way that would minimize their interface with conventional dwellings. (This requirement has resulted in a less-than-optimum orientation—more commercial than residential—for the Banister Street townhouse live/work neighborhood.)

Rancho Mission Viejo contributed the land for Ladera Ranch from the historic 30,000-acre cattle ranch controlled by the O'Neill/Moiso family since the 1880s. As master developer, DMB Ladera is responsible for master planning, obtaining approvals and entitlements, putting in community infrastructure (including storm drains and roads), ensuring that community buildings (schools, fire stations, and sheriff's facilities) are constructed, and delivering almost finished sites to homebuilders.

The various homebuilders are responsible for neighborhood infrastructure (including paving streets; the construction of sewers, water lines, and storm drains; and the provision of utilities), landscaping, and house construction. They manage their own sales programs within an umbrella marketing program directed by DMB Ladera.

Calculating the price of the Front Street tract was a challenge for DMB Ladera because no comparable products existed from which the developer could derive the residual land value. In the end, the developer discounted the land cost to Standard Pacific by about 10 percent because Front Street was a small project and the fixed costs had to be absorbed by only 22 units. If this had been a 75- to 100-unit project, it could have more easily absorbed full land costs.

With an untested product like suburban live/work residences, pricing the units is a challenge. Standard Pacific thought that homebuyers might place a lower value on the unit's commercial square footage than on its residential square footage and thus expect to pay less than for a similarly sized conventional house. However, buyers proved willing to price all the square footage equally and from the start demand exceeded the limited supply of Front Street units.

Unit prices in the first phase of the Front Street development were in the $600,000 to $625,000 range and, by the time the last house closed escrow in January 2004, the price had escalated to over $700,000. (The 24 live/work townhouses on Banister Street went on the market in May 2004, with prices starting in the high $500,000s.)

Design

The live/work houses on Front Street are a product innovation—and for DMB Ladera and Standard Pacific, they represented a giant leap of faith. Their design was inspired by the older houses that often line the main street leading into the downtown of traditional small towns, stately houses that today are adorned with the shingle of a local attorney, accountant, or architect. The development team sought to create a new product line that is residential in character—with elegant detail and classical elevations—but also including modest signage and extra parking in order to accommodate a mix of small, professional businesses.

DMB Ladera developed the general concept and design criteria for the neighborhood, while Standard Pacific Homes designed the units. For inspiration, the homebuilder looked to other live/work developments in southern California, including Chapman Avenue in Old Towne Orange, downtown Tustin, and areas of Long Beach.

Front Street differs from other live/work communities in its overall look and feel—a traditional suburban neighborhood—and in its inclusion of the area intended for work uses on the same level as the living area. (A loft option for the work area is also available.) To passersby, the commercial component of the neighborhood is subtly indicated by the shingles that announce the businesses and by larger windows in the work areas, which can be used as display windows.

The Front Street enclave is located at the intersection of Sienna Parkway and Daisy Avenue within the Avendale Village of Ladera Ranch. The units are grouped around a 20,000-square-foot, wedge-shaped park, which provides an outdoor setting for neighbor-to-neighbor or business-to-client interaction. Visitors and employees of the home-based businesses park around the perimeter of the park, and residents park in their own rear-facing garages. Entry to the public parking area is provided from Sienna Parkway and Gilly Flower Street.

Front Street houses come in four architectural styles—Cape Cod, Monterey, Italianate, and classic colonial, of which the latter proved to be the most popular—and in four models:

- 2,901 square feet of living space with three bedrooms and 456 square feet of work space;

- 2,763 square feet of living space with four bedrooms and 450 square feet of work space on the ground floor or second floor;

- 2,711 square feet of living space with four bedrooms and 598 square feet of work space; and

- 2,942 square feet of living space and 692 square feet of work space.

Homebuyers could mix and match unit elements, choosing from front entry or private rear entry work space, ground-floor or second-story work space, one-story or two-story work space, and second-story or rear

living quarters. The two-story work space option is designed with loft space overlooking a downstairs open area, providing space upstairs for administrative work and downstairs for client-oriented or assembly work.

Importantly, a unit's dedicated business area does not intrude into its dedicated living area. Each area has its own entrance, and these are located on opposite sides of the house. The business area and living area are divided by a reinforced fire-resistant wall. The work area can be accessed from inside the house.

The Banister Street live/work townhouse units now under development in Ladera Ranch's newest village of Terramor are designed with the work space and garage on the ground floor and the living area on the two upper stories. At 420 to 460 square feet, their work areas will be somewhat smaller than those in the Front Street units. Available in two different styles—English cottage and American heritage—each townhouse will have approximately 2,100 square feet of living space with up to three bedrooms.

Target Market and Resident/Business Profile

DMB Ladera and Standard Pacific Homes saw two potential markets for the Front Street live/work units:

- two-earner couples with children, with one spouse able to work from home and be with the children; and

- independent professionals who provide one-on-one services and want a high-quality office setting.

The average age of householders in the Front Street project is 35 years, and three-fifths of the households include children. The target market for housing units in Ladera Ranch as a whole is much broader, ranging from young couples to older families with children (parents in the late 30s to early 50s age range).

Standard Pacific Homes identified three different kinds of home-based businesses in which it expected the occupants of the live/work units to engage:

- public businesses, such as accountants or insurance brokers, with clients who visit the office and thus require a front office;

- businesses, such as jewelry makers, that produce and distribute a product and do not receive clients and thus can be accommodated in a rear office; and

- businesses, such as distributors, that may occasionally receive clients and can be accommodated in either a front or rear office.

The unit configuration with a front office proved to be the most popular. Among the initial businesses operating in the Front Street live/work units are the following: seven real estate agencies, two property management companies, two photography studios, two daycare operators, a recording studio, a wedding magazine publisher, a computer software designer, a computer consultant, a financial adviser, an insurance agent, a house cleaning service, a hair salon, and a trophy manufacturer.

Marketing and Management

A Ladera Ranch Web site constitutes the centerpiece of DMB Ladera's marketing strategy. Newspaper, magazine, and direct-mail ads steer prospects to a Web site, on which visitors can register and create a personal folder of information about Ladera Ranch—its neighborhoods, amenities, and available units. The master developer keeps in touch with an interest list that has always exceeded 8,000 people.

An online survey of people on the Ladera Ranch interest list conducted by Standard Pacific Homes revealed hundreds of prospects expressing interest in the live/work units. The builder stayed in touch with these potential buyers, sending them updates on the progress of construction and information about the grand opening.

Common areas at Ladera Ranch, including those within the Front Street neighborhood, are maintained by LARMAC, the homeowners association. The base fee for housing units within Ladera Ranch is about $155 monthly. Front Street residents pay an additional $36 per month for the maintenance of the interior park, landscaping, and neighborhood parking areas.

Experience Gained

■ Nascent trends outside a developer's market can be potentially adapted into a niche product that succeeds in the developer's market. DMB Ladera and Standard Pacific thought that they could successfully adapt the national trend in urban live/work environments to a suburban residential location. The risk they took in developing a new niche housing product was rewarded

with strong market acceptance.

■ Opportunities to push the envelope in terms of residential design are always present, but patience is required. Standard Pacific now has models for single-family and attached live/work units that it can use in other locations.

■ Inflexible local building codes can hinder the introduction of a new product, even if it conforms to the designated zoning classification, as did the Front Street live/work units. Live/work should be recognized in local building codes as a hybrid product that takes elements from both commercial and residential codes.

■ Although the Front Street live/work enclave has had market success, it does not generate the degree of urban activity and energy that had been envisioned by the planners. Front Street is, in fact, a quiet neighborhood of residential character. In order to enliven a village core with urban and pedestrian activity, developers should consider a more straightforward live/work product that includes obvious commercial storefronts. This solution, however, can add significant risk for the developer.

■ The Internet works well as a marketing tool for large, master-planned communities. Standard Pacific was able to successfully market its niche product by tapping into Ladera Ranch's interactive Web-based prospects list.

The Townhouses at Banister Street, a second live/work neighborhood at Ladera Ranch inspired by the success of the Front Street home-based business enclave.

CONTACT INFORMATION

DEVELOPERS

DMB Ladera LLC (Master Developer)
Ladera Ranch
P.O. Box 9
San Juan Capistrano, California 92693
949-240-3363
www.laderaranch.com

Standard Pacific Homes (Builder)
15326 Alton Parkway
Irvine, California 92618
949-789-1600
www.standardpacifichomes.com

ARCHITECT

Bassenian/Lagoni Architects
2031 Orchard Drive, Suite 100
Newport Beach, California 92660
949-553-9100
www.bassenianlagoni.com

OTHER KEY TEAM MEMBERS

Fuscoe Engineering Inc.
16795 Von Karman, Suite 100
Irvine, California 92606
949-474-1960
www.fuscoe.com

Summers/Murphy & Partners Inc.
(Landscape Architect)
34197 Pacific Coast Highway, Suite 200
Dana Point, California 92629
949-443-1446
www.smpinc.com

DEVELOPMENT SCHEDULE

Site Purchased:	January 2002
Planning Started:	January 2002
Construction Started:	July 2002
Sales Started:	March 2003
Project Completed:	December 2003
Sales Completed:	January 2004

LAND USE INFORMATION

Site Area:	3.4 acres
Dwelling Units:	22
Residential Density:	6.5 units per gross acre
Parking:	4 spaces per housing unit

LAND USE PLAN

	ACRES	PERCENT OF SITE
Housing	2.15	63 %
Streets and Parking	.78	23
Open Space	.47	14

DEVELOPMENT COST INFORMATION

SITE ACQUISITION COST AND PARTICIPATION	$3,723,833
SITE IMPROVEMENT COST	1,302,988
CONSTRUCTION COSTS	
Indirect	604,698
Direct	4,089,317
TOTAL	4,694,015
SOFT COSTS	
Interest and Fees	150,000
Consultants	158,911
Model Units	783,315
Selling Costs	757,151
Other Soft Costs	300,086
TOTAL	2,149,463
TOTAL DEVELOPMENT COST	$11,870,299
Development Cost per Unit	539,559
Development Cost per Square Foot	160

RESIDENTIAL UNIT INFORMATION[1]

| UNIT TYPE | AVERAGE LOT SIZE (SQUARE FEET) | UNIT SIZE (SQUARE FEET) | | | NUMBER OF UNITS | | INITIAL BASE SALE PRICE |
		ENTIRE UNIT	LIVING SPACE	WORK SPACE	PLANNED	BUILT	
Plan 1[1]	4,348	3,357	2,901	456	5	5	$645,000
Plan 2[2]	4,348	3,213	2,763	450	6	6	625,000
Plan 3[3]	4,348	3,309	2,711	598	6	6	639,000
Plan 4[4]	4,348	3,634	2,942	692	5	5	681,000

1. *Front office entry; first-floor office space only; rear living entry. Styles: Italianate or Monterey.*
2. *Rear office entry; optional second-story office space; front living entry. Styles: classic colonial or Italianate.*
3. *Front office entry; first-floor office space only; rear living entry. Styles: Cape Cod or classic colonial.*
4. *Rear office entry; optional second-story office space; front living entry. Styles: classic colonial or Monterey.*

DEMOGRAPHIC PROFILE

	PERCENT OF ALL HOUSEHOLDS	TYPE OF HOME-BASED BUSINESS
AGE RANGE		
25–34	9 %	—
35–44	41	—
45–54	36	—
55–64	9	—
65+	5	—
HOUSEHOLD TYPE		
Singles with Children[1]	9	real estate agent; financial adviser
Singles without Children	14	real estate agent; property management
Couples with Children[2]	65	house cleaning service; real estate agent; daycare operator; insurance agent; photography studio; hair salon; recording studio; magazine publisher; computer software designer
Couples without Children	12	computer consultant; real estate agent; trophy manufacturer
GENDER[3]		
Male	80	—
Female	20	—

1. *Both single-parent households consist of divorced males with children living at home part time.*
2. *Including one couple with adult children living at home.*
3. *Gender of single-person and single-parent households.*

FIRST FLOOR   SECOND FLOOR

This floor plan is versatile, offering studio/ground-floor workspace with an optional mezzanine office as well as options for using residential space for different purposes.

Fruitvale Village

OAKLAND, CALIFORNIA

SIGNIFICANT FEATURES

- Developed by a non-profit, neighborhood-based community development corporation

- Transit-oriented development

- Retail, community services, office, and residential uses

- Market-rate apartments for low- to middle-income households

Fruitvale Village is a mixed-use retail/office/residential complex on four acres forming the core of a planned 19-acre transit village in Oakland's Fruitvale neighborhood about 4.5 miles south of downtown. Developed by the Fruitvale Development Corporation (FDC), an entity created for this purpose by the Unity Council, a community development corporation, the project consists of two buildings containing 40,000 square feet of ground-floor retail space; 115,000 square feet of office space primarily for various social services and civic operations, including a Head Start child-development center, a seniors' center, a public library, and a health clinic, but also available for leasing by businesses; and 47 rental apartments, ten of which are reserved for low-income households. It is located next to the Fruitvale Bay Area Rapid Transit (BART) station and features a central plaza designed to lead pedestrians from the station to stores along International Boulevard.

Site and Surroundings

The project lies within the Fruitvale Village redevelopment area between 33rd and 35th Avenues to the north and south, the BART station to the west, and East 12th Street to the east. A car-free pedestrian plaza along 34th Street at the center of the project continues on the other side of East 12th Street to create a pedestrian path between the transit station and International Boulevard.

Before the Nimitz Freeway (I-880) was constructed in the late 1950s, International Boulevard (then known as East 14th Street) was one of the main north/south roads, connecting Oakland to the cities of San Leandro and Hayward. Within Oakland, ethnic and immigrant neighborhoods line the boulevard. Within the Fruitvale District, the street is lined with two- and three-story buildings constructed before World War II that are occupied by stores and businesses providing goods and services to the neighborhood's Latino population. About 43 percent of Fruitvale's population is Latino and the remaining 57 percent is mostly Asian or African American.

Named for the orchards planted by 19th-century German settlers, Fruitvale became Oakland's "second downtown" before World War II by virtue of its stores, mansions, and a rich inventory of Victorian houses. During the war, the district attracted many factories (and factory workers). After the war, many of the factories closed and Fruitvale—along with all of Oakland—entered an era of economic decline.

The construction of the Fruitvale BART station in 1972 brought more changes—the demolition of buildings and houses, the reconfiguration of the street grid, and the

Site plan.

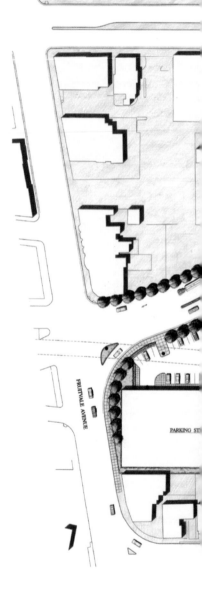

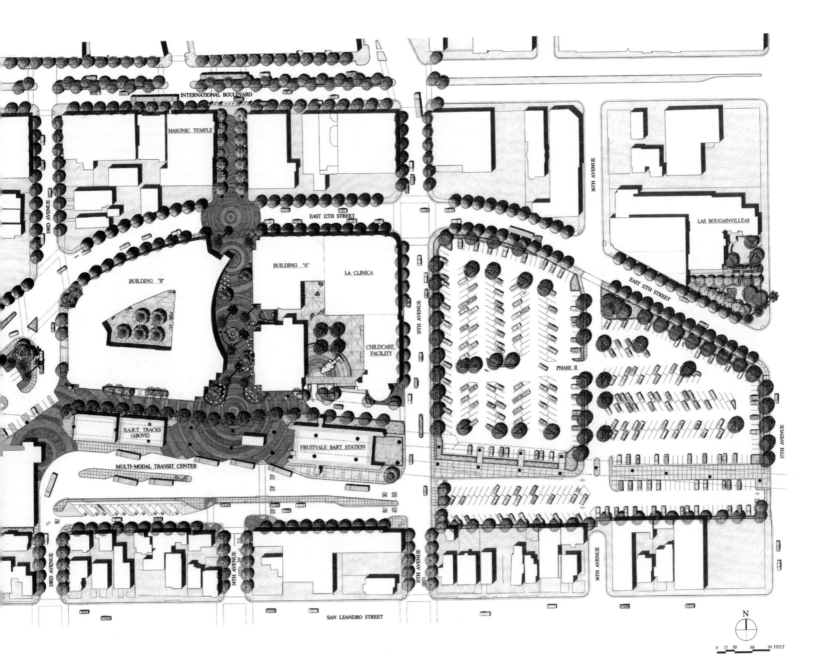

INTERNATIONAL BOULEVARD

MASONIC TEMPLE

3RD AVENUE

BUILDING "B"

EAST 12TH STREET

BUILDING "A"

LA CLINICA

CHILDCARE FACILITY

34TH AVENUE

35TH AVENUE

B.A.R.T. TRACKS (ABOVE)

FRUITVALE BART STATION

MULTI-MODAL TRANSIT CENTER

PHASE II

36TH AVENUE

EAST 12TH STREET

LAS BOUGAINVILLEAS

37TH AVENUE

SAN LEANDRO STREET

N

0 15 30   60   90 FEET

addition of giant surface-parking lots for commuters. Free BART parking brought many people to the Fruitvale neighborhood, but all they saw was parking and the service entrances and backsides of the East 14th Street retail strip. Within the region, Fruitvale was viewed as an unsafe, unattractive, and economically depressed area. Visitors did not take time to shop or explore the neighborhood. To make matters worse, the residents of Fruitvale were not shopping there either.

A decade's worth of neighborhood revitalization initiatives had started to take effect by the time that the Fruitvale Village project got underway. Along International Boulevard, the results of the Unity Council's facade improvement and streetscape plans are evident. Aged and deteriorated storefronts have been replaced or restored. Newly planted trees line the sidewalks. Traffic-calming median strips make crossing the boulevard much safer.

A second phase of Fruitvale Village, comprising a mix of up to 250 affordable and market-rate multifamily units, will occupy the site of a large surface-parking lot south of the existing development. A five-story parking garage for BART commuters designed to complement the Fruitvale Village complex lies north of the project.

Other transit services—stops for Alameda County Transit (AC Transit) buses, taxi stands, and kiss-and-ride facilities—are located on the west side of the BART station. Farther west of the BART station and San Leandro Boulevard, Victorian houses and aging industrial and warehouse buildings predominate.

Development Process

In the early 1990s, BART proposed the construction of a four- to five-story, concrete parking garage to replace a surface parking lot at its Fruitvale station. The community was overwhelmingly opposed. Around the same time, a team of graduate students from the University of California (UC) at Berkeley's City and Regional Planning Department conducted a study of the Fruitvale area that suggested the creation of a pedestrian link between the BART station and International Boulevard.

The nonprofit Unity Council was founded in 1964. Its mission is to enhance and improve resources and assets (both human and physical) in the Fruitvale district

through the provision of social services and through economic and real estate development. It has organized and sponsored many programs related to homeownership, job training, daycare, seniors, and literacy. In addition, it has developed a number of projects in the neighborhood, among which are the 100-unit Posada de Colores and the 68-unit Las Bougainvilleas, both affordable housing projects for seniors.

With the UC–Berkeley study in mind, the Unity Council held a series of community meetings and forums to find an alternative to the proposed parking garage. This neighborhood initiative convinced BART that the train station would benefit if transit-oriented development occurred around it. With the help of a $185,000 community development block grant (CDBG) from the city of Oakland, the Unity Council then held community meetings, design meetings, and a symposium that resulted in a new vision: Development around the Fruitvale BART station would take the form of a mixed-use transit village and would be a catalyst for the economic revitalization of the whole neighborhood. Furthermore, the primary tenants of the nonresidential portions of this project would be social-service agencies.

The Unity Council's Main Street Program established a design committee that oversaw the development of design guidelines for a facade improvement program. Through its Main Street Program and CDBG funding, the council provided technical, financial, and physical assistance to shops along International Boulevard and nearby commercial streets.

Impressed by the community's idea of integrating the transit station into the surrounding community, U.S. Secretary of Transportation Federico Peña helped the Unity Council secure $470,000 in U.S. Department of Transportation (USDOT) funds in the fall of 1993. By 1995, most of the concept plans, environmental assessments, traffic studies, and feasibility studies were underway or had been completed.

To oversee the Fruitvale Village project, the Unity Council created the Fruitvale Development Corporation (FDC) with Arabella Martinez serving as the CEO for both entities. The scope of the project necessitated the involvement of many governmental agencies, including the city of Oakland, BART, AC Transit, the Metropolitan

The presence of an elevated BART train station encouraged the design of Fruitvale Village as a transit village incorporating affordable rental housing.

Transportation Commission (the San Francisco Bay Area's metropolitan planning organization), the Alameda County Congestion Management Agency, and many others. Most of the agencies involved were very supportive in terms of providing grants and loans and working with the FDC to obtain approvals for the project.

Initially, the FDC considered forming a partnership with a local for-profit developer. During its "auditioning" process for a development partner, however, the FDC realized that it had more in-house expertise than it had thought, as well as specialized knowledge about the neighborhood and the local market. Bringing on a private developer, it surmised, would have not added much additional expertise to the project and would have decreased its share of the equity. The decision was made not to bring in a private developer.

The development of Fruitvale Village required close coordination between the city of Oakland and the FDC. To legitimize high-density, mixed-use development in the transit district, the city created a new overlay zone (S15) allowing for higher densities around transit, providing density bonuses, and lowering parking requirements. (However, the project's construction start had to be delayed until the rezoning was adopted.) The city also worked with the FDC on associated traffic issues. East 12th Street stood in need of traffic calming to enhance pedestrian safety. The street was realigned with narrowed lanes, and special pavers and signage were installed to signal to drivers that they must yield to crossing pedestrians. A segment of East 12th Street was realigned to help divert traffic from it and Fruitvale Avenue to 37th Avenue. In addition, 33rd and 34th Avenues on the western side of the BART tracks were opened up in order to reroute buses and automobiles from East 12th Street to San Leandro Boulevard.

Financing and Public Sector Partnerships

Forming a partnership with BART was of paramount importance, because the transit agency owned most of the land around the station. Believing that their long-term goal of increasing ridership was best served by the transit village concept, planners at BART assisted in the planning process. BART required that the FDC replace all of the parking that the project would eliminate—at a total cost that exceeded $12 million. Funding for replacement parking was obtained through a $7,561,000 grant from USDOT, a portion ($4.2 million) of a transportation bond approved by Alameda County voters, and several other grants for surface parking. The Unity Council loaned BART $975,000 to complete the fifth level of its parking structure in exchange for control of the BART parking lots between 35th and 37th Avenues for the development of Fruitvale's second phase. A land exchange swapped some more developable BART properties on the east side of the station for Unity Council land on the station's less marketable west side. The council owns the land on which the pedestrian plaza and the project's southern building sit and it rents the land on which the northern building sits under a 95-year lease with BART.

As a nonprofit developer without ready access to debt financing, investment capital, or in-house funds, the Unity Council faced many financing challenges. The FDC and the council had to raise a substantial amount of grant dollars before they could obtain the requisite debt financing. The process of securing adequate financing and equity investment from 30 different sources—including development and construction grants, land swaps with the city and BART, and its own reserves—lasted four years. Not able to risk a gap between the construction and permanent financing, the development team sought a lender that was willing to provide both.

Thanks largely to the efforts of city councilman Ignacio De La Fuente, Fruitvale was designated a tax-increment financing (TIF) district, allowing the project to receive TIF funding, which supported a $4 million bridge loan from the Local Initiatives Support Corporation (LISC), at that time the largest bridge loan that LISC had ever approved. Through the city of Oakland, the project received a $3.3 million economic development initiative grant under the auspices of the U.S. Department of Housing and Urban Development's (HUD) Enhanced Enterprise Community program, which was matched by a $3.3 million HUD Section 108 loan. The city of Oakland issued $19.8 million in tax-exempt 501(c)(3) bonds, for which Citibank provided the credit enhancement, thereby lowering the interest rate paid by the FDC. The city then approved a $4.5 million 20-year prepaid lease that allowed the FDC to pay down the 501(c)(3) bonds

Top left: The pedestrian plaza that goes through the center of Fruitvale Village links the BART station to the neighborhood's main commercial street.

Top right: Housing on the third and fourth levels of the two mixed-use buildings promotes activity on the streets outside of normal business hours and enhances neighborhood safety.

Bottom left: A playground serving households with children, which make up one-third of households at Fruitvale Village.

Bottom right: De Colores, a Head Start child-development center, helps fulfill one part of the vision for this project—that the primary nonresidential tenants would be social-service agencies.

Left: The private entrance to the residences. Fruitvale Village targets low- and moderate-income households needing convenient access to transportation and services.

Right: Fruitvale Village's 47 one- and two-bedroom rental lofts and flats help alleviate a shortage of affordable housing in this densely populated district.

by $2 million soon after the completion of construction and reduce its interest payments and fees.

Planning and Design

Based on the participation of McLarand Vasquez Emsiek & Partners (MVE) in an FDC-sponsored community design workshop, the FDC selected MVE as the project's architect and planner. The developer and architect sought to integrate Fruitvale Village into the larger community, in order to give community residents a sense of ownership and pride in the development. To accomplish this, they listened carefully to community input and designed a project that is similar in scale and massing to the buildings nearby. Thus, the buildings were kept to four stories—even though the zoning would have allowed more—so that the project would not, for example, obscure residents' views of nearby St. Elizabeth Church.

As a whole, the architect sees Fruitvale Village as a collage that represents the variety of building styles and cultures found along International Boulevard. A contemporary blending of California's design heritage, the project contains elements that evoke the Mission style and elements that are more influenced by local reinterpretations of Mediterranean and Mexican styles. The palette that was selected creates a festive atmos-

phere with colors that have historic and cultural precedents in the region.

Fruitvale Village currently consists of two mixed-use buildings with a pedestrian plaza between them. Each building contains an at-grade parking garage for a combined total of 150 parking spaces and a second-floor patio above the garage. The patio in the southern building includes a play area for children in the Head Start program housed in the building and a courtyard for Unity Council use. The patio in the northern building is for the use of the seniors' center, the library, and the residential tenants.

In an effort to create a pedestrian environment that appeals to BART commuters, the majority of the project's retail shops are oriented to the plaza or East 12th Street, while most of the office space is located on the second floors of the buildings and most of the market-rate housing on the top two floors. The eastern half of the pedestrian plaza, called De La Fuente Plaza, acts as a gateway to International Boulevard. It is framed by a former Masonic temple owned by the Unity Council on the north and a small grocery store with three floors of apartments above it on the south. The temple and plaza will become the venue for a public market incubator program that includes a farmers' market that began operations in May 2005.

In addition to the public library and the seniors' center, the northern building contains 22 market-rate apartments, two affordable apartments, an additional 20,200 square feet of office space, and a free bicycle parking garage—the Fruitvale Bike Station—with space for more than 200 bicycles. Cosponsored by the Unity Council, BART, the city of Oakland, and Alameda Bicycle (a local bicycle shop), the Fruitvale Bike Station is one of the largest bike garages in America. The southern building contains the Unity Council headquarters, the Head Start center, a community health clinic (La Clínica de La Raza), 15 market-rate apartments, and eight affordable apartments.

Entrances and elevators and stairwells have been located to keep the project's uses separated. La Clínica de La Raza and the Head Start center have private entrances and their own elevators and stairwells. The Unity Council and the residential units in the southern building share an elevator and a staircase. In the northern building, the office space, seniors' center, and residential units share an elevator and staircase. The second-floor library is accessed through a small foyer on the ground floor at the northeastern corner of the building served by an elevator and a stairwell shared by the library and the residential units above.

The 37 market-rate apartments and four of the affordable units are laid out as one- and two-bedroom lofts. The six remaining affordable units are one- and two-bedroom flats designed to be fully wheelchair accessible. Every residential unit comes with a washer and dryer, energy-efficient electrical appliances, granite countertops, and a balcony or patio.

Marketing and Resident Profile

Fruitvale Village targeted low- and middle-income, transit-using households. The global firm that was hired at first by FDC to market the project was unfamiliar with marketing challenges in a low-income community, and the developer found that its own knowledge of the neighborhood made it more effective at marketing the village without the firm's help. In early 2003, the FDC canceled the contract with this firm, retained a full-time leasing consultant, and took on all marketing tasks in-house.

The economic downturn has slowed the leasing of the retail and office space, but the residential component is fully leased. While the ten affordable and handicapped-accessible units have a waiting list with more than 300 names, lease-up of the market-rate units took longer than expected due to the readjustment of rents throughout the Bay Area in the wake of the economic downturn.

Fruitvale Village has attracted a resident group ranging in age from 25 to 64 and exhibiting a diversity of ethnic backgrounds. Most renters (49 percent) are singles without children. Couples without children (19 percent), couples with children (17 percent), and single parents (15 percent) together make up half of the occupants. Among single-person households, females are somewhat more numerous (57 percent) than males (43 percent).

Experience Gained

■ Initial small grants for community planning made this project possible. The CDBG funds ($185,000) and the grant from USDOT ($470,000) were critical to the project's success. While the overall revitalization of the Fruitvale district would end up costing upward of $100 million, the initial planning funding enabled the development team to later obtain the necessary larger funding.

■ Depressed inner-city neighborhoods can offer great development potential. Despite a market study early in the development process that showed little demand in the Fruitvale district for commercial services, the latent market was huge. Fruitvale Village was able to uncover this market by providing a mix of uses, making the village and the district a distinctive place, and creating pedestrian connections that attract commuters into the community.

■ The Unity Council's deep roots in the community enhanced the project's acceptability. The council's long history of service in the community has engendered a high level of trust among residents, merchants, and other stakeholders, and this was invaluable in moving the development forward.

■ The staffs of many nonprofit community development organizations possess a range of skills, expertise, and knowledge of community dynamics that can make them excellent developers and potentially good development partners. Like the Unity Council, such organizations may have greater development expertise in-house than they think they have when they set out to develop a major project.

■ The challenge that nonprofit associations face in obtaining funding and financing makes partnerships with for-profit developers difficult. The hurdles experienced by the FDC in securing project financing prolonged the development process longer than expected.

■ As an economic development catalyst and social-service project, Fruitvale Village has been a success. Vacancy rates on International Boulevard are near 1 percent, down from a high of 40 percent when the project was first conceived. Among Oakland's districts, Fruitvale now yields the second highest sales tax revenue. The centralization of social services in a location accessible by public transportation has made their delivery more efficient and client friendly.

CONTACT INFORMATION

PROJECT WEB SITE

www.fruitvalevillage.net

DEVELOPERS

Fruitvale Development Corporation
1245 34th Avenue
Oakland, California 94601
510-534-5841
www.fruitvalevillage.net

Unity Council
3411 East 12th Street, Suite 200
Oakland, California 94601
510-535-6900
www.unitycouncil.org

ARCHITECT/PLANNER

McLarand Vasquez Emsiek & Partners Inc.
350 Frank Ogawa Plaza, Suite 100
Oakland, California 94612
510-267-3189
www.mve-architects.com

PUBLIC PARTNERS

Bay Area Rapid Transit
300 Lakeside Drive, 18th Floor
Oakland, California 94612
www.bart.gov

City of Oakland
250 Frank Ogawa Plaza
Oakland, California 94612
510-444-2489
www.oaklandnet.com

COMMUNITY PARTNERS

La Clínica de La Raza
1515 Fruitvale Avenue
Oakland, California 94601
510-535-4000
www.laclinica.org

Fruitvale Bike Station
3301 East 12th Street, Building B, Suite 141
Oakland, California 94602
510-536-2200
www.bartbikes.com

DEVELOPMENT SCHEDULE

Planning Started:	1992
Site Acquired from BART:	August 2001
Construction Started:	January 2002
Sales/Leasing Started:	fall 2002
Fruitvale Village Completion:	2006

LAND USE INFORMATION

Site Area:	4 acres
Building Area:	
Office	114,509 square feet
Retail	39,612 square feet
Residential	52,716 square feet
Parking	50,150 square feet
Courtyards	23,382 square feet
TOTAL	280,369 square feet
Covered Parking Spaces:	150

RESIDENTIAL UNIT INFORMATION

UNIT TYPE	UNIT SIZE (SQUARE FEET)		NUMBER OF UNITS	INITIAL MONTHLY RENT RANGE
MARKET RATE				
1 Bedroom/1.5 Baths (Loft)	828–	911	20	$1,250–$1,425
2 Bedrooms/2 Baths (Loft)	969–	1,287	17	1,450– 2,300
AFFORDABLE UNITS				
2 Bedrooms/1 Bath (Flat)	795–	823	6	1,029
1 Bedroom/1.5 Bath (Loft)	828–	860	4	486– 860

DEMOGRAPHIC PROFILE

	PERCENT OF ALL HOUSEHOLDS
AGE RANGE	
18–24	1%
25–34	25
35–44	30
45–54	44
HOUSEHOLD TYPE	
Singles with Children	15
Singles without Children	49
Couples with Children	17
Couples without Children	19
GENDER (SINGLE-PERSON HOUSEHOLDS)	
Male	43
Female	57

DEVELOPMENT COST INFORMATION

Site Acquisition	$500,000
Site Improvement	1,291,931
Construction[1]	39,539,275
Soft Costs	17,907,643
Health Clinic Development	9,761,151
TOTAL DEVELOPMENT COST	**$69,000,000**

1. *Not including costs of the surface and structured parking lots, the street improvements needed to reroute traffic away from East 12th Street, and the multimodal transit stop adjacent to the BART station*

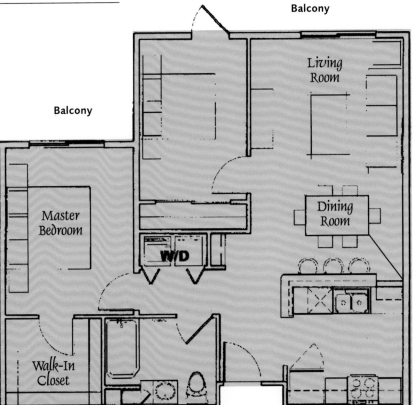

Floor plan for an affordable apartment.

Greenwood Avenue Cottages

SHORELINE, WASHINGTON

Greenwood Avenue Cottages is a community of eight tiny houses located on just four-fifths of an acre. The brightly colored houses range in size from 780 to 1,000 square feet and are clustered around a landscaped community green and garden. Each house has its own private yard that is surrounded by a low fence and accessible through a garden gate. Garages and visitor parking are located on the perimeter of the site—a design feature that encourages neighborliness by ensuring that residents walk through the central common to get to their houses. The development also features a communal building that includes a 400-square-foot room for community use and storage lockers.

The project is one of five "pocket" neighborhoods developed in the Puget Sound area by the Cottage Company, a Seattle-based developer, and Ross Chapin Architects. Their concept of pocket neighborhoods is that they provide an option for people seeking well-designed, but not-so-big houses and a sense of community. The Greenwood Avenue cluster fits comfortably into a larger, established neighborhood of single-family houses.

The project was developed under the city of Shoreline's Cottage Housing Code (CHC), which allows this type of infill development in single-family residential areas.

Development Process

The city of Shoreline is a first-ring suburb of Seattle located on Puget Sound just beyond the city limits. It is largely built out with post–World War II Craftsman style houses on large lots. Seeking to accommodate growth by increasing density and to provide options for detached in-town housing without compromising the town's character, the city of Shoreline adopted its CHC in 2000 in an ordinance that is similar to one enacted in 1995 by the nearby town of Langley.

The CHC permits higher densities—four to 12 single-family dwellings per acre—for houses that do not exceed 1,000 square feet of living space. Under the code, cottage housing is specified as a conditional use in single-family neighborhoods. The conditions cottage housing must meet include covered front porches facing a central green space, detached parking, architecture that is compatible with the surrounding

SIGNIFICANT FEATURES

- Single-family cottages each under 1,000 square feet

- Central courtyard and a communal building

- Developed under a code that allows pocket cottage neighborhoods within lower-density single-family neighborhoods

- Target market of single women and empty nesters

Most Greenwood Avenue residents are single, professional women drawn to the cottage community's intimate scale.

neighborhood, and maximum roof heights (18 feet for a flat roof and 25 feet for a pitched roof).

In early 2001, Jim Soules of the Cottage Company and architect Ross Chapin bought a vacant .8-acre infill site located off Highway 99, Shoreline's main drag, amid a leafy expanse of meandering suburban development. The site had previously been approved for four 7,200-square-foot lots, but under the new CHC, Soules could develop something very different.

The Cottage Company's first pocket neighborhood development, Third Street Cottages in Langley, had been completed in 1998. The success of this and two later projects led Soules to look for a similar opportunity in Shoreline.

A project in Seattle—Pine Street Cottages—inspired Soules's cottage housing projects. The Craftsman style Pine Street Cottages were built as housing for blue-collar workers in around 1915. They were rehabilitated in 1992 as 400-square-foot, one-bedroom houses clustered about a courtyard, with detached parking.

It was not only the beautiful gardens, the sense of neighborhood, and the feeling of security at the Pine Street Cottages that spoke to Soules, but also the fact that such a marketable project—which was snatched up by eager buyers at high prices and profiled in the national media—could not be legally built under single-family zoning in most localities. Noting that more than half of U.S. households consist of one or two people, Soules saw a market for single-family housing for small households

Soules established the Cottage Company and began working with Chapin out of a recognition that there is a market for high-quality, small single-family houses. That this market is underserved is indicated by the high—$750,000—sale price of 1,100- to 1,200-square-foot Craftsman houses on Queen Anne Street in Seattle.

Soules and Chapin's application for the development of cottage housing on the Greenwood Avenue site triggered neighborhood meetings. Neighbors worried that rental or student housing was being proposed (the site is near a community college), that traffic would become worse, and that property values would decrease.

The success of the Third Street Cottages helped smooth the approval process. Eventually, many members of the city council, planning commissioners, and neighbors visited Third Street Cottages in Langley to better evaluate what the Cottage Company was espousing for Shoreline.

Zoning approval came fairly easily with just a few minor difficulties, the biggest of which was providing a turnaround for fire trucks. The site's slope away from the existing storm drain forced the developer to install a deep storm drain that would keep water from running to the east, where residents would not grant a stormwater easement.

Requiring only minor street improvements and being tucked behind existing homes, the project kept a low profile during construction. Upon completion, the project won ready acceptance. The city cosponsored with the Cottage Company its nomination for a regional design award and adopted it as the standard by which it would like other cottage neighborhoods developed. Since the completion of Greenwood Avenue Cottages, two other cottage housing developments have been completed in the city and another is going through the approval process.

Financing

The Cottage Company is a development company that forms separate limited liability partnerships for each of the projects that it undertakes. For Greenwood Avenue, the partnership was called the Cottage Company LLC with the Cottage Company and the architect Ross Chapin as 50/50 partners.

The project was financed conventionally with a local bank construction loan at 80 percent of appraised value and the balance of the equity coming from the Cottage Company and Chapin. Arriving at an appraised value was problematic, because there were no comparable products in the local market to offer pricing guidance. The appraiser estimated value by pricing the cost of buying a small fixer-upper and bringing it up to the assumed quality of the cottage houses.

The first house closed in March 2002. Seven of the eight houses were sold within two months, and the last sale occurred in June. The smallest unit is 780 square feet; it sold for $275,000. The 1,000-square-foot properties sold for $280,000 to $290,000.

Private frontyards are defined by low wood fences and gates. Porch railings are "sitable."

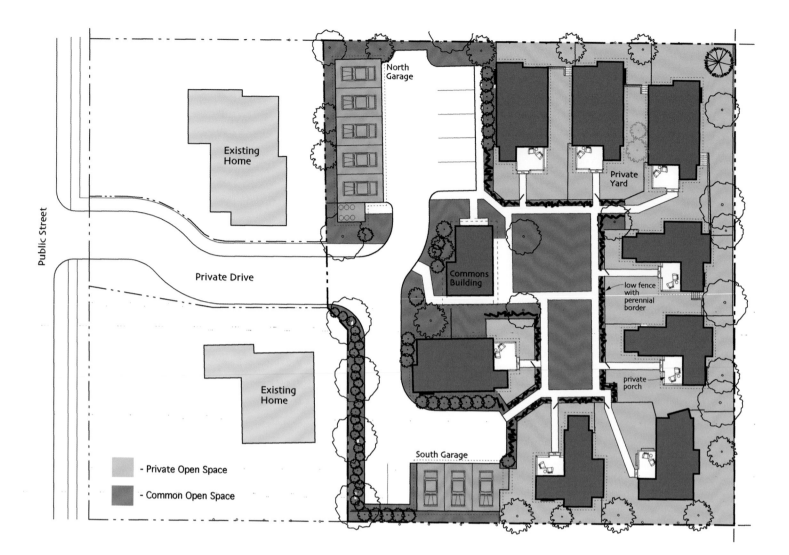

Labels on the site plan:

North Garage

Existing Home

Private Yard

Public Street

Private Drive

Commons Building

low fence with perennial border

private porch

Existing Home

South Garage

- Private Open Space

- Common Open Space

Site plan.

Neighbors were initially concerned that the small houses would degrade the value of nearby houses. In the end, however, $300,000 is comparable to the selling price of neighboring 30-year-old, 1,700- to 2,000-square-foot houses on 7,200-square-foot lots. On a square-foot basis, the Greenwood Avenue cottages are twice as expensive as older houses in the neighborhood.

Planning and Design

Early 20th-century bungalow courtyards inspired the design of the cottages. Seattle has some examples, but far more are found in southern California. These are usually configured with eight to 12 one- or two-bedroom houses clustered around a landscaped courtyard. They were built with the quality and details of Craftsman res-

idences—fine millwork, stained glass, built-ins, ceramic tile, and so forth.

In keeping with the classic cottage, which is one and one-half stories tall, the Greenwood Avenue cottages feature a loft that overlooks the living areas. The lots are approximately 32 feet wide and 45 feet deep. The smallness of the houses and lots makes it necessary to address real and perceived notions of public and private space. The cottages have a yard on one side and abut the lot line on the other side, leaving ten to 14 feet between them. Each cottage has a small private frontyard defined by a two-foot-high picket fence. All the cottages have an 80- or 100-square-foot covered porch.

Concerns about height, privacy, and character informed the design. Site planning was key. Eight houses clustered on four-fifths of an acre require a precise plan. The challenge of getting the houses to nest together was addressed through interior and exterior design.

For the most part, windows open to the south to the house's private yard. No windows are placed on the north side or they are situated high or take the form of skylights that bring in light without looking directly into the bedroom of the house next door.

Parking is accommodated as unobtrusively as possible. Two detached garages are located on the western edge of the site—one with three spaces and the other with five. Visitor parking is provided near the parking garages. After parking, residents and visitors walk through the common area to enter the private yards. Chapin calls this movement from public space to private space "layering."

A good example of the preciseness in the layering design that is normally not noticed at first but has been an immensely successful feature is the porch railing. Although the railing sets a boundary, it rises only 30 inches tall, which means it is "sitable." If it were 36 inches or 42 inches high, the railing would have been a barrier instead of a seating opportunity that promotes neighbor-to-neighbor visits. Success is in the details. An energy-efficient, blown-in insulation in the units provides for a high level of sound reduction. The more active rooms, such as the dining area, face the common, allowing residents to keep track of who is on the grounds. The more private rooms are toward the back. The creation of zones within the living space and the clear differentiation between public and private spaces make these small houses function as if they were larger.

Ample natural light that varies throughout the day will make a small house feel larger and more dynamic and vital. The Greenwood Avenue units are designed to bring in daylight wherever possible. For example, the eating alcoves have windows on three sides. In the evening, these windowed alcoves become lanterns that illuminate the common.

The units lack (space-wasting) hallways. Taking advantage of the slope of the land, two cottages have basements that can be used for storage.

Fiber cement (a product made from recycled sawdust) and other low-maintenance materials are used on the exterior of the units instead of wood. Fiber cement endures, needs little maintenance, and holds paint well.

The common area was designed to feel like everyone's front yard. It is encircled by a landscaped border that along with the low picket fence (the wood was scrap from an old cedar mill) separates the common from private space. It features two different concepts: a multipurpose lawn and a formal walking garden—the "knot" garden—with a sculpture.

Target Market and Resident Profile

The Cottage Company did not want the cottages to be perceived as retirement housing, starter housing, or low-cost housing. The assumption by some city council members that 1,000-square-foot houses would cost half as much as a 2,000-square-foot house had to be laid to rest. Sewer fees, electrical service, and water connections cost about the same for small and large houses.

The developer's target market was single, professional woman and empty-nester couples. Buyers fit this

Top: The "pocket" neighborhood is designed to fit comfortably into its suburban context.

Bottom: Parking for residents and visitors is accommodated unobtrusively on the edge of the site

target precisely: 63 percent of the homeowners are single women and 27 percent are empty nesters. All households include a working professional, among which are a college professor, a commercial appraiser, and a nurse. One single-parent household includes two children, the only resident children. One single woman shares her cottage with her elderly mother.

Compared with households in the surrounding area, Greenwood Avenue Cottage residents are older. Many of them are homeowners in their 50s or 60s who have decided to downsize.

Greenwood Avenue homebuyers were attracted by the project's high quality and attention to detail. The detached house format was also attractive, offering an alternative to apartment condominiums. A further attraction was the seamless integration of this project into its surrounding single-family residential neighborhood.

Marketing and Management

Publicity and the reputation of the Cottage Company marketed this project. The developer did a limited amount of advertising, held a home tour in June 2002, and placed a sign out front.

As the first cottage neighborhood to be built under the Shoreline code, the development was well covered by the local press. Greenwood Avenue Cottages was included in a couple of feature articles in the real estate section of the *Seattle Times*. Furthermore, the Cottage Company has earned a reputation for innovative development and people express interest in its projects before actual development starts.

The developer's Web site attracts thousands of visitors a month. Some of this traffic is due to widespread interest in the idea of cottage housing from all over the United States and Canada as well as from other places around the globe.

The Cottage Company directly sells all its cottages. They are not listed with brokers or multiple listing services. The developer does not provide selling commissions to brokers who come in with a buyer. The company feels that it is important to be a direct seller—it wants to understand how the buyers of its houses live and what they are looking for. This gives it key information for selling its next development.

The common grounds take up very little area and no third-party property manager is required. The homeowners set up a garden and facilities committee, which established a monthly homeowners association fee. They decide how much work to do themselves and how much is to be done by a gardener. The committee creates a list of chores—including a once-a-week inspection of the common buildings.

Experience Gained

■ The task of providing a level of comfort to neighbors and educating the city's planning staff on the suitability of putting eight houses on a site that ordinarily would fit only four was challenging. With this experience under its belt, the developer expects that its ability to invite the residents of functioning cottage communities to the planning meetings for future cottage housing projects and to arrange for decision makers to visit actual communities will facilitate this task.

■ Including a small private yard for each unit simplifies operations. The common areas for two subsequent cottage projects in Shoreline that have no private yards are too large for resident maintenance and thus must be maintained by outside management companies.

■ Homebuyers did not appreciate some of the important, underlying features of the Greenwood Avenue Cottages development—for example, the superior ventilation system with an inaudible fan, the high-quality insulation, and an innovative stormwater management system—because they were not well explained by the developer.

■ It would probably have been better to start serious marketing earlier to capture market interest at the beginning stages of the project when it was getting a lot of press.

■ In order to end up with neighborhoods to which residents are personally attached and willing to contribute time for maintenance, cottage housing clusters should not have more than 12 houses. The residents of the eight-unit cluster at Greenwood Avenue illustrate the degree of neighborliness that can be achieved by the fact that they celebrate many holidays together in the common room.

Interior views. Although only 780 to 1,000 square feet in size, each cottage contains two bedrooms and usable loft space, as well as a living room, kitchen, and dining nook.

CONTACT INFORMATION

DEVELOPER

The Cottage Company LLC

8215 41st Avenue NE

Seattle, Washington 98115

206-527-9128

www.cottagecompany.com

ARCHITECT

Ross Chapin Architects

P.O. Box 230

Langley, Washington 98260

www.rosschapin.com

DEVELOPMENT SCHEDULE

Site under Contract:	May 2000
Planning Started:	June 2000
Construction Started:	June 2001
Sales Started:	September 2001
First Closing:	March 2002
Construction Completed:	May 2002
Sales Completed:	June 2002

LAND USE INFORMATION

Site Area:	34,755 square feet (.8 acre)
Dwelling Units:	8
Residential Density:	10 units per gross acre

LAND USE PLAN

	SQUARE FEET	PERCENT OF SITE
Housing	9,355	27 %
Streets	5,900	17
Common Open Space	9,900	28
Private Open Space	9,600	28

RESIDENTIAL UNIT INFORMATION

UNIT TYPE	SIZE (SQUARE FEET)	NUMBER OF UNITS	INITIAL SALE PRICE RANGE
2 Bedrooms/ 1 Bath	780–1,000	8	$275,000– $289,000

DEMOGRAPHIC PROFILE

	PERCENT OF ALL HOUSEHOLDS	NUMBER OF RESIDENTS
HOUSEHOLD TYPE		
Singles	50 %	4
Singles with Children	13	3
Couples without Children	37	6
GENDER[1]		
Male	—	3
Female	—	10

1. *Gender of 11 adult residents and two children.*

DEVELOPMENT COST INFORMATION

SITE ACQUISITION COST	$310,200
SITE IMPROVEMENT COST[1]	185,000

CONSTRUCTION AND SOFT COSTS	
Structures[2]	690,000
Plumbing/Gas/Water Heaters	76,000
Electrical	63,000
Finishes	193,000
Hardscape[3]	32,000
Landscape	34,000
City Fees and Permits	36,000
Engineer/Consultants	35,000
Supervision	45,000
General Conditions	27,000
Loan Fees and Interest	87,000
Architectural Services	36,000
Development Services	48,000
Other Costs[4]	23,000
Direct Marketing	10,000
TOTAL	1,435,000

TOTAL DEVELOPMENT COST	$1,930,200
Development Cost per Unit	241,275

1. *Includes grading, sewer, water, stormwater, curbs, gutters, sidewalks, and paving.*
2. *Includes foundations, framing, roofing, siding and trim, drywall, insulation, doors, windows, and porches.*
3. *Includes walks, fences, and benches.*
4. *Includes administration, insurance, legal services, and condominium costs.*

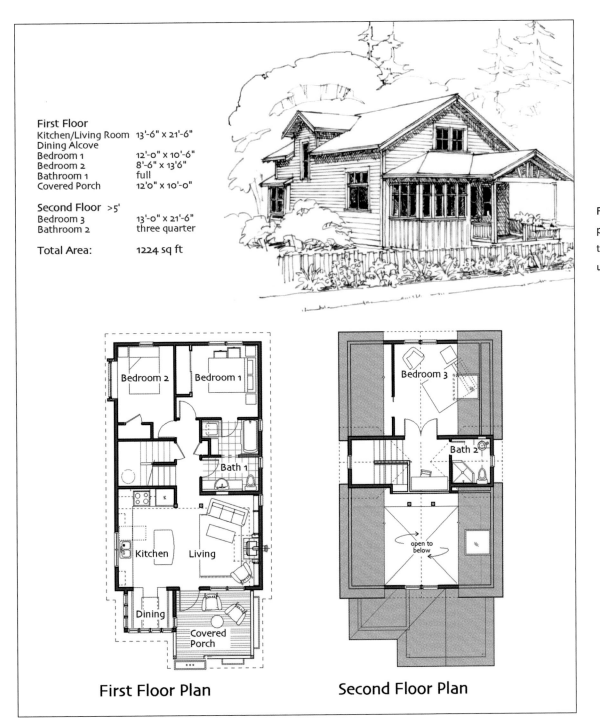

First Floor
Kitchen/Living Room 13'-6" x 21'-6"
Dining Alcove
Bedroom 1   12'-0" x 10'-6"
Bedroom 2   8'-6" x 13'6"
Bathroom 1   full
Covered Porch   12'0" x 10'-0"

Second Floor >5'
Bedroom 3   13'-0" x 21'-6"
Bathroom 2   three quarter

Total Area: 1224 sq ft

First- and second-floor plans for one of the cottages; the loft space is used for a third bedroom.

First Floor Plan

Second Floor Plan

Hearthstone

DENVER, COLORADO

Developed by Wonderland Hill Development Company, Hearthstone is a cohousing community of 33 townhouses located three miles northwest of downtown Denver. The 1.6-acre project is part of Highlands' Garden Village (HGV), a 27-acre new urbanist infill development that offers a mix of market-rate and affordable housing, neighborhood parks, and a civic and commercial center.

Cohousing is a development model in which future residents play an active role in the planning and design of the community, the community is designed to facilitate interaction among its residents, and residents are expected to be closely involved in the community's long-term management. A cohousing neighborhood is typically a compact cluster of 15 to 35 housing units organized around a network of pedestrian pathways and pedestrian-friendly activity nodes. It features a "common house" that is programmed by the residents and that may include a community kitchen and dining room, children's play spaces, guest rooms, laundry facilities, and a library or sitting room. Resident parking is usually located at the periphery.

About 85 cohousing communities have been built in the United States and Canada since the late 1980s. The first of these were developed by their eventual residents, who in the main were seeking an alternative to typical suburban housing developments lacking a strong sense of community. More recently, many cohousing initiatives have sought out professional development partners and a number of developers, including Wonderland Hill, have taken the lead in the collaborative development of cohousing projects. Wonderland has completed 13 cohousing projects in Colorado, California, Washington, and Arizona. Hearthstone is the first such project it has developed that is part of a planned unit development (PUD). It has proven profitable for both Wonderland and HGV developer Perry Rose. It also exceeds Colorado's Built Green program guidelines and has received the U.S. Environmental Protection Agency's Energy Star rating

Development Process and Financing

In 1998, Perry Rose LLC purchased the 27-acre site, which had been the location—until its shuttering four years earlier—of the Elitch Gardens Amusement Park, a once popular entertainment destination for Denver residents. The site was surrounded by declining residential neighborhoods and was a designated urban renewal area. Based on a mixed-use, new urbanist master plan prepared by planner Peter Calthorpe of Berkeley-based Calthorpe Associates, Perry Rose took the commercially zoned site

Top: Highlands' Garden Village mixes different product types, including Hearthstone cohousing (at left), multifamily housing (left background), and townhomes (middle).

Bottom: An aerial view of HGV. The development of the 1.6-acre Hearthstone cohousing neighborhood within HGV promoted the new urbanist goals of the larger community.

through a two-year public review process to get the project rezoned as a planned unit development (PUD).

The HGV plan envisioned a walkable, traditional neighborhood development designed in an environmentally sustainable manner with a mix of housing and commercial and civic activity. Perry Rose would develop the infrastructure and some amenities, including the restoration of several historic structures, and sell lots for development by local partners.

Jonathan Rose and Charles Perry approached Jim Leach, president of Wonderland Hill, about developing cohousing townhouses in a transitional area between neighborhoods designated for single-family houses and four-story multifamily apartments—a somewhat uninspiring area that is defined on its northeastern edge by a major arterial intersection at West 37th Avenue and Winona Street. Leach's spin-off company, Wonderland Homes, had already been selected to develop some of HGV's single-family and townhouse neighborhoods. Leach was well known for his instrumental role in developing the Colorado Built Green program, and he had completed six cohousing neighborhoods in the state. The HGV partners thought that cohousing could bring design and housing diversity to this portion of the site and contribute high-quality density to the overall PUD.

Perry, however, had some reservations. Noting that Leach's cohousing projects had done well in "progressive" areas of the state like Boulder but had been untried in Denver, he wondered if a cohousing component would take a development that was already risky and cutting-edge "over the top." However, most of his fears were allayed by Leach's description of his streamlined business model for cohousing development—a model that incorporates the participation of the (future) residents into a conventional project structure.

Leach argued that a cohousing project would give HGV a jump-start on housing sales and plant seeds leading to the establishment of a vital HGV community. Cohousing buyers are proactive and civic-minded, he noted, and would be positively inclined toward the mixed-income housing that was planned for next door. His business model projected that 70 percent of the cohousing units would be presold before the start of construction.

Perry Rose gave Wonderland Hill a one-year free option on the townhouse site, during which time the developer would refine the cohousing concept and organize a resident group. If cohousing was found to be feasible, the developer would purchase the site and agree on a profit share. In September 2000, Wonderland Hill purchased the site for $752,800.

Under the PUD zoning, the 1.6-acre Hearthstone site was designated a clustered housing zone for up to 70 units and a minimum of 1.5 parking spaces per unit. In accordance with a compromise negotiated by Perry Rose early in the public review process, the density of housing on this site was limited by a 35-foot height limit and a restriction against stacked units or flats. Wonderland Hill did not have to take the project through a separate public review process, but the developer met with local planning staff and held meetings with the West Highlands' Neighborhood Association.

Wonderland Hill worked with Perry Rose to integrate the cohousing plan into the new urbanist master plan. Development on the site was regulated by the master plan's guidelines on building design, roadways, and landscaping. All buildings at HGV were required to meet or exceed Colorado's Built Green program guidelines.

Development of the cohousing was financed by equity investment from Wonderland Hill Development, the resident group, and a private investor. They fell four units short of their goal of 70 percent presales before closing on the construction loan, but in the winter of 2000 the equity investors decided together to move forward with construction. Compass Bank provided the construction loan.

The developer and the resident group shared in the benefits as well as the risks associated with the project. Resident members invested incrementally in the project from the predevelopment stage to construction—including monthly dues and workshop fees, a 3.5 percent equity investment just before Wonderland secured the construction loan, and a 5 percent down payment due by the start of construction. Some residents chose to invest more into the project in return for discounts on their units, which sold for between $154,000 and $268,000. The project generated a 13 percent profit, which was split among

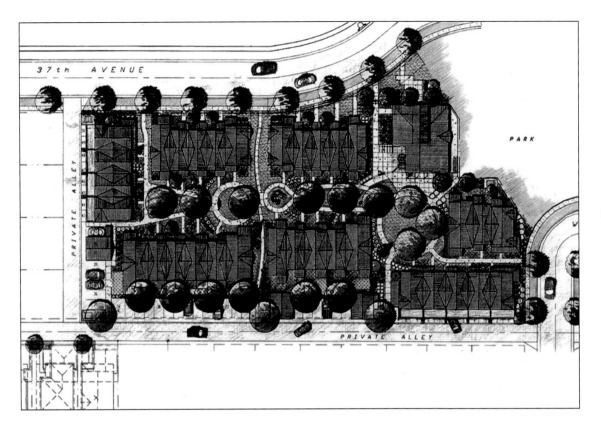

Site plan.

- Wonderland Hill Development, 37 percent;
- Perry Rose, 26 percent;
- the private investor, 18.5 percent; and
- the resident group, 18.5 percent, with this share going into the budget of the homeowners association.

After the completion of the townhouses and common house in early 2002, the resident group finalized its purchase of the project from the developer. The last two units were sold in the summer of 2002. The townhouse units are individually owned as condominiums, with the public spaces owned by the Hearthstone Home Owners Association.

Community Planning and Design

The development team worked collaboratively with HGV site planner Peter Calthorpe and Hearthstone's (future) resident group to plan and design Hearthstone. HGV's new urbanist guidelines were consistent with the key elements of village design for a cohousing development. A central design challenge was to create permeable boundaries that would respond meaningfully to neighborhood conditions and help establish Hearthstone as an identifiable community. In the course of the planning and design process, the Cohousing Company, the conceptual architect, organized three collaborative programming workshops with the resident group, at which the architect presented a series of design options.

The site plan that emerged from this process locates townhouse clusters around a linear community green. Landscaped gaps and pathways between the buildings provide attractive, narrow view lines; connect the townhouses with each other, to peripheral carports and garages, and to the common house; and connect Hearthstone to the surrounding neighborhoods. The buildings are arranged to create neighborhood definition and privacy. The community green—which is 50 feet or less in width from front porch to front porch—invites informal interactions among neighbors and provides a safe place for children to play. Most residents have a direct view to the common house from their front porch. Parking is provided in carports and garages along alleys (driveways)

shared with HGV at the edges of the Hearthstone site. Because this arrangement does not require interior driveways, more space is made available for shared community uses.

The common house, located at the northeastern edge of the site, marks the meeting point between Hearthstone and the adjacent neighborhood and buffers the community green from a park and playground shared by all HGV residents to the east. The common house is designed to look like a community building. A relatively wide path on its west side indicates arrival into the Hearthstone community. A patio opens out onto the eastern end of the community green.

The character of the housing derives from traditional village design as well as the cottage, Victorian, and bungalow architecture of Denver's older neighborhoods. Hearthstone's housing is distinguished from neighboring housing by its up-close and friendly scale, relaxed internal boundaries, bright colors, and simple but articulated facades. Its high-pitched roofs contribute to a villagelike feel.

The project's community amenities include generous outdoor spaces and walkways well separated from vehicular traffic, a tot lot, and a bike-storage shed. Local grasses and plants are used for landscaping in most of the common areas, minimizing water use and lowering maintenance requirements.

The 4,800-square-foot common house serves as the center of the community, symbolically and in practice. Its finished 2,400-square-foot main floor features a large kitchen, a dining (and meeting) room for 70 people, a sitting room with a fireplace, a small library, a playroom, a bathroom, and a laundry room. Mail boxes are located in its entry area, which also offers a large coat and mud room, bins for recycling junk mail, announcement boards, and assigned cubbies into which residents can put notes or small items. Residents use the common house for classes, clubs, community meetings, community dinners and brunches, as well as for family events and parties. The basement of the common house is unfinished, and residents are currently deciding what they will do with it.

Hearthstone residents also can take advantage of access to a number of HGV community amenities, including a community garden, a playground, parks, and the civic and commercial center. A restored carousel with labyrinth and the HGV concert green are located only a two-minute walk from the Hearthstone common house.

Unit Design

The project's 33 compact townhouses are designed to be resource-efficient and to provide gradations of privacy and flexibility in use over time. All front doors face a community open space or pathway. Kitchens are located in the front, and have a generous window above the sink looking out on community open space. The dining and living rooms extend in an open plan toward the back, providing more privacy. The bedrooms are also tucked away at the back or located on the second story. Each house has a 6.5-foot-wide covered front porch, which is wide enough for a small table and several chairs, and a more private back deck or porch.

The design and housing mix reflects the developer's extensive work with the (future) resident group on ascertaining preferences and housing needs. Units range from 1,304 to 2,146 square feet and contain one to three bedrooms plus unfinished basement space that can be adapted for bedrooms or other uses.

Environmentally advanced features are integrated into every unit. These include energy-efficient mechanical systems, a high-efficiency boiler and hydronic radiant heat, high-performance insulation and windows, resource-efficient Energy Star appliances, low-impact materials such as bamboo floors and natural linoleum, low VOC paints, and fiber cement siding.

Certain upgrades—such as hardwood floors, higher-end cabinetry, operable skylights, and advanced environmental features—were optional. The residents were instrumental in pushing the developer to include as standard certain design and mechanical elements that were not originally proposed. They felt, for example, that some of the finishes specified by the architect were too plain and so formed a committee to find alternatives. A group of residents who were planning to opt for hydronic radiant heat as an upgrade persuaded the others to invest in it as a standard feature. The residents as a whole advocated for handicapped-accessible features.

Top left: The common house, which has a kitchen, dining room, and meeting rooms, is the practical as well as the symbolic center of the cohousing community

Top right: Hearthstone's 33 townhouses face a central green, while their garages and backyards face the site's perimeter.

Bottom: Townhouse exteriors. Cohousing appeals to people seeking an alternative to typical suburban subdivisions lacking a strong sense of community. Homebuyers helped design the site plan and houses.

Book club meetings, group meals, and resident-taught classes are among the activities that take place regularly in the common house, which is maintained and managed by Hearthstone residents.

Marketing

The marketing for a cohousing project is essentially an ongoing community-building process that involves collaborative planning and programming, workshops, and outreach. At Hearthstone, as prospective residents became more interested, they could elect to become decision-making members of the (future) resident group. The monthly dues and workshop fees they paid were put toward their house purchase and community amenities.

Cohousing marketing relies primarily on word of mouth, advertising in lifestyle media, and efforts to get the word out at the grass-roots level—for example, at grocery stores, schools, libraries, churches, and public civic events. At Hearthstone, the developer and members of the resident group members worked side by side to promote interest in the project. To help the resident group work effectively, the developer provided consensus training, facilitated meetings, and assisted in the formation of task committees.

Wonderland Hill notes that although its investment in marketing and community support activities in cohousing projects comes at the beginning of the development process rather than at the end, the marketing budget is the same as for more conventional projects. Once the collaborative planning and marketing process is set in motion, (future) residents become effective marketers for the project.

Target Market and Resident Profile

Potential cohousing homebuyers are easier to categorize by using psychographics than by using conventional demographics. The target market comprises people in all age groups and households of all types. Basically, cohousing homebuyers tend to be middle-income households that put as much or even more value on the qualitative aspects of a neighborhood—especially its walkability and neighborliness—than on the size and style of their individual housing units. People who are attracted to cohousing are willing to take an active role in creating neighborly communities and are often enlivened by the prospect.

The emerging market of cohousing buyers is made up of "cultural creatives"—that is, well-educated individuals with a strong sense of social and environmental stewardship; people who seek out cross-cultural experiences and are driven to act creatively in the world; people who express their values in positive, meaningful ways, often through active engagement in political and civic life; people who shop at alternative retailers and eat at local restaurants, who buy hybrid cars and gravitate toward green-built housing.

Cultural creatives tend to feel disconnected from conventional housing choices. At cohousing organizing meetings, the parents of young children often talk about feeling a lack of connection to extended family and friends in their current neighborhood, and about the relentless cycle of auto-dependence and structured play dates. Empty nesters and retirees talk about their frustration with age-segregated communities and a forced culture of leisure and consumption. Singles, especially single women, talk about the isolation they feel in their neighborhoods. These diverse kinds of households all see cohousing as an attractive, viable alternative to conventional housing choices.

Hearthstone has attracted a diverse mix of residents that enhances the economic and household diversity of the HGV neighborhood. The homebuyers at Hearthstone range in age from their late 20s to their early 80s. Of the community's 68 residents, 46 percent are between 25 and 44 years old; 21 percent between 45 and 54; and 10 percent 55 and over. Fifteen children live in the community.

Of the 53 adults living at Hearthstone, 19 are single and 34 are living in couples. Most of the single residents are women. Residents are highly educated.

A number of regular activities are well attended, including twice a week dinners at the common house, brunches, a book club, resident-taught classes, and a lace stitching group. Residents have organized a twice monthly parents night out with parents taking turns watching the children. Hearthstone residents hold monthly general meetings. They maintain and manage the common areas, including the common house.

Experience Gained

■ The market for cohousing is particularly strong among young families, single women, and active older adults. The developer's next project, Silver Sage Village in Boulder, will be a cohousing project geared to seniors and located across the street from a multigenerational cohousing community.

■ Collaborative planning translates into sales. The stronger the decision-making and problem-solving capabilities of the cohousing resident group, the stronger the project will be.

■ The success of the Hearthstone project suggests a productive meeting ground for new urbanist place making and the cohousing model of community development. According to the developer of HGV, Hearthstone demonstrates not only that cohousing involves no extra risk for a master-planned community, but also that it represents a good way to introduce economic and housing diversity into a new urbanist community and to enhance the sense of place, a result that is perhaps symbolized by the use of Hearthstone's common house for HGV homeowner association meetings.

■ The preference of the Hearthstone resident group for a compact community, enabled HGV to achieve a higher residential density.

■ In the opinion of HGV developer Charles Perry, Perry Rose had better financial results from sharing the cohousing profits than they would have had from putting a conventional townhouse development on the lot.

■ A collaborative development process with future residents helps a developer create a better product. As Leach says: "Community is the way to go if you want to develop projects that are environmentally sustainable and architecturally high quality."

■ The business model developed for Hearthstone effectively shared risk and profit between the resident group and the developer. Resident investment covered most predevelopment costs and contributed to the project's cash flow. The residents supported—and even pushed for—design innovation. As advocates for their future neighborhood, the residents became their own sales force.

■ Working with customers almost on a daily basis from the start of a project can be difficult for the developer. The developer needs to provide ongoing customer education and to carefully manage expectations.

■ Trying to sell housing based primarily on community value rather than on the value of the individual unit is a risk-filled endeavor. Because the extent of the cultural creatives demographic is still largely unknown, each cohousing project is a step into an untried market. Leach's experience, however, suggests that the market for cohousing is strong in urban communities and university communities—as long as the local planning department is innovative.

■ Although the zoning did not allow multifamily flats, there would have been a market for one-bedroom apartments at Hearthstone.

CONTACT INFORMATION

PROJECT WEB SITES

www.whdc.com

www.denvercohousing.com

DEVELOPER

Wonderland Hill Development Company

745 Poplar Avenue

Boulder, Colorado 80304

303-449-3232

www.whdc.com

HEARTHSTONE PROJECT INFORMATION

ARCHITECTS

The Cohousing Company (Conceptual Architect)

1250 Addison Street, #113

Berkeley, California 94702

510-549-9980

www.cohousingco.com

Synergy Design (Unit Design)

917 Cottonwood Circle

Golden, Colorado 80401

303-278-1880

www.synergyhomeplans.com

GENERAL CONTRACTOR

Lennar Family of Builders

9990 Park Meadows Drive

Lone Tree, Colorado 80124

303-430-9080

www.lennar.com

DEVELOPMENT SCHEDULE

Master Planning Started:	January 1997
Cohousing Planning Started:	January 1999
Sales Started:	January 1999
Site Purchased:	September 2000
Construction Started:	December 2000
Project Completed:	February 2002

LAND USE INFORMATION

Site Area:	1.576 acres
Dwelling Units:	33
Residential Density:	20.9 units per gross acre
Parking Ratio:	1.5 spaces per housing unit

LAND USE PLAN

	SQUARE FEET	ACRES	PERCENT OF SITE
Buildings[1]	31,344	.72	46 %
Parking	4,941	.11	7
Open Space	32,365	.74	47

1. *Including porches and garages.*

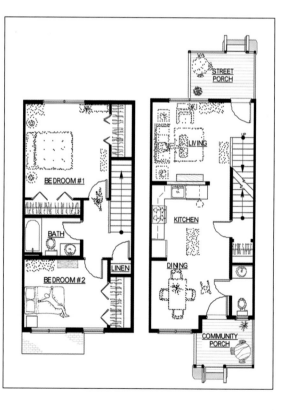

Floor plan for a 1,568-square-foot townhouse. Every townhouse features a porch, passive solar design, and open floor plan.

RESIDENTIAL UNIT INFORMATION

UNIT TYPE[1]	UNIT SIZE (SQUARE FEET)	NUMBER OF UNITS BUILT	SOLD	INITIAL SALE PRICE[2]
A: 1 Bedroom/1 Bath	1,304	3	3	$154,000
B: 4 Bedrooms/3 Baths	2,112	4	4	249,000
C: 3 Bedrooms/2.5 Baths	1,568	12	12	183,000
D: 4 Bedrooms/3.5 Baths	2,060	5	5	238,000
E: 4 Bedrooms/3.5 Baths	2,146	4	4	259,000
F: 4 Bedrooms/3.5 Baths	2,024	2	2	241,000
G: 4 Bedrooms/3.5 Baths	2,112	3	3	259,000

1. Unit types B, C, D, E, F, and G include unfinished space equivalent to one bedroom and one bathroom; thus, for example, B units contain three finished and one unfinished bedroom and two finished and one unfinished bathroom.
2. Base price; does not include buyer options and upgrades or lot premiums.

DEMOGRAPHIC PROFILE

	PERCENT OF ALL RESIDENTS OR HOUSEHOLDS
AGE RANGE	
<18	22 %
18–24	1
25–34	25
35–44	21
45–54	21
55–64	4
65+	6
HOUSEHOLD TYPE	
Singles with Children[1]	9
Singles without Children[2]	40
Couples with Children[3]	33
Couples without Children[4]	18
GENDER (SINGLE-PERSON HOUSEHOLDS)	
Male	26
Female	74

1. Singles with children living at home.
2. Four single-person households "without children" have children living away from home.
3. Couples with children living at home.
4. One couple household "without children" has children living away from home.

DEVELOPMENT COST INFORMATION

SITE ACQUISITION	$752,800
CONSTRUCTION COSTS	
Residential Units	2,695,391
Common House	301,846
Common Elements[1]	198,401
Garages and Carports	68,621
Field Overhead	212,177
Contingency	114,249
General Conditions[2]	412,929
Options and Change Orders	327,581
TOTAL	4,331,195
SOFT COSTS	
Design/Engineering	274,912
Permits and Fees	157,855
Administrative/Legal/Miscellaneous	80,647
Community Allowances3	24,800
Community Marketing Budget	150,640
Project Management Fees	382,700
Financing Costs	255,979
Costs Incurred at Closing	171,260
Warranty Costs	25,000
Project Contingency	20,000
TOTAL	1,543,793
TOTAL DEVELOPMENT COST	$6,627,788

1. Includes landscaping, sidewalks, and paving.
2. Includes contractor profit.
3. Includes landscape allowance ($6,000) and common facilities allowance ($18,800).

Jefferson Commons at Minnesota

With student enrollment in degree-granting higher educational institutions projected to reach approximately 17.5 million by 2011—an increase of 16 percent over ten years—student housing continues to be a lucrative proposition, both on and off campus. The good news for developers specializing in this product is that the need will remain strong for years to come.

In recent years, on-campus housing has satisfied only 30 percent of undergraduate student demand. JPI, a multifamily residential developer headquartered in Irving, Texas, entered the student housing market in 1994 in response to that need. Since then, the privately held, 1,000-person company has developed 28 off-campus student apartment communities in 14 states. All but two of these have "Jefferson" in their name. Most of them are called "Jefferson Commons"—JPI's brand for this particular housing product, which is always located close to a major college or university. JPI also has an on-campus division that has developed 11 student housing projects in tandem with university clients.

Jefferson Commons at Minnesota is a garden apartment complex in downtown Minneapolis, three blocks from the University of Minnesota campus. It features four four-story residential buildings containing 164 apartments (480 bedrooms); 38 one-car garages in three detached buildings; 206 surface parking spaces; a clubhouse; an outdoor Jacuzzi; bike storage facilities; and leasing and management offices.

JPI rents individual bedrooms—not units—to students, with lease terms of 12 months. It began leasing activities more than a year before project completion in fall 2003. The complex has been 95 percent occupied on average since opening, despite stiff competition. Encouraged by its success in a new market for its student housing, JPI is considering developing a second site in Minneapolis.

Site and Surroundings

The 4.17-acre site, which lies a mile east of the revitalized downtown business district, was formerly occupied by an industrial building with three tenants. The building was razed to make way for Jefferson Commons, which shares its immediate environs with older single-family neighborhoods, commercial and retail uses, and several competi-

SIGNIFICANT FEATURES

- Off-campus rental housing for university students

- Branded housing product

- Individual furnished bedrooms as the lease unit

- Hiring program for tenants in project maintenance and management work

Front view of clubhouse and two of the complex's four garden apartment buildings.

tors. Located one-eighth mile east of the University of Minnesota–Twin Cities campus, the site fronts Huron Boulevard, a major artery to the campus. Classrooms and the Stadium Village retail/entertainment strip, a popular student hangout featuring retail and dining venues, are within a seven-minute walk.

City buses stop in front of Jefferson Commons on Huron, and university buses stop on Huron three blocks west (toward the campus). Many local and chain restaurants (including Burger King, Starbucks, Subway, and Blimpies) and stores (including Blockbuster Video, a university book store, a copy center, a bank, and other student-oriented shops) are within easy walking distance.

Development Process and Financing

The property was zoned as an Industrial Living Overlay District (ILOD), a classification that the city of Minneapolis created for its warehouse districts primarily along the Mississippi River downtown and adjacent to the University of Minnesota campus. The ILOD allows multifamily housing as a conditional use. In order to

meet an aggressive production schedule and project pro forma, JPI elected to proceed with the highest-density project it could fit on the site without rezoning, rather than applying for variances that would have permitted higher densities. Local height limitations, floor/area ratios, and construction costs also contributed to the decision to limit the development to four-story buildings.

The core of the site consisted of several privately owned parcels, which JPI acquired by negotiation. The site adjoins federal highway I-94 and Huron Boulevard, which connects to the highway. In order to meet minimum lot size requirements and gain control of the edges of the site, JPI had to acquire approximately two acres of excess right-of-way from the Minnesota Department of Transportation. MnDOT was required to first offer the land to the parties from which it had been originally acquired, unless the city asked for the land for public purposes. JPI applied to the Minneapolis Community Development Agency, the city's redevelopment authority, to ask MnDOT to convey the land to the city, with subsequent reconveyance to JPI.

On-site surface parking. Noting that the project would have more than three times as many beds as apartment units, the city of Minneapolis upped its parking requirement.

Because of the notice and hearing periods required to establish the public purpose for which the city would acquire and reconvey the land, the municipal application and acquisition process took two months. Because MnDOT had to determine that the right-of-way was in fact "excess" and had to obtain state and federal authorization for the sale, its acquisition process took longer.

JPI's approach on this type of project is to spend predevelopment dollars to get the land titled to its purpose and then go to settlement with building permits already in place. According to Derrick J. Turnbull, the JPI vice president and area partner responsible for developing this project: "In a best-of-all-possible-worlds scenario, we would have entitlements and permits so we could close the deal one day and start moving land the next. There is no slack in our construction schedule, which is based on the school year. Student housing must be ready for occupancy by the start of fall semester, period."

JPI projects, including Jefferson Commons at Minnesota, are financed through an investment venture with General Electric Capital Services. GE Capital has committed more than $650 million in equity to this venture, making JPI one of the largest private multifamily real estate companies in the country. JPI has a bank capacity of $2.5 billion and a net worth estimated at $484 million.

Planning

The development of Jefferson Commons involved two closely related critical planning issues—the project's impact on the surrounding residential neighborhood and its impact on parking. In that the city's zoning ordinance does not address student housing per se, the zoning administrator was permitted to apply multifamily housing

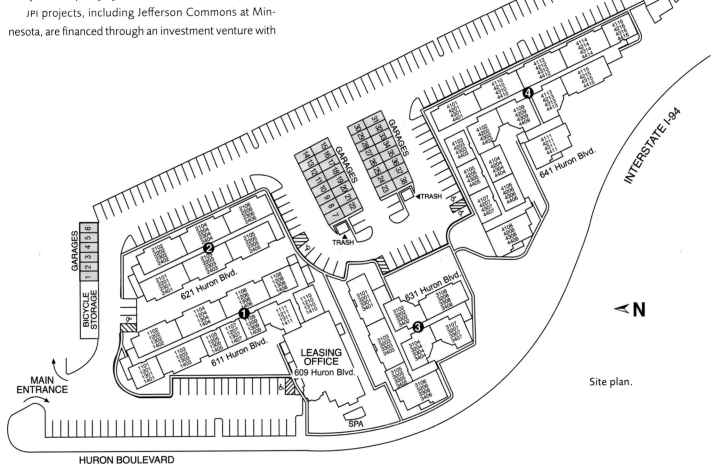

Site plan.

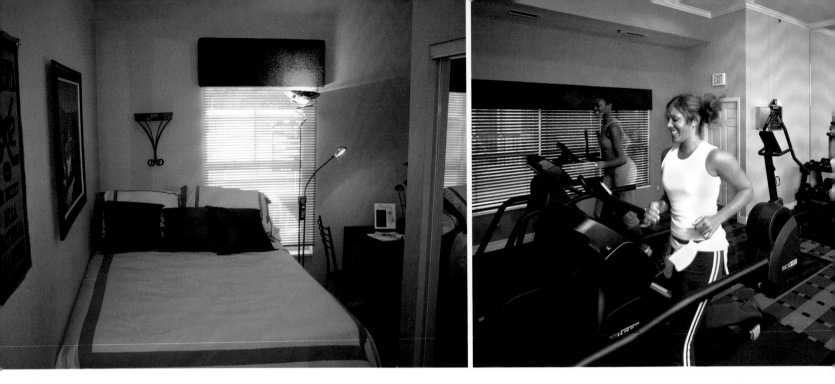

Left: A bedroom. Jefferson Commons features unit layouts, finishes, and custom furnishings that offer more privacy and personal space than a typical student dorm.

Right: Inside the fitness center room. The developer's surveys indicated that students would be willing to pay rent premiums for in-unit washers and dryers, a location near campus, effective sound-proofing, and fitness facilities.

standards. Thus, parking was the only planning issue that required special administrative attention.

The conditional use permit process under which Jefferson Commons was approved gave the city authority to require more than the one stall per unit of on-site parking required under the city's multifamily ordinance. The city deemed one stall per bed excessive for a project that was proposed to have a maximum of 555 beds in 164 units—and it deemed one stall per unit inadequate. It thus required JPI to prepare a travel demand management plan to help the city establish a parking ratio appropriate for the proposed use. Based on JPI's plan; an existing study of available travel alternatives to cars, including transit, walking, and biking; and traffic counts at similar facilities, the city established a parking ratio for this project of 1.46 spaces per unit—or .43 per bed. Five percent of parking spaces are reserved for visitors.

The city's planning process mandates the review of proposed projects by designated neighborhood associations. The determinations made by these associations are only advisory, but they exercise a significant impact on the decisions of the planning commission and the city council. East and west of the historically industrial project site lie residential neighborhoods, including a relatively affluent area of single-family homes owned by professors and professionals.

However, the site is separated from the single-family neighborhood by a low-income housing project, topographical changes, and an arterial street—so neighborhood association concern about the visual impact of Jefferson Common was minimal. On the other hand, the possibility that students would park on neighborhood streets to avoid paying an additional $75 per month for an on-site surface stall or $125 per month for a garage was of concern. In the end, the neighborhood association was satisfied that the developer's travel demand management plan demonstrated that the project would supply adequate parking on-site for students with cars.

Design

Capitalizing on market acceptance and brand recognition of the Jefferson Commons program, JPI uses the same basic design plan for each of its student communities, tailored to meet the specific needs of each location. The developer's student communities in suburban areas are built in a garden style configuration, with buildings encircling a landscaped courtyard and clubhouse/pool area. Suburban projects typically range in size from 150 to 300 units with 550 to 850 bedrooms, and they are built at a density of 15 to 20 units per acre. JPI also offers an urban garden apartment product that ranges from 40 to 60 units per acre and a high-rise

product that attains up to 100 units per acre.

The site plan for Jefferson Commons at Minnesota departs from the norm because of the parcel's long and somewhat narrow shape. Here the main entrance is located at the northwestern tip of the site just off Huron Boulevard. The northernmost third of the site is occupied by Buildings 1 and 2 and the leasing office/clubhouse and spa. The central portion of the site houses Building 3, most of the garages, and most of the outdoor trash receptacles. Building 4 occupies the southeastern end of the site. Surface parking is located along the eastern edge.

Prior to designing a student community, JPI surveys students to determine what amenities they would be willing to pay for in the form of rent premiums. A Web survey involving 600 or so University of Minnesota–Twin Cities students indicated that they would place a high priority on washers and dryers in apartment units (96 percent), a location within walking distance of the campus (96 percent), soundproofing (90 percent), air conditioning (85 percent), and an on-site fitness center (84 percent). Fewer of these students indicated a willingness to pay for a walk-in closet (78 percent) or resort style pool (66 percent).

Local zoning codes, construction costs, and the city's inclement winter weather were factors in the exterior design of buildings. The design features wood-frame construction, vinyl siding, and brick accents, and porticoes above the building entrances providing protection from the elements. The exterior palette is neutral—gray with white trim. A more vibrant color scheme differentiates interior public spaces, such as the lobby of the leasing office, the business center, the game room, and the fitness center.

The unit layouts are intended to accommodate a variety of living arrangements and budgets. Jefferson Commons at Minnesota offers four basic apartment types ranging from one to four bedrooms. Three different layouts of the popular two-bedroom/two-bathroom alternative are available.

JPI's student apartment communities are essentially dorms, and the unit layouts, finishes, and custom furnishings are designed to accommodate a student lifestyle. Seeking to provide each tenant with as much private space as possible, the design emphasizes privacy and clear boundaries with respect to each tenant's bed, desk, closet, and storage space. Although on-site management staff works to match potential roommates, five strangers may find themselves sharing living quarters— underlining the importance of privacy issues. In that students tend to be hard on their living quarters, the design specifies finishes that are relatively easy to maintain and inexpensive to replace.

Apartments are outfitted with utilitarian yet funky

Left: High-speed Internet access and phone and cable TV connectivity are essential amenities for student renters.

Right: To meet security concerns, unit break-in alarms are hardwired to the front desk; entry into each building is controlled by a passcard; and a security officer lives on site.

and attractive living-room, dining-room, and bedroom furniture, much of it designed specifically for JPI; a full-size washer and dryer; kitchen appliances; and ready wiring for phone, cable, and data/modem lines in the living room and bedrooms.

Security is a concern to both parents and students. Each unit is equipped with an audible intrusion alarm that can be connected to a central monitoring station for a nominal monthly fee. Additionally, a security officer lives on site and entry into each building and the clubhouse is controlled by passcards.

Target Market and Market Analysis

JPI targets its Jefferson Commons developments for locations with an established major university with a minimum of 15,000 students and a stable enrollment base; a relatively low supply of high-quality, off-campus student housing; and available sites with easy access to the university campus.

The target market (and resident profile) for these projects is easily defined—undergraduates. Full-time freshmen are a particular target, because they represent potential renewals over several years. JPI determines eligibility for tenancy by university enrollment—tenants must be enrolled as students—and financial ability to pay rent. There is no age limit. Apartment units have all female or all male tenancy. For all JPI's Jefferson Commons developments in 2004, females made up 65 percent of tenants and males 35 percent.

JPI performs extensive research before entering a new market. For Jefferson Commons at Minnesota, it evaluated university growth trends, the local economy, and the rental market. The university's Office of Institutional Research provided evidence of recent and projected growth in enrollment. The developer used Economy.com—a provider of economic, financial, and industry data—as its source on the metropolitan area's demographic and economic trends. *Apartment Trends*, a quarterly report issued by GVA Marquette Advisors, provided information on historic and projected occupancy rates, supply forecasts, options for off-campus student housing, and rental rates. Finally, JPI identified a number of competing properties and analyzed them based on their location, number of units, unit type,

number of bedrooms, amenities, and rental rates.

Marketing and Management

Most students start looking in the fall for a place to live the following school year. Leasing activity heats up in March, April, and May. JPI's goal is to be 70 percent pre-leased by the end of the spring semester for the following school year.

More than a year before Jefferson Commons at Minnesota was completed, JPI mounted a comprehensive advertising and marketing campaign with a budget of about $200,000. It located its leasing office strategically within a popular retail strip on Huron, next to a Subway and a pizza joint—guaranteeing lots of foot traffic. And it put up signs at the construction site that directs students to its Web site and leasing office.

Other marketing efforts in which JPI engaged include the distribution of flyers on campus, ads in the programs of sports events, event sponsorships, bus and bench ads, the distribution of flyers through campus kiosks, and an open house and grand opening

Management of Jefferson Commons at Minnesota requires four full-time administrative employees and two full-time and five part-time maintenance employees. The maintenance full-timers are handymen who make basic plumbing, drywall, and fixture repairs. Major repairs and services, like electrical services, are subcontracted out. The maintenance part-timers are students in JPI's community assistants program, who must work 16 hours per week. Their tasks range from office work to light maintenance chores. Groundskeeping is contracted with a local landscaping company.

Experience Gained

■ Off-campus student rental housing is in its own product category. Its developer must be sensitive to the requirements not only of the target tenants, but also of whoever is paying the rent—usually their parents.

■ Although JPI has 28 student rental apartment projects under its belt and several more in the planning stage, it invests in good market research before planning each project. The University of Minnesota student survey for this project identified the services and amenities valued by this target market and for which they were willing to pay. The findings from this survey were used to establish the building and management program.

■ Many brokers like to focus on income-producing properties rather than the difficult business of land brokerage. Rather than use a land broker, JPI generally looks for its own sites and shops the comps—except in certain tough markets in which the company keeps selected brokers on retainer.

■ For student apartments, a flat monthly fee per bedroom that encompasses all services and utilities except for telephone greatly simplifies the leasing, move-in, and payment processes.

■ In urban areas where opportunities for extracurricular activities abound and part-time and summer jobs are widely available, students tend to remain in their apartments throughout the year. In the more rural areas, they are more likely to leave during school breaks.

■ Student tenants are harder on a building than is any other type of tenant. Student rental buildings should use materials and finishes that are least easily vandalized and most easily repaired.

■ Wide corridors are not a good design element, because they encourage students to congregate in them.

■ Balconies are a good design element. They are universally popular and they provide a place other than inside the apartment for tenants or visitors to smoke.

■ JPI's experience with allowing pets in student rental properties has been negative; no pets are allowed in JPI student housing.

Project Update

In November 2004, JPI sold Jefferson Commons at Minnesota for $31 million to Evergreen Development LLC, a company based in Santa Ana, California. The occupancy rate at the time of sale was 93 percent. Evergreen Development renamed the project Fulton Avenue Commons and will lease to graduate students. Luke McCarthy, chief executive of Evergreen, said in a statement: "Investors see value in the continued constant demand in the university environment and security in the creditworthiness of working graduate students with parents as cosigners on 12-month leases."

Model apartment. JPI has developed 28 off-campus student housing projects. The company looks for locations near large universities with a relatively low supply of attractive rental housing.

JEFFERSON COMMONS AT MINNESOTA PROJECT INFORMATION

CONTACT INFORMATION

OWNER
(as of November 2004)
Evergreen Development LLC
1851 East 1st Street, Suite 900
Santa Ana, California 92705

DEVELOPER
JPI
600 East Las Colinas Boulevard, Suite 1800
Irving, Texas 75039
www.jpi.com

ARCHITECT
Humphreys & Partners Architects
5350 Alpha Road
Dallas, Texas 75240
972-701-9636
www.humphreys.com

LAND USE ATTORNEY
Leonard, Street and Deinard
150 South Fifth Street, Suite 2300
Minneapolis, Minnesota 55402
612-335-1500
www.leonard.com

DEVELOPMENT SCHEDULE

Planning Started:	summer 2001
Site Purchased:	December 2001
Construction Started:	spring 2002
Leasing Started:	fall 2002
Project Completed:	August 2003
Project Sold:	November 2004

LAND USE INFORMATION

Site Area:	4.17 acres
Dwelling Units:	164
Parking:	
Surface Spaces	206
One-Car Garages	38
Parking Ratios	1.49 spaces per housing unit; .43 spaces per bed
Residential Buildings:	
Number	4
Leasable Area	154,748 square feet
Common Area	45,252 square feet
Total Area	200,000 square feet

LAND USE PLAN

	PERCENT OF SITE
Buildings	30%
Roads/Parking	47
Landscaping/Open Space	22
Other Uses	1

RESIDENTIAL UNIT INFORMATION

UNIT TYPE	UNIT SIZE (SQUARE FEET)	NUMBER OF UNITS	AVERAGE RENT PER BEDROOM
1 Bedroom/1 Bath	501	16	$899
2 Bedrooms/2 Baths	727	36	659
2 Bedrooms/2 Baths	905	28	835
4 Bedrooms/2 Baths	1,111	72	554
4 Bedrooms/4 Baths	1,205	12	625

Site Acquisition	$2,545,000
Construction	16,700,000
Soft Costs	7,800,000
TOTAL DEVELOPMENT COST	$27,045,000
Development Cost per Unit	185,240
Construction Cost per Net Rentable Square Foot	108

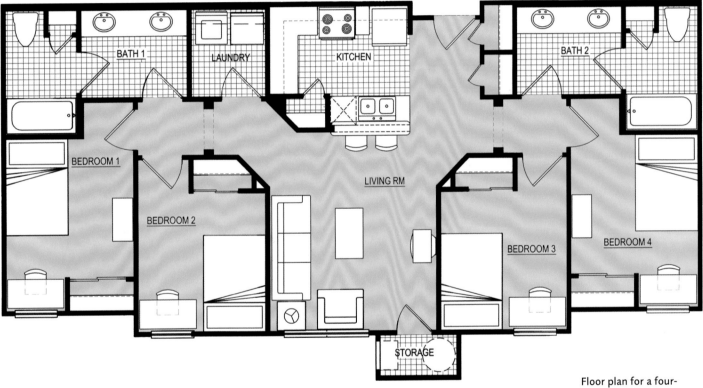

Floor plan for a four-bedroom, two-bath unit.

Lasell Village

SIGNIFICANT FEATURES

■ College-affiliated continuing-care retirement community (CCRC)

■ Site zoned for mixed residential and educational uses

■ Residency requirement includes 450 hours of "active learning" a year

■ Independent living apartments and skilled nursing care facility

To enable Lasell Village residents to meet their annual active learning commitments, each building contains an educational element, such as a classroom, a fitness studio, or an art studio.

Lasell Village is a continuing-care retirement community (CCRC) adjoining the campus of Lasell College in Newton, Massachusetts. Eight miles west of Boston, Newton is an upscale suburb known for its quality of life, a well-educated and progressive-minded citizenry, outstanding public schools, and several institutions of higher learning. The 171-unit development on 13.2 acres combines the standard amenities of an independent-living CCRC with a nonstandard educational program that residents consistently say is the most important aspect of their life at Lasell Village. As part of their residency, Lasell Villagers commit to an annual 450 hours of "active" learning and physical fitness programs—the equivalent of an undergraduate course load at the college. Part of the active learning requirement involves residents' participation in intergenerational programs with Lasell College students and elementary-school students in Newton.

The project was developed by Lasell College in partnership with CareMatrix at a time when the college was looking for a new educational niche and a much needed income stream. Completed in 2000, Lasell Village has in fact distinguished the college as an educational innovator—and it has exceeded the college's financial goals for its development as well. Lasell Village's design as a clustered village supports its educational mission and provides opportunities for resident interaction. The Village is three minutes by foot from the college campus and five minutes from a light-rail station serving Boston. Its walkability and accessibility to the college, public transportation, and local amenities make it possible for residents to stay independent as they age. Lasell Village has attracted a base of enthusiastic residents—average age 83—who want to stay intellectually engaged, value the convenience and security of a CCRC, and welcome the opportunity to be part of an intergenerational learning community.

Development Process and Financing

Lasell College was founded in 1851 as Auburndale Female Seminary and renamed Lasell Junior College in 1932. Until its recent restructuring as a four-year coeducational institution, it had been the nation's oldest two-year women's college.

The college began planning the development of a retirement community in 1988, soon after Thomas de Witt had been brought on board as president to turn around the fiscally struggling institution, whose enrollment had declined to a 32-year low. De Witt's rescue plan involved a major restructuring of operations, programs to enhance the college's image, the establishment of a four-year academic curriculum, and educational innovation. In 1988, an opportunity presented itself to de Witt and the col-

Site plan and an
aerial view.

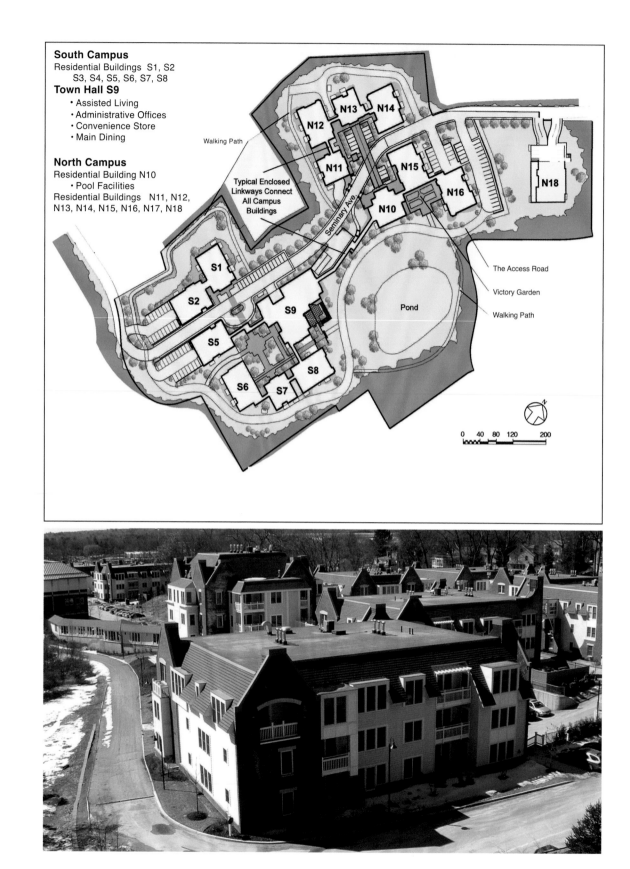

South Campus
Residential Buildings S1, S2
  S3, S4, S5, S6, S7, S8
Town Hall S9
  • Assisted Living
  • Administrative Offices
  • Convenience Store
  • Main Dining

North Campus
Residential Building N10
  • Pool Facilities
Residential Buildings N11, N12,
N13, N14, N15, N16, N17, N18

Walking Path

Typical Enclosed
Linkways Connect
All Campus
Buildings

N13 N14
N12
N11 N15
N18
N16
N10

Seminary Ave

The Access Road

Victory Garden

Walking Path

Pond

S1
S2
S9
S5
S8
S6 S7

0 40 80 120 200

lege's board of trustees when development restrictions on a donated 13.2-acre tract of land expired. The college's first thought was to develop the site for single-family houses, but de Witt prevailed on the trustees to envision a higher and better use with potential educational synergies.

Following a public RFP process, the college proposed that a for-profit, 206-unit residential tower targeted to retirees be built on the site—a project requiring a special permit. However, the town's aldermen voted down the proposal after some last-minute neighborhood resistance surfaced. Determined to make the project work, de Witt commissioned college and outside experts to conduct a study of intergenerational learning. The findings corroborated his conviction that there exists a growing market for active intergenerational learning among older adults and that Lasell could address this niche by developing an associated education-based CCRC.

De Witt turned to a little-known piece of state legislation, the Dover Amendment, that had been adopted in the 1950s. The Dover Amendment precludes local and state jurisdictions from using zoning to unreasonably limit the growth and development of educational and religious institutions. Asserting that an educational community on this site was an as-of-right land use under this law, the college sued the city.

In 1991, de Witt negotiated an agreement for judgment with the city. This stated that in return for the right to develop the site under mixed-use, educational institution zoning, the college would make a payment in lieu of taxes to the city and guarantee the continued use of the property for nonprofit educational purposes.

To make good on this guarantee, Lasell included an active education program in the CCRC plan. The centerpiece of this program was a requirement that residents participate in "active" learning at least 450 hours a year. Other initiatives undertaken by the college that are related to the educational purpose of Lasell Village include the establishment of a research center on aging and intergenerational learning, the engagement of the wider community in active learning, and the programming of intergenerational activities involving college students and Lasell Village residents. "The mandatory learning requirement was a real gamble," notes de

Witt. "No one had ever required that of retirement-community residents."

Also included in the agreement with the city was the maintenance of a 60-foot-wide vegetative barrier between village structures and the upscale single-family neighborhoods that border the site on three sides. (Compared with the original proposal to develop a single apartment building, the scale of the new cluster plan was more in keeping with the surrounding neighborhoods—which further placated the neighbors.)

The proposed project was redesigned as an "educational village" containing mixed-use residential clusters (or minicampuses) connected by enclosed corridors. Each mixed-use building contained a programmed educational space, keeping the project within zoning guidelines.

In March 1993, the Massachusetts Land Court upheld the negotiated agreement and the as-of-right use of the site for a nonprofit educational village. Five years of legal challenges followed, culminating in an unsuccessful appeal by interveners to the Massachusetts supreme court. The college prevailed and secured the right to permit and develop the project.

The as-of-right zoning for this site allowed mixed-use educational institution use and a maximum of 200 residential units. The site's development potential was also affected by the city of Newton's strict floor/area ratio (FAR) and setback requirements, the presence of wetlands, state regulations related to environmental protection, and public health regulations related to skilled nursing facilities. Also complicating the process is the fact that a portion of the northern campus cluster falls within the boundaries of a state historic district.

Because of the arduous permitting process, Lasell College had expended half of a $3 million endowment fund that it was using for initial predevelopment activities, when the trustees directed the college president to negotiate a joint venture with a for-profit developer willing to put money at risk. Several developers expressed interest but then shied away from the perceived marketing risk of the educational requirement.

Finally, one and a half years after permits had been secured, de Witt negotiated a contract with CareMatrix, a national development and management company with a portfolio of 50 assisted-living facilities but no experience with CCRCs. At the end of 1998, CareMatrix helped to secure a $56 million bond issue that was largely unsecured and required a 60 percent presale of units.

The initial agreement with CareMatrix stipulated that CareMatrix would develop, market, and manage the project under a five-year management contract with Lasell. In return, the college would receive $4 million in ground-lease income. However, by the start of construction in 1999, CareMatrix was experiencing major financial problems unrelated to this project, and the college found itself handling most of the marketing and media—and making development decisions. CareMatrix would eventually go bankrupt, but well before that event Lasell College's trustees decided to buy out the developer. Lasell College continues to own and manage the CCRC.

Phase 1 of Lasell Village opened in 2000 with 70 percent of its 162 independent living units presold. In 2003, a 15th mixed-use building that contains nine housing units was added. A 16th building with 17 units is scheduled for completion in 2005.

The rescue of the CCRC project has proven to be a financial boon to the college. Lasell Village Inc., the nonprofit entity created by the college to manage the project, pays about $1 million annually to the college in the form of management fees, education fees, and ground rent on a long-term lease. In addition, the college has been able to combine or coordinate many of its administrative, technology, communications, purchasing, and groundskeeping functions with those of Lasell Village and thus achieve economies of scale.

Community Design and Educational Program

Lasell Village is designed to support the independent-living and continuing-care functions of the CCRC as well as its educational mission. No precedent was available for programming this "living and learning" community. The design team often took a personal approach to the task, asking, in the words of project architect Jana Silsby, "How would we like to retire? What would we like to be doing?"

The 14 original three-story, garden style apartment buildings—each of which contains at least one classroom, art studio, computer laboratory, or other learning

space in accordance with the project's designation as a mixed-use development—are arranged in two seven-building "campuses" off a central curved driveway. They are connected by open and enclosed pathways. The raised walkways between two buildings frame the entry to the community. The southern cluster is anchored by a building known as "Town Hall," which contains community dining, educational, and medical facilities and is distinguishable by its greater height and clock tower. This cluster is centered around an active central courtyard, while the northern cluster centers around a community "victory" garden and quieter outdoor spaces. The newer 15th building is located next to the northern cluster. Pathways connect the Village to the college and surrounding neighborhoods; and half the parking is located underground to maintain a walkable environment.

The steep, wooded site and the presence of a small pond and wetlands area on its eastern side presented some development constraints. Because of the wetlands, the center of the property had to be left undeveloped, which led to the design of Lasell Village as two campuses—north and south. The pond/wetlands area was restored and a soft pathway and seating installed around it, creating a community amenity. The victory garden was sited on the eastern edge of the north campus with views downhill to the pond. The mixed-use buildings were designed to the maximum allowable height within the parameters dictated by FAR and setback requirements.

The development program combines typical CCRC facilities and educational facilities. The three-story Town Hall combines a number of uses—Lasell Village's management and educational offices, a central lobby, the concierge desk, dining rooms, a café, a convenience store, a bank, a wellness center and medical facilities, a multipurpose ballroom, several libraries, and six living units—that make it the center of Village life.

The lobby's carpeting and oversize couches suggest an informal inn or a resort hotel rather than an institutional building. The design team's decision to locate the community's 38-bed skilled nursing facility, known as Lasell House, in Town Hall was initially disputed by CareMatrix, which advocated for the facility's location in a separate building because its presence in Town Hall

Left: One of the Village's 15 mixed-use buildings. About half of the independent living units feature balconies or private outdoor patios.

Right: Enclosed walkways between buildings (top) and open pathways (middle) create a walkable environment and provide links to Lasell College and public transportation. The northern cluster of buildings centers around quiet outdoor spaces (bottom).

A community reading room and a classroom. Lasell Village taps into a growing market for active learning among older adults.

could be "upsetting" to the independent residents. This decision was based on economics, but the convenient central location of the care facility has also proved popular with residents who visit spouses and friends there.

Among residents, the educational program is one of the highest-rated services provided by the CCRC. The Village offers at least 25 classes in every trimester—plus special programs. The Village has its own academic dean, Paula Panchuck, who was formerly chair of education and interim dean of academic affairs at Lasell College. She meets with each new resident to create an individualized educational plan. Residents participate in educational programs for as long as they are intellectually and physically able.

The 450 hours of active learning each year required of residents can be met through a variety of activities and programs, including classes at the Village and the college, individual creative work, public service, continuing employment, cultural excursions, educational travel, gardening, physical fitness classes, special lectures, concerts, and cross-generational programs with Lasell College and elementary school students. As Panchuck says: "A lot of what counts is already in residents' lifestyles. We don't create active learners. We sustain them."

The Village's educational program was created by Panchuck in collaboration with prospective residents and focus groups. It was initially modeled after the Lasell College undergraduate curriculum, but making the program meaningful to seniors meant making it more flexible and responsive to their lifestyles. Many Village residents who travel, for example, prefer course sessions lasting only six to eight weeks. Seniors who are not interested in pursuing professional degrees are more likely to prefer a wide array of short courses in the liberal arts and humanities over Lasell College courses that lock them into two or three class meetings a week over an entire semester. Lasell Village class scheduling takes into account the preferences of seniors on medication and sleep schedules for classes at certain times of the day.

The Village's educational program is highly varied. In a typical week, the offerings might include a continuing Spanish class or a new bioethics class; a class on navigating the Internet; various exercise, stretch, or balancing classes; individualized computer training from a fellow resident; a sketching class; a pain management seminar; a cello performance; or a presentation on British poets of the First and Second World Wars. In an annual countdown, residents tally learning and fitness hours completed—with the average participation totaling 540 hours of learning and fitness activities.

The Lasell Village program has catalyzed new research activities at the college and the establishment of a graduate degree program in the management of eldercare services. In 2001, Lasell College established the Rosemary B. Fuss Center for Research on Aging and Intergenerational Studies. The center, which is located at Lasell Village, is dedicated to enhancing the quality of life of older adults through research, teaching, and participation in community partnerships focused on aging, lifelong learning, and intergenerational learning programs. About half of Lasell Village residents and a quarter of Lasell College students participate in intergenerational learning experiences each year, including student professional internships at the Village.

Unit and Building Design

The CCRC's independent living units range in size from 544 square feet to 1,933 square feet and in style from modest one-bedroom units to large two-bedroom apartments with dens. Natural light is plentiful in the apartments as well as throughout the project—in part because of its therapeutic effects. About half of the living units have balconies or private outdoor patios and 70 percent are corner units that receive ventilation and light from two sides. The units have open floor plans, are handicapped accessible, and can be adapted by residents for assisted living.

All the buildings are based on a 60-by-64-foot template, which is expandable with an additional 30-foot module. This design technique was chosen to create architectural variety within a very limited budget. Durable, solid building materials—brick, precast concrete, vinyl, and metal—are used. The apparent mass of the buildings is reduced by the use of oversized windows and siding, and the height of the third floors is minimized by the use of sloping roofs with dormers.

Marketing and Sales

Marketing focuses on Lasell Village's "living and learning" theme and its association with Lasell College. Its demographic is defined as senior "active learners" who want to be part of an engaged intellectual community and who are willing to make a commitment to their own ongoing education. A preopening survey of prospective residents revealed that the development's location, college affiliation, mandatory education program, and opportunities for multigenerational interaction were its biggest draws.

The original 162 units sold out within four months of completion. Lasell Village currently has a waiting list of 104 potential residents for its now 171 units. Prospects continue to be drawn by the Village's edu-

cational reputation, the quality of the living environment and continuing-care services, and opportunities to interact with young people. Its location in Newton and proximity to Boston public transit continue to be attractions as well.

Residents invest in Lasell Village via an entry fee of $240,000 to $775,000 based on the size of their unit. They or their estate recoup 90 percent of the entry fee should they leave or die. Residents also pay a monthly fee of $2,000 to $4,000, which covers services standard to CCRCs and the educational program.

To qualify for residency, prospects must be at least 65 years old, have earned a high-school diploma or its equivalent, have the physical and intellectual capacity (at the beginning of their residency) to participate in the Village's educational programs, and be financially qualified.

Resident Profile

The resident base consists of middle- and upper-middle-income, highly educated, retired professionals—77 percent have at least a baccalaureate and 21 percent have a doctorate. Observing that "for many of these residents, continued learning was a prerequisite to their professional success and people like that do not shut off their minds at 65," de Witt sees the resident profile at Lasell Village as an indicator of a growing market of seniors who want to stay physically and intellectually engaged and active.

Residents range in age from 67 to 97. They have an

Town Hall has become the center of Village life, offering not only independent living units, a wellness center, and a 38-bed skilled nursing facility, but also dining venues, educational facilities, lounges, and a convenience store.

average age of 83. Most have moved to Lasell Village from within Massachusetts, with 38 percent moving from elsewhere in Newton—a city with a high degree of professional and educational attainment. Of the community's 207 residents, 125 are single or widowed and 82 live as couples. Almost three-quarters of the residents are women.

Experience Gained

■ Academic institutions with a development opportunity have a chance to leverage their educational missions to create special projects and tap niche markets. The development of this "living and learning" community for lifelong learners has put Lasell College on the map of educational innovation—and helped revitalize it academically and financially.

■ The success of Lasell Village as a living and learning environment prompted the college to establish the Lasell Consulting Group in 2004, with Paula Panchuck as its principal. This group specializes in planning college-affiliated development projects—residential communities or other programs—targeted to older adults and incorporating lifelong learning and intergenerational exchange in their design, financing, marketing, and implementation.

■ The mandatory educational requirement agreed to by Lasell College as part of the approval process was considered the project's most risky gamble, but it proved to be a marketing draw.

■ Standard CCRC approaches to programming and design are based on medical, institutional, and hospitality models and they fail to account for the educational, physical, or social needs of active older adults. Such standard approaches were not generally useful in the programming and design of Lasell Village.

■ The number of dwelling units that could be developed under the site's zoning, FAR, and setback requirements is too small for Lasell Village to comfortably support its extensive CCRC program. Lasell College thinks that such a facility is economically optimized at 300 to 400 units. However, the college has found some compensation in the form of the economies of scale realized by shared facilities management and administration with the Village.

Anchored by Town Hall, which is distinguished by its clock tower, the south minicampus encircles an active central courtyard.

CONTACT INFORMATION

PROJECT WEB SITE

www.lasellvillage.com

DEVELOPERS

Lasell College
1844 Commonwealth Avenue
Newton, Massachusetts 02466
www. lasell.edu

CareMatrix Corporation (initial phase)
197 First Avenue
Needham, Massachusetts 02194

ARCHITECT

Steffian Bradley Architects
100 Summer Street
Boston, Massachusetts 02110-2106
617-305-7100
www.steffianbradley.com

DEVELOPMENT SCHEDULE

Site Leased:	November 1998
Planning Started:	1988
Sales/Leasing Started:	1996
Construction Started:	1998
Project Completion:	
Phase 1 (162 units)	2000
Phase 2 (9 units)	2003
Phase 3 (17 units)	2005[1]

1. Scheduled.

LAND USE INFORMATION

Site Area:	13.2 acres
Dwelling Units:	171
Residential Density:	12.2 units per gross acre
Parking:	
Spaces	242
Parking Ratio	1.4 spaces per housing unit

LAND USE PLAN

	ACRES	PERCENT OF SITE
Buildings	2.2	17 %
Streets and Parking	1.7	13
Landscaping/Open Space	9.3	70

DEMOGRAPHIC PROFILE

	PERCENT OF ALL RESIDENTS OR HOUSEHOLDS
GENDER	
Male	29 %
Female	71
EDUCATIONAL LEVEL[1]	
High School or Equivalent	15
Post–High School [2]	8
Bachelor's Degree	37
Master's Degree	19
Doctorate	21
HOUSEHOLD TYPE	
Married Couples	40 %
Single/Widowed Men	9
Single/Widowed Women	51
MOVED TO LASELL FROM . . .	
Newton	38
Elsewhere in Massachusetts	46
Elsewhere in New England	4
New York State	6
Elsewhere	6
AGE OF RESIDENTS	
Range	67–97 years
Average	83 years

1. Highest educational level completed by resident.
2. Includes residents with an associate's degree.

RESIDENTIAL UNIT INFORMATION

UNIT TYPE	SIZE RANGE (SQUARE FEET)	NUMBER OF UNITS		CURRENT ENTRY FEE RANGE
		BUILT	OCCUPIED	
1 Bedroom	544– 860	54	54	$240,000–$410,000
1 Bedroom With Den	990– 1,145	39	39	400,000– 480,000
2 Bedrooms	875– 1,145	49	49	430,000– 560,000
2 Bedrooms With Den	1,175– 1,933	29	29	550,000– 775,000

DEVELOPMENT COST INFORMATION

PHASE 1	
Soft Costs	$29,000,000
Hard Costs	32,600,000
TOTAL DEVELOPMENT COST	$61,600,000
Development Cost per Unit	380,500
Development Cost per Square Foot	107

PHASE 2	
Soft Costs	720,000
Hard Costs	4,500,000
TOTAL DEVELOPMENT COST	$5,220,000
Development Cost per Unit	578,000
Development Cost per Square Foot	145

Floor plan for a one-bedroom unit.

Santana Row

SAN JOSE, CALIFORNIA

SIGNIFICANT FEATURES

■ Conversion of a conventional shopping center site to a higher-density, mixed-use urban village

■ Design and land use criteria focused on creating a lively, pedestrian-friendly street scene

■ Luxury rental housing targeting young professionals

■ Units designed with conversion to condominium in mind

Santana Row is an 18-block urban village comprising housing, restaurants, and shops oriented around a main street. A grayfield development located five miles southwest of downtown San Jose, the mixed-use project replaces a 1960s era single-story, suburban style shopping center—ten buildings surrounded by a sea of parking lots—with a high-density, multistory (yet low-rise) urban style neighborhood. When complete, Santana Row will include 680,000 square feet of retail and restaurants, as many as 1,201 dwelling units, two hotels, and seven parks.

Site and Surroundings

Located on Stevens Creek Boulevard, Santana Row has direct access within a half mile to I-880, I-280, and Route 17. These heavily traveled highways make the site easily accessible from the East Bay, Peninsula, South Bay, downtown San Jose, and the airport.

Directly across Stevens Creek Boulevard is Valley Fair Mall-Westfield Shoppingtown, one of the most profitable indoor malls in the country based on sales per square foot. Santana Row's western boundary is formed by Winchester Boulevard, a major north/south thoroughfare hosting a mélange of commercial uses. A famous Bay Area tourist attraction, the Winchester Mystery House, is within walking distance.

On the southern perimeter are two office buildings and an assisted-living facility. To the southeast lies Santana Park, the public park from which the development derives its name. At the eastern edge are residential properties and to the northeast there is a mix of residential and commercial uses.

Development Process

The vision for Santana Row evolved from Federal Realty's positive experience with a smaller mixed-use project—Bethesda Row—that it had developed in downtown Bethesda, Maryland, just outside of Washington, D.C. Founded in 1962 and headquartered in Rockville, Maryland, Federal Realty Investment Trust is an equity real estate investment trust (REIT) specializing in the ownership, management, development, and redevelopment of shopping centers and street retail properties in major metropolitan markets on the East and West Coasts.

In March 1997, when the developer purchased the property, Silicon Valley was a world capital for the high-tech industry. Dynamic corporate growth had precipitated a population increase in a region lacking the housing and retail capacity to support it. Demand exceeded supply, providing an attractive scenario for a developer about to

Oriented around a main street, most of the buildings within Santana Row contain retail space on the ground floor topped by residential units.

embark on a mixed-use project with a significant residential component.

In addition to the lessons learned from Bethesda Row, the developer borrowed from the design and operation of successful destination streets in the San Francisco region and Europe and incorporated lessons learned from an examination of local history, economic and cultural trends, and vernacular architecture to create the Santana Row concept. Above all, Federal Realty wanted to create a memorable main street experience that would realize long-term value and equity in this project.

The development of a fully integrated mixed-use project in the site's essentially suburban setting would require rewriting current zoning ordinances. In early 1998, the concept of razing the site and redesigning it to accommodate Santana Row and achieve optimum connections with surrounding neighborhoods and infrastructure was submitted to the city of San Jose as a general development plan (GDP). The specific plan was entitled in June 1998, and from 1999 to 2003, the project received a number of other major entitlements that supported its special features.

The approval process was not without controversy. While many downtown merchants and real estate interests fought against the project, seeing it as a threat to their livelihood and the value of retail land, it had some strong proponents in city government. Federal Realty worked through the offices of two former councilmen and the mayor to steer the project through an elaborate political and community process. It posted a dedicated Web site and issued a newsletter for helping neighborhood residents keep up with the project, and these neighbors attended public hearings and collaborated with Federal Realty on finding solutions to their concerns.

In order to assure that permits could be issued in a timely manner, Federal Realty collaborated with San Jose's planning staff to develop preapproved design and building standards that would facilitate decisions. The city's planning staff ran interference with other city agencies involved in the permitting process to expedite approvals. Among the solutions for various environmental issues that came up were the relocation of an endangered species of burrowing owl, the moving and replanting of 17 50-year-old oak trees at a cost of $30,000

per tree, and the design of outdoor lighting to prevent its interfering with the Lick Observatory. The developer also had to find solutions to inappropriate elements within the zoning ordinances by, for example, obtaining approvals for shared parking between uses, redefining the parameters for parks and open space to fit the project's urban context, and rewriting the ordinance governing lighting, signage, and graphics.

Santana Row would need the right balance of features to attract and retain both residential and retail market share. Focusing on an upscale market, the planners sought to combine high-quality rental housing that would fill a void in the Silicon Valley real estate market with high-end fashion and lifestyle retailers not found elsewhere in the Bay Area. The overall goal was to create a lively, pedestrian-oriented urban village offering people a sense of discovery and adventure in a comfortable and safe environment.

Three key development strategies were adopted to implement Santana Row. First, in a departure from the REIT's historically conservative approach to growing its portfolio, Federal Realty maintained control over all aspects of the project by taking on 100 percent of the financial risk. The development of such a large and complex project without public funding or financial partners constituted an unprecedented risk for the publicly traded company.

Second, in order to reduce financial risk yet capitalize on momentum, the developer delivered the project in phases. In Phase 1, Federal Realty was determined to deliver the critical mass of retail, residential, and restaurant products necessary to validate Santana Row as a legitimate destination that would attract renters, retailers, and visitors. The phasing strategy resulted in nine blocks of residential and retail development—Phase 1—being completed simultaneously.

Third, Federal Realty had built its reputation on retail—not residential—development and it did not envision retaining the residential component of Santana Row as a long-term asset. Thus, a financially beneficial exit strategy from the housing component was necessary. Anticipating eventual conversion, the developer had the housing units "condo mapped" at the outset, which provided the flexibility to market them as rentals

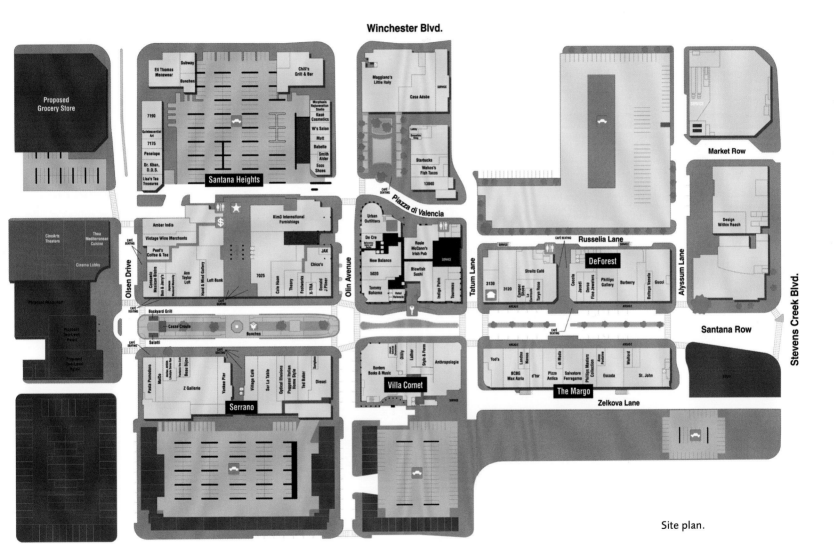

Site plan.

The siting of restaurants and cafés around the Plaza di Valencia (and other open spaces) encourages outdoor dining.

or as a turnkey condominium conversion at any time.

The development of Santana Row experienced three major blows between the start of construction (June 2001) and opening day (November 2002)—the bottom dropped out of the high-tech industry, hitting Silicon Valley's economy hard; the ripple effects of the September 2001 terrorist attacks weakened the region's retail, tourism, and investment markets; and, just 30 days before the originally scheduled grand opening, an eight-alarm fire destroyed 36 shops and 242 luxury townhouses and flats in the nearly completed Santana Heights building, the largest of nine buildings on the site at that time.

Insurance covered the fire damages and rebuilding began almost immediately. Federal Realty faced the region's economic decline head-on by reducing the average rent on residential units from an anticipated $3.07 per square foot to $2.05 per square foot and by negoti-

ating easier lease terms—such as shorter leases—with retail tenants to reduce their risk. Also, the REIT became an investor in six restaurants in order to help them achieve successful, on-time openings—and all six remain profitable, with sales ranging between $700 and $1,000 per square foot.

Financing

Federal Realty paid $42 million in cash for the initial 39-acre parcel and later paid cash for three adjacent acres. In April 2001, the REIT closed on a $295 million construction loan for Phase 1 from Fleet National Bank in partnership with six international banks. The interest rate and Federal Realty's guarantee of the loan were subject to step-down provisions based on the satisfaction of specified conditions. After 18 months, Federal Realty decided it did not want to bear the debt and, using internal reserves, it paid off the loan, which had had a three-year term with two one-year extension options. Phase 1 involved demolition of the entire site, installation of new infrastructure for the entire project, and the modification of seven off-site intersections—and thus cost proportionately more than the subsequent phases, which the REIT financed internally

Community Planning and Design

The big planning decisions were made first. Maximum densities and floor/area ratios were established based on the findings of a traffic study that evaluated the capacity of existing roadways. Blocks were initially organized in a 30-by-30-foot grid pattern to create a sense of structure around the retail and residential spaces and to allow flexibility in how these spaces would be apportioned as development proceeded.

Santana Row—the main street—and Olin Avenue were designed as the most prominent streets. Wide sidewalks adorned with outdoor seating for restaurants and cafés give the main street a sense of vibrancy, and establish it as a promenade for strolling. Santana Row Park sits inside the wide median at the south end of the main street between Olin Avenue and Olsen Drive.

On either side of Santana Row Park the street is lined with shops. The residential portions of the Serrano and Santana Heights buildings sit atop and behind the shops on their respective sides of the street. Further down the main street, the residential portions of the Villa Cornet, the DeForest, and the Margo also sit atop high-end shops. Midway on Santana Row, between Olin Avenue and Tatum Lane, sits the Hotel Valencia, which, like the other buildings on this street, contains fashionable ground-floor retail establishments and restaurants topped by 213 luxury hotel rooms. Behind the Hotel Valencia lies the Plaza di Valencia, a park sporting a water feature and bordered on two sides by restaurants.

Four strategies guided the development team in determining the use mix and location of uses in this plan:

■ Retail spaces would provide a sense of rhythm on the street level. Tenants were carefully selected and placed in strategic locations. Anchor stores, entertainment venues, and the hotel were given locations with visual prominence, auto and foot traffic, and parking. Best Buy, the Container Store, and Crate and Barrel, for example, are located along Stevens Creek Boulevard where exposure to automobile traffic is highest. Most of the high-end luxury shops are located on Santana Row, while most of the smaller independent shops and convenience stores are along Olsen Drive and Olin Avenue.

■ Residential uses would add life to the streets. Housing was placed where it would have the strongest impact on street life. The high-density DeForest and Margo loft units were placed in the most urban location in Santana Row a block away from Stevens Creek Boulevard. The Villa Cornet—offering the most expensive units—is at the center of the development directly across from the Hotel Valencia. Townhouses are placed at the edges of the development and along the less busy side streets, giving their residents a more private and quiet location.

■ Parks and restaurants would be important gathering spots. The two most popular outdoor gathering places—Santana Row Park and the Plaza di Valencia—feature a variety of seating accommodations, activities, and uses. Restaurant uses are concentrated around these parks, while restaurants are also sprinkled throughout the development in order to energize every block. Per the merchants' request, the luxury shopping area contains the fewest restaurants.

■ Well-located parking would support all uses and contribute to the pedestrian experience. Each building is designed to promote pedestrian activity and conceal its parking facilities. Parking is generally located in garages that are ringed with retail, in underground garages, or in garages located on top of a podium. Surface parking lots occupy future development sites. Visitor parking is easy to locate, whereas resident parking is accessed from secondary streets. Parallel parking along all the streets buffers the sidewalks and promotes their use for dining, strolling, and shopping. Service areas are tucked behind buildings and accessed from side streets and lanes to reduce conflict.

Retail tenant selection criteria included not duplicating what is offered at the mall across the street; targeting a sophisticated customer demographic; seeking a 60/40 ratio of credit tenants to regional and local tenants; including some destination tenants that people would be willing to drive a distance to get to; and including convenience stores and personal services in response to residents' needs. The developer established a program to help incubate exciting local retail concepts that otherwise might not have had the resources to locate at Santana Row.

Urban design guidelines and architectural standards created for the project aim at optimizing the pedestrian experience. In order to encourage original and creative exterior design solutions, especially for the retail facades and gallerias, these guidelines are not overly detailed. In this way, the development team hoped to mirror the way a city street evolves, to give the blocks an "evolutionary" feel—as if they had been built over time by different owners.

Through myriad details, ranging from a 200-color paint palette to a super-sized chess board in Santana Row Park (see photo on opposite page), Federal Realty sought to give Santana Row a sense of place. Artists have been commissioned to create original works for the project's streets and buildings. Among the pieces now in place are 16 ceramic mosaic fountains, a retail arcade ceiling mural showing phases of the moon, and many freestanding sculptures.

Unit Design

The design of the residential component was driven by market research indicating that people who seek the amenities and convenience of a mixed-use living environment—urbanites—would be most attracted to Santana Row. The development targeted high-income renters who would value privacy, security, convenience, and comfort along with a location offering an active street environment and synergistic nonresidential land uses.

To promote mixed-use synergies while minimizing potential conflicts, resident and nonresident parking areas were separated; rear or underground access from parking areas to residential buildings was provided; key-card access to building lobbies and parking was provided; private garages were attached to townhouses; and the general living space within units was oriented to the street or more public views, while bedrooms were put in the rear away from the streets.

Podium-level outdoor spaces are provided in the Serrano and Santana Heights buildings for resident use.

Situated on the first level above the street, these neighborhood common areas feature access streets (including street addresses for the townhouses), landscaped parks, and open space.

The goal for the residential component of Santana Row was to present something that would appeal to all segments of the targeted demographic. This required a variety of types of units, sizes and layouts, price ranges, and locations vis-à-vis street views and other views. The choices offered include flats, lofts, townhouses, and villas, as follows.

Flats—At buildout, there will be 160 flats, all with private terraces, in the Santana Heights building inside a perimeter ring of townhouses. The flats are viewed as an alternative to lofts for people who prefer partitioned rooms to an open floor plan; and as an alternative to townhouses for people who prefer one level to three levels. Floor plans range from 822-square-foot units with one bedroom and one bathroom to 1,284-square-foot units with three bedrooms and two bathrooms. Parking will be provided in an underground garage with elevator access to the building or the podium level.

Lofts—Lacking old warehouse buildings that can be converted to lofts, San Jose has a scarcity of loft apartments, which drives demand. Santana Row offers lofts in two buildings, the DeForest (98 units) and the Margo (100 units), designed on a 15-by-46-foot module along double-loaded corridors. In the three-story Margo, one-story lofts are located above retail uses with two-story lofts above them. The DeForest has two levels of two-story lofts. Lofts range from 700-square-foot, one-level units with one bedroom and one bathroom to 2,133-square-foot, two-level units with three bedroom and three bathrooms. The rear-facing, first-level units in the DeForest feature terraces over the retail podium, while only a few other lofts in either building—units located in the center or at the corners—have balconies. Parking is handled differently in each loft building. Parking for Margo tenants is in an underground garage below the retail. Parking for DeForest tenants is in the basement of the public parking structure at the rear of the building in a section with key-card access. These tenants must walk outside the garage to access their elevator lobby.

Santana Row Park, a popular gathering space, features a variety of seating accommodations, fountains, and artwork.

Townhouses—Townhouses are provided in the Serrano building (36 units) and the Santana Heights building (96 units) at each building's perimeter starting at the top of the retail podium. All have private balconies and attached two-car garages, which are accessed at podium level via a gated ramp from the street. Four layouts are offered at the Serrano, ranging from a 1,228-square-foot unit with two bedrooms and two bathrooms to a 1,537-square-foot unit with two bedrooms, a den, and two and one-half bathrooms. Nine floor plans will be offered at Santana Heights, ranging from a 1,228-square-foot unit with two bedrooms and two bathrooms to a 2,271-square-foot unit with four bedrooms, a den, and three bathrooms.

Villas—The Villa Cornet building offers 21 luxury villas. The largest and most expensive of Santana Row's residences, the villas were designed to appeal to well-heeled renters, such as local sports celebrities. Each villa contains three levels—with two private terrace/gardens on the first level—and features a private gated entry through a landscaped courtyard that is accessed via an elevator lobby. Parking is underground with direct elevator access to the building. Villas range from 2,102-square-foot units with three bedrooms and three and one-half bathrooms to 3,876-square-foot units with four bedrooms and four bathrooms.

Target Market and Resident Profile

Federal Realty engaged a market research firm to perform a feasibility study and help the developer define Santana Row's residential component in terms of unit types, number and mix of units, general floor plans and features, lease terms and rental rates, and phasing for the release of products.

It was determined that a mix of lofts, flats, villas, and townhouses could offer an attractive range of choices to renters seeking an alternative to the automobile-oriented, garden style apartment complexes that are common in the South Bay area. Santana Row's target renter already lived and worked in the South Bay, preferred a more urban lifestyle, was 50 years old or younger, and had an annual household income in the six figures range.

The tenant demographics suggest that Santana Row has been successful in reaching its target market. About

Opposite: A pedestrian-friendly environment attracts retailers like Borders (top) and an active street scene attracts tenants to projects like the Margo building (bottom) featuring loft and two-story apartments above street-level retail.

Santana Row offers an urban lifestyle alternative to San Jose's generally suburban style housing market. The residents of these high-end apartments are mostly young—average age 36—and single.

Above: The apartments in the Villa Cornet building command some of the highest rents in the South Bay area. Prominently located atop high-end shops, the three-level villas feature gated entrances from a landscaped courtyard.

Opposite: A rooftop townhouse neighborhood located on the top of the retail podium of the Serrano building features an interior courtyard, streets, attached parking, and small park areas.

two-third of the tenants are younger than 40 years, and the average age is 36. Most households—60 percent—are single or divorced persons and only 5 percent of households are families with children.

Marketing and Performance

Santana Row is marketed as a single retail/entertainment/residential entity with myriad attractions. Marketing tools include a Web site; ads in newspapers, on TV and radio, and in lifestyle magazines; and a media/public relations program. The marketing effort includes the programming of a variety of on-site events and community outreach initiatives. Advertising for the rental units has been cut back, because 90 percent of prospects are walk-ins.

Retail and specialty tenants are always marketed as a group. When differentiation is necessary, Federal Realty uses the following categories: fashions, accessories, home, and specialty.

Two operating management entities have been established. Federal Realty handles the administration, maintenance, and leasing of all the nonresidential components—the streets, the common areas, the parking garages, and the retail. An outside management company has been subcontracted to manage the residential component. It is responsible for leasing, tenant relations, and property management inside the residential buildings. Residential leases have six-, eight-, and 12-month terms. The annual turnover rate is approximately 65 percent, mostly because many tenants purchase homes or relocate out of the area.

Available retail space is currently 92 percent occupied and space that will be available in the future is being preleased. Only second-level space was slow in filing up. Turnover has been around 10 percent since the project opened. Average retail sales are around $600 a square foot, which far exceeds the national average, and restaurant sales are even higher.

Experience Gained

■ Encouraged by the popularity and financial success of Santana Row, Federal Realty plans to continue to develop mixed-use residential projects. However, it will take a slightly different approach, as indicated by some of the lessons learned that are listed in the following bullets.

■ Financial risk can be reduced by partnering with government entities or private developers.

■ Development should be phased to capitalize on equity and momentum, to allow project changes over time in response to shifting markets, to control costs, and to simplify construction management.

■ Ideas and details can be refined as the project matures and the learning curve flattens.

■ The clarity of the relationships between uses should be maintained at all times.

■ Shopping streets need to mix things up to remain vital. The street activity around the cluster of luxury retail tenants without restaurants on Santana Row contrasts sharply with the street's livelier areas where uses are more integrated.

■ The creation of a superior street experience establishes significant value for commercial as well as residential uses. Residential tenants will pay a premium for a view overlooking a memorable street.

■ Preparing the residential units for conversion to condominiums provided Federal Realty with an effective exit strategy for the residential component.

CONTACT INFORMATION

PROJECT WEB SITE

www.santanarow.com

DEVELOPER/OWNER

Federal Realty Investment Trust
1626 East Jefferson Street
Rockville, Maryland 20852
301-998-8100
www.federalrealty.com

**SANTANA ROW
PROJECT
INFORMATION**

MASTER PLANNER/ENVIRONMENTAL DESIGNER

Street Works LLC
30 Glenn Street
White Plains, New York 10603
914-949-6505
www.street-works.com

Maestri Design Inc.
217 Pine Street
Seattle, Washington 98101
206-622-4322

ARCHITECTS

SB Architects
One Beach Street, Suite 301
San Francisco, California 94133
415-673-8990
sbarch@sandybabcock.com
www.sandybabcock.com

BAR Architects
1660 Bush Street
San Francisco, California 94109
415-441-4771
www.bararch.com

MBH Architects
1115 Atlantic Avenue
Alameda, California 94501
510-865-8663
www.mbharch.com

LANDSCAPE ARCHITECT

The SWA Group
55 New Montgomery Street, Suite 888
San Francisco, California 94105
415-836-8770
www.swagroup.com

RESIDENTIAL CONSULTANT

Group Interland Management
411 Borel Avenue, Suite 600
San Mateo, California 94402
650-574-9200
www.interlandusa.com

CONSTRUCTION MANAGEMENT

Bovis Lend Lease Inc.
33 New Montgomery Street, Suite 220
San Francisco, California 94105
415-512-0586
www.bovislendlease.com

DEVELOPMENT SCHEDULE

Site Purchased:	March 1997
Planning Started:	March 1997
Construction Started:	June 2001
Residential Leasing Started:	spring 2002
Completed:	
Phase 1	November 2002
Phase 2	February 2003
Phase 3	August 2004
Phase 4	January 2006[1]

1. *Expected.*

LAND USE INFORMATION

Site Area:	42 acres
Retail Space:	
Planned	680,000 square feet
Completed	555,270 square feet
Dwelling Units:	
Planned	1,201
Completed[1]	511
Hotels:	
Planned	404 rooms
Completed	213 rooms

1. *Through 2006, upon completion of the Santana Heights building.*

RESIDENTIAL UNIT INFORMATION

UNIT TYPE	UNIT SIZE (SQUARE FEET)	NUMBER OF UNITS		INITIAL MONTHLY RENTS
		BUILT	LEASED	
Lofts (DeForest and Margo)	700– 2,140	198	193	$1,846–$4,400
Townhouses (Serrano)	1,228– 1,537	36	33	2,662– 3,575
Townhouses (Santana Heights)	1,228– 2,271	961	0	2,750– 4,400
Villas (Villa Cornet)	2,102– 3,876	21	18	4,400– 7,500
Flats (Santana Heights)	822– 1,284	160[1]	0	1,963– 2,950

1. The Santana Heights building is currently under construction with completion expected in 2006.

LAND USE PLAN[1]

	PERCENT OF SITE
Residential	45%
Retail	43
Hotel	4
Streets and Parking	2
Open Space	6

1. Reflects entitlement for the development of different land uses, not necessarily what will actually be built.

DEMOGRAPHIC PROFILE

	PERCENT OF ALL HOUSEHOLDS
AGE	
18–21	1%
22–29	21
30–37	38
38–49	29
50+	11
HOUSEHOLD TYPE	
Singles	60
Couples	40
GENDER (SINGLE-PERSON HOUSEHOLDS)	
Male	60
Female	40

DEVELOPMENT COST INFORMATION

Site Acquisition	$55,000,000
TOTAL DEVELOPMENT COST	532,000,000[1]

1. Estimated costs at project completion.

Level 2

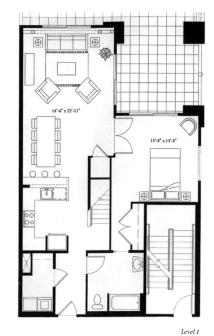

Level 1

Floor plan for a two-story loft unit in the DeForest building.

Solivita

POINCIANA, FLORIDA

SIGNIFICANT FEATURES

- Master-planned community targeted to retirees

- Affordable country club lifestyle

- Extensive and varied recreational facilities

- Amenities developed before residential sales began

Solivita is an active adult community on 4,000 acres in central Florida. It is being developed by Avatar Properties, a newcomer to this type of residential community. Its target market is retirees 55 and older who desire a country club lifestyle at a reasonable price.

At buildout, Solivita will have 6,500 single-family dwellings occupying 40 percent of the site—with the remaining 2,400 acres devoted to a variety of community amenities, including conservation areas, parks, open space and lakes, two 18-hole golf courses; and a social and recreational activities hub called the village center.

Site and Surroundings

Poinciana is a strategic location—an essentially rural setting that is less than 35 miles south of Orlando International Airport and Disney World and less than 100 miles east of the Gulf coast and 100 miles west of the Atlantic coast. This central location is a major consideration for retirees anticipating visits from children and grandchildren.

Before development, part of the site lay in a floodplain and most of it was covered by the scrub growth, oak trees, and other plants indigenous to central Florida. In its developed state, Solivita strikes a balance between the preservation of the natural landscape as a shared amenity and the shaping of the landscape to accommodate a programmed and built environment.

As might be expected in a community of 16,000 people spread over 73 square miles, Solivita feels far from the madding crowd. However, much commercial and residential development is springing up within a five-minute drive—including a recently completed Wal-Mart store; the Poinciana Towne Center with nearly 50 retail stores and businesses, including two major supermarkets; and the new Promenade Shopping Center featuring national brand name retailers. Kissimmee, a town immediately east of Poinciana, has a Home Depot, an enclosed retail mall, and a historic downtown district with more than 70 shops and restaurants.

Development Process

In 1970, Avatar purchased 3,300 acres and more recently made two additional land purchases that bumped the Solivita site to just under 4,000 contiguous acres. In 1998, the developer deemed the market ripe for an affordable, country club–lifestyle community targeted to active adults. This represented a departure from the developer's usual product—single-family subdivisions aimed at a broad market.

Master plan.

Solivita was internally financed. A less solvent company would not have been able to phase the development as Avatar did. Its innovative phasing involved the completion of the village center and the first golf course (a second golf course will open in summer 2005) and the preparation of 1,100 lots for construction before the first sales contract was signed.

Planning and Design

The master plan is based on traditional neighborhood design (TND) planning principles and a respect for the site's topographic and environmental conditions. The idea was to preserve the best characteristics of the site while resolving the less desirable ones. Ten neighborhoods were planned to be released in eight phases.

Marketing factors influenced the planning. Solivita was literally shaped to appeal to buyers looking for the convenience of the suburbs and the pleasures of nature—for the best of both worlds. Existing hammocks that serve as wildlife habitat were carefully preserved. More than 700 mature live oaks were relocated for the duration of initial site construction to a tree farm created by the developer. Lakes in addition to Lake Polk, which 40 years ago was a borrow pit for the Poinciana Racquet

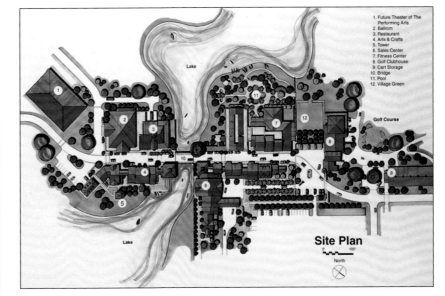

1. Future Theater of The Performing Arts
2. Ballrom
3. Restaurant
4. Arts & Crafts
5. Tower
6. Sales Center
7. Fitness Center
8. Golf Clubhouse
9. Cart Storage
10. Bridge
11. Pool
12. Village Green

Site Plan

North

Typical homebuyers consider their investment in Solivita's active lifestyle as important as their purchase of a house. The community offers a wide variety of recreational options, including two golf courses (center top) and a village center (far left, center bottom, and site plan) with stores, restaurants, and a wellness center and spa.

Club, were constructed to handle stormwater runoff—and provide the fill needed to engineer the site out of the floodplain.

This environmental stewardship approach to development has resulted in a community that looks more mature than it is. Canopies of old oak trees cover portions of roadways, trails, and golf-cart paths. In order to encourage residents to enjoy Florida's outdoors, shade trees large enough to use for streetscaping are also planted at individual homesites. View amenities are placed in key locations to make the best vistas available to everyone, rather than limiting them to premium lots along lakefronts, woodlands, and golf fairways. The number of premium lots and their placement are determined accordingly.

Among the TND design principles incorporated into the master plan are lots that are small relative to typical lot sizes elsewhere in the market area, lots with street frontage of varying widths, short streets that encourage walking, community parks, widely distributed pocket parks, and an ample number of green spaces that can accommodate active and passive recreation.

The design theme for public buildings and individual houses is distinctly Mediterranean, which underscores the subliminal message of the word "Solivita"—a word (and future brand) coined by Avatar to suggest the connection between "sun" and "life."

The 105,000-square-foot village center on a 15.5-acre site acts as Solivita's main street. Its buildings exude an old-world charm while providing state-of-the-art interior spaces that fulfill specific functions. The use of cobblestones, aged wood, stucco, and mature landscaping creates the overall illusion that the village center has been around for a long time. This old-world atmosphere works to great effect as the entry sequence to the sales center.

Color plays a key role in lending vibrancy to Solivita, in welcome contrast to many early active adult communities that tended toward monochromatic facades and featureless architecture that made wayfinding difficult. The village center offers a palette of warm, Tuscany-inspired hues (see photos on opposite page). Homebuyers are offered a selection of creative combinations of colors for their units.

The typical Solivita buyer wants plenty of floor-plan and design options. To date, six different housing products have been offered, providing something for everyone from snowbirds wanting a small second home to professionals wanting a home office in their residence. A duplex model that was offered in the first neighborhood has been discontinued because of buyer preferences and Avatar's long-range vision for the community. One of the most popular models, the Bolero (in the Classical series), features a separate guesthouse.

Three to seven models are offered in each of the five available product lines—Vineyards, Musical, Classical, Symphony, and Tuscany—for a total of 25 different models. The same basic construction package is used for each model in a product line, but each model offers a different range of upgrades chosen to reflect the variety of tastes and price sensitivities among active adult households.

Target Market and Resident Profile

When it first contemplated the active adult housing market, Avatar not only diligently researched buyer preferences, but also acquired two companies—a builder specializing in custom homes in South Florida

and a firm that had built thousands of homes for seniors in Florida over the last 30 years—in order to gain expertise and credibility.

The developer hired three firms to independently conduct market research, including seven focus groups around the United States. Baby boomers who would be reaching retirement age in increasing numbers within the next decade were the focus of this research. Their feedback on what would constitute an ideal retirement community helped shape the concept for Solivita's development. As did the findings from an analysis of the competition, which was tackled by Avatar's design development team.

The market research revealed that while baby boomers do not all think alike—after all, they number nearly 78 million—they tend to hold in common a number of preferences and expectations about retirement housing, lifestyle, and the homebuying process. One of the most significant commonalities that showed up was a preference for living in a community, not a development. Baby boomers want to live in an environment that facilitates social connections among people with similar values, tastes, and lifestyles. As homebuyers, they are not willing to take risks and are not even tremendously comfortable with change. They tend, paradoxically, to crave the familiar within new surroundings.

As is typical for active adult communities in Florida, Solivita's residents are mainly from New York, New Jersey, and Florida (with many of the Floridians having earlier migrated from other parts of the country). Midwestern states like Illinois, Michigan, and Wisconsin account for a number of the community's other residents, and there are a smattering from other states. The homebuyers here are solidly middle class. Although Avatar offers a range of products priced from the low $100,000s (Vineyards) to more than $400,000 (Tuscany), this is a community inhabited by the financially comfortable rather than the wealthy.

In broad terms, Solivita buyers tend to be primarily Caucasian couples in their early to mid-60s who are not first-time homeowners. They may be downsizing or simply looking for a lifestyle change. Their collective attitude is "I've paid my dues and the kids are raised and gone. Now it's time for me." In response, Avatar has

gone to great lengths to provide a choice-oriented purchasing process that stops short of actual customization, but gives buyers control over the finishes and system upgrades that help personalize a house.

Typical homebuyers at Solivita consider their investment in the community's lifestyle as important as their purchase of a house. Unlike many active adult communities where the golf clubhouse is, in effect, the only center of social interactions and recreational activities, Solivita caters to the preferences of its target market for choices by providing a wide variety of other recreational options—physical and intellectual activi-

The country club–lifestyle options include the lakefront village center, which is designed to have the feel of a European main street (top left) and features a waterfront board-

walk and terraced steps to the water's edge (top right); a state-of-the-art wellness center and a spa (bottom left); and a high-end restaurant in the golf clubhouse (bottom right).

ties, indoor and outside activities. In addition to golf, these options include bike paths, miles of walking trails, boating, fishing, neighborhood recreational facilities and pools, parks, a community pool, three restaurants, a 30,000-square-foot spa and fitness center, an art studio and art classes, a computer center, an investment center, and a ballroom that easily converts to a 500-seat movie theater.

Feedback from residents continues to influence the community's recreational programming. Calling Solivita "a living, breathing thing," John Corners, vice president for administration at Avatar, notes that the activities cal-endar—including club formations, special courses, and guest speakers—has grown tenfold over the past four years in response to the interest expressed by residents. "We create amenities our residents will enjoy," says Cor-ners, "and try to adapt community facilities to meet their needs, within reason."

Marketing

Marketing has been aggressive, using an arsenal of tools such as a Web site, ad placement in regional newspa-pers, direct mail, and promotional packages called "Dis-covery Days" involving on-site visits by prospective homebuyers, who are put up at a local hotel for two nights, given lunch, and offered complimentary use of the golf course and other recreational facilities.

Keeping customers satisfied is the best and least expensive marketing strategy. Solivita has a full-time construction staff that has been known to waive warranty dates for items that were initially covered or were within the scope of the builder's responsibility. The hard work that the developer has devoted to making residents happy has reaped marketing dividends. Solivita has a strong, 35 percent referral base. In fact, people who knew each other prior to moving to Solivita make up sizable sections of some neighborhoods.

The development phasing—amenities before housing—was a successful marketing strategy. When the first prospects came to Solivita, key recreational venues, including the golf course and the village center, were fully staffed. As soon as prospects sign a sales contract, they are given a membership card and allowed unrestricted use of community facilities while they wait for their house to be built.

In keeping with the target market's strong interest in lifestyle issues, the developer told prospects that the participation and input of residents would be sought as the community evolved. Residents have not been disappointed in this respect. To keep the lines of communication open, the Solivita activities director hosts Monday coffee talks, which are attended by hundreds of residents. The homeowners association meets monthly. A 20-page monthly newsletter is produced. And staff maintains an open-door policy.

Management

The recreational amenities that have attracted residents to Solivita are to be managed and maintained in perpetuity by Avatar. The facilities covered in the Club Plan—which addresses all the community's land and facilities with the exception of residential property, streets, the conservation areas, and commercial enterprises—will be retained by Avatar. (A homeowners association maintains the community areas not included in the Club Plan.)

Avatar opted to take this calculated departure from the tradition that the ownership, governance, and management of community facilities are eventually transferred from the developer to a homeowners association in order to assure continued quality control and protection of natural and constructed community resources; and also to not put a burden on Solivita's residents who are more interested in recreational activities than they are interested in facilities management.

Experience Gained

■ Development for the active adult market is in some ways distinctly different from development for the primary housing market. It is about creating a community, not a subdivision.

■ Buyers at Solivita tend to have a literal interpretation of what they see. If the sales staff displayed upgrades in a model that were not actually available in that model, buyers got upset.

■ At the beginning, the sales staff furnished some models inappropriately to the price point and likely buyer profile, thus turning off potential buyers.

■ Active adults present a very challenging buyer profile—they are demanding, opinionated, and high maintenance. Developers targeting this market cannot adopt the staffing formulas used by production builders. They need more staff to meet the heightened expectations of active adult buyers. This may be the last house they will ever buy, and they want it to be perfect.

■ It is important to provide enough models within the product lines—which must be priced and designed to appeal to the target market—to accommodate different tastes and lifestyles.

■ There are subtleties to this market. Rules that worked for their parents do not work for baby boomers, especially the younger ones. Not all boomers think alike, which adds to the challenge.

■ Putting amenities in up-front can aid sales. Selling a vision is much easier if it can be tied to something tangible. Also, residents obtain immediate enjoyment and satisfaction, which gets the owner/seller relationship off to a positive start.

■ It is advisable to question every decision made, even if it was based in documented, accurate research. There will always be surprises and developers should be ready and willing to make adjustments accordingly.

Left: Homes priced from the low $100,000s to more than $400,000, make the community's country club–style amenities available to middle income households. Small lots, short streets, and community parks promote recreation and social interaction.

Right: The developer preserved critical wildlife habitat and relocated more than 700 mature live oak trees to create shady areas along roads, trails, and golf-cart paths.

CONTACT INFORMATION

PROJECT WEB SITE

www.solivita.com

DEVELOPER

Avatar Properties Inc.
201 Alhambra Circle, 12th Floor
Coral Gables, Florida 33134
305-442-7000
www.avatar-holdings.com

SOLIVITA PROJECT INFORMATION

VILLAGE CENTER ARCHITECT

Spillis Candela DMJM
800 Douglas Entrance
North Tower 2nd Floor
Coral Gables, Florida 33134
305-444-4691
www.spilliscandela.com

PLANNER

Canin Associates
500 Delaney Avenue, Suite 404
Orlando, Florida 32801
407-422-4040
www.canin.com

GOLF COURSE ARCHITECT

Ron Garl
704 South Missouri Avenue
Lakeland, Florida 33815-4738
863-688-8383
www.rongarl.com

DEVELOPMENT SCHEDULE

Site Purchased:	1970
Planning Started:	1988
Construction Started:	1999
Sales/Leasing Started:	2000
Completed:	
Phase 1	2003
Buildout	2009[1]

1. *Expected.*

LAND USE INFORMATION

Site Area:	3,974 acres
Dwelling Units:	
Planned	6,500
Completed (2004)	1,453
Residential Density:	
Gross	1.62 units per acre
Average Net of Amenities	1.74 units per acre

LAND USE PLAN

	ACRES	PERCENT OF SITE
Buildings	1,300	32 %
Streets/Surface Parking	306	8
Landscaping/Open Space	2,100	53
Golf Course	268	7

RESIDENTIAL UNIT INFORMATION

UNIT TYPE	LOT DIMENSIONS (FEET)	UNIT SIZE (SQUARE FEET)	NUMBER OF UNITS			CURRENT SALE PRICE RANGE
			PLANNED	BUILT	SOLD	
Duplex	—	1,200– 1,350	74	74	74	—
Vineyards	40 x 110	891– 1,504	651	203	300	$105,000 – $145,000
Musical	55 x 110	1,314– 1,826	1,500	500	639	150,000 – 174,000
Classical	65 x 110	1,714– 2,317	1,500	450	441	174,000 – 208,000
Symphony	70 x 110	2,274– 2,701	200	126	126	211,000 – 238,000
Tuscany	80 x 125	2,275–3,000	300	100	107	272,000 – 312,000
TBD[1]	—	—	2,275	0	0	—

1. Product types to be determined.

DEMOGRAPHIC PROFILE

	PERCENT OF ALL HOUSEHOLDS
AGE RANGE	
45–54	10 %
55+	90
HOUSEHOLD TYPE	
Singles without Children	14
Couples without Children	86
GENDER (SINGLE-PERSON HOUSEHOLDS)	
Male	34
Female	66
USE OF SOLIVITA UNIT	
As Primary Residence	78
As Second Home	22

DEVELOPMENT COST INFORMATION

SITE ACQUISITION	$17,000,000
SITE IMPROVEMENT COSTS	
Excavation/Grading	4,000,000
Sewer/Water/Drainage	4,300,000
Paving/Curbs/Sidewalks	4,500,000
Landscaping/Irrigation	7,000,000
Fees and General Conditions	300,000
TOTAL	20,100,000
CONSTRUCTION COSTS (VILLAGE CENTER)	
Superstructure	21,600,000
HVAC	650,000
Electrical	500,000
Plumbing/Sprinklers	650,000
Finishes	3,000,000
Graphics/Specialties	100,000
Fees and General Conditions	500,000
TOTAL	27,000,000
SOFT COSTS	
Architecture/Engineering	1,000,000
Project Management	400,000
Marketing	3,000,000
Legal/Accounting	600,000
Taxes/Insurance	1,000,000
Title Fees	200,000
TOTAL	6,200,000
TOTAL DEVELOPMENT COST	$70,300,000
Development Cost Per Unit[1]	10,816
Construction Cost Per Square Foot[2]	255

1. Based on the 6,500 units planned at buildout.
2. For village center.

Spring Island

BEAUFORT, SOUTH CAROLINA

Spring Island is a development paradox. Although it has earned accolades and awards, it defies definition and true emulation. There is simply nothing quite like it, perhaps because its concept was born more from a sense of place than a response to a market opportunity. In fact, there was no discernable market for Spring Island, which was one of the biggest challenges its developer faced.

Chaffin/Light Associates purchased Spring Island in 1990 from the Walker family for $15 million. The 3,000-acre island is located in the coastal region of South Carolina's storied Lowcountry. From the time of its first private ownership in 1706 until 1991, when it was connected to Callawassie Island and thus to the mainland by a $2.3 million causeway, Spring Island had basked in the isolation that had made development too difficult and expensive to undertake.

Jim Chaffin and Jim Light had been long acquainted with and enamored of Spring Island's stunning natural attributes and rustic charm. They foresaw a singular second-home community positioned to attract highly discriminating buyers who were willing to take a major leap of faith based on the developer's word and reputation alone. The prospect was daunting, but like many who believe strongly in both their vision and their ability to execute it, the partners moved forward.

They created a master plan that originally proposed 500 homesites and was later pared down to 407 sites—in contrast to the 5,500 dwelling units that had been approved by the county when the island's previous owner proposed developing it. Forty percent of the island is devoted to open space. Strict covenants ensure that all structures lie lightly on the land.

Fifteen years after its inception, Spring Island flourishes as an exclusive community where like-minded residents live in voluntary harmony with nature and participate in land stewardship to preserve the island's ancient beauty for future generations.

Site and Surroundings

Crossing the quarter-mile long and typically deserted causeway above a marshland teeming with wildlife is transformational. A primeval forest of live oaks draped in Spanish moss looms at its terminus. True to the developer's vision, much of Spring Island remains in its virgin state and the built environment has been skillfully—and intentionally—camouflaged.

Originally called Cochran's Island after its first owner, John Cochran, the island was later renamed after the spring-fed ponds that dot it. In addition to the ponds, a

Spring Island's Old Tabby Links is considered one of the best golf courses in the country.

small waterfall, and abundant wildlife, the island also boasts a 400-acre live oak forest that is said to be the largest in the southeastern United States.

The 1.5-by-6.5-mile island is framed by vast salt and freshwater marshes, which are in turn encircled by the Colleton and Chechessee Rivers. Development had bypassed it due in large part to its ownership history and relative remoteness. Once a thriving plantation, the property had become an exclusive hunting preserve where the main attraction was quail by the time Chaffin/Light arrived on the scene.

No retail establishment exists on the site, and none is planned. Residents must travel two causeways—Spring to Callawassie Island, and Callawassie to the mainland—to reach a small general store where they can pick up a jug of milk or loaf of bread. Most choose to do their major shopping in the historic town of Beaufort 13 miles away.

By car, Spring Island is 30 miles from the open ocean off Hilton Head Island. By boat, the Atlantic is nine miles away via the Chechessee River and Port Royal Sound.

Development Process and Financing

Chaffin and Light started out together at the Sea Pines Company under the direction of the late Charles Fraser, who developed Sea Pines Plantation, Hilton Head Plantation, and Kiawah Island in South Carolina and Amelia Island in Florida. In 1978, they began developing their own residential resort projects in Colorado, Washington, North Carolina, and South Carolina. When they were working on a preretirement community at Callawassie, which was launched in 1985, they became familiar with and then enamored of Spring Island.

Shortly after the purchase of Spring Island in 1990, Chaffin/Light invited eight high-profile developers to visit the island and offer opinions on how it should be developed. The consensus view recommended at least 3,000 housing units and three golf courses. Chaffin/Light rejected this as too dense.

Armed with a "conventional wisdom be damned, we're going to do this anyway" attitude, the developer hired design and planning professionals and a market research firm to begin testing the financial and marketing logic of a program defined as a "community within

The Golf House serves daily meals and can be reserved for special events.

One-third of Spring Island's 3,000 acres are dedicated as a nature preserve and only 400 homes will ever be built on the site. The community's well-heeled buyers are attracted by the island's natural beauty and the certainty that it will remain an untamed refuge.

a park." Five hundred homesites turned out to be the magic number for creating an economically sound development without compromising mission and concept.

At the request of Spring Island residents, who put the matter to a vote in 1998, the total number of housing units has been reduced by 90 lots to 407. With 95 percent of residents in favor, the current residents agreed to each pay a special one-time assessment to buy out Chaffin/Light's interest for $7 million.

The initial due-diligence financing was provided internally. A six-month presale program of 36 waterfront estate lots for $300,000 apiece, as well as a small piece of acquisition debt financing, provided the primary funding for purchasing the island.

Development has been carried out in 14 major phases. As of June 2004, 14 of the original lots were left for sale; 175 houses had been built; 25 were under construction and another 25 were undergoing the review process; and 48 resale lots were on the market.

Planning and Design

The master plan took shape as the developer began to define the target market. As a high-end preretirement, second-home community in the Deep South, Spring Is-

land would likely attract mostly wealthy buyers older than 50 who expect to enjoy year-round active and passive leisure activities. Some buyers would want the proverbial cabin in the woods and others would prefer more of a neighborhood feel. Buyers would embrace the developer's vision of a community within a park and want to live in harmony with nature.

The master plan set forth five main elements: residential neighborhoods, community open space, trails, a golf course, and nature preserves. For the residential neighborhoods it defined two types of homesites:

Estate homesites—ranging in size from two to five acres and typically surrounded by other estate homesites, open space, or nature preserve. There are 275 estate lots, which are located south of Walker Landing at the island's perimeter or around the nature preserves in the interior. Estate lot owners must retain wooded buffers and set back structures 150 feet from the road and 50 feet from the side property line. Houses cannot exceed 4,500 square feet, although additional small guest houses and garage studios are permitted.

Cottage homesites—ranging in size from a quarter to a half acre. There are 135 cottage lots, which are located in the Walker Landing, Old Tabby Links, and Bonny Shore areas. These homesites appeal to buyers who prefer a more intimate neighborhood, a location within walking distance of amenities, and less yard to maintain. Structures on a cottage lot may not exceed 3,500 square feet and must be set back 50 feet from the road and 25 feet from the side property line.

Spring Island lot buyers get an accessible lot with utility hookups. When they are ready to build a house they hire their own architect and construction contractor. All proposed structures must be evaluated and approved by the Habitat Review Board. Most landowners have been conscientious about their house design and have attempted to stay true to local and regional architectural traditions. Several houses on Spring Island have won design awards and have been featured in national magazines.

As part of Chaffin/Light's goal of giving residents psychological ownership of edges, amenity areas were sited to take advantage of the best views of the island's interior and of the marshland and rivers surrounding the island. The community's amenity areas include the following:

■ *Walker Landing*. Located at the northern tip of the island on the west side facing Chechessee Creek, Walker Landing is the social nexus of the community. It comprises River House, which is a restaurant and reception hall; the nature center; a recreation center; a swimming pool; an equestrian center; a community vegetable garden; a softball/Frisbee field; community docks; tennis courts; four guest cottages; and the sales center and administrative offices. In a clever bit of behavioral engineering, the residents' mailboxes are located at Walker Landing, which encourages frequent social encounters.

■ *Old Tabby Links*. The golf course and Golf House, a facility at which meals are served daily and special events can be held, are located in the middle of the east side of the island adjacent to the tabby ruins of a former owner's mansion. ("Tabby" is a cement made of lime, sand or gravel, and oyster shells.) Close by is the "cathedral," which is a statue of St. Francis reverently framed by a barrel vault of live oaks.

■ *Bonny Shore*. A gazebo on top of a bluff overlooking a community dock and pier is located on the south-

Top: Master plan.

Bottom: The island's 35 miles of trails wander through open fields and a 400-acre live oak forest, and along marshes and ponds.

western tip of the island with a view to the Colleton River. Bonny Shore provides perhaps the best vista on Spring Island.

■ *Chechessee and Colleton Nature Preserves and Duck Ponds.* Twelve hundred acres of forests, fields, and ponds occupy much of the interior of the island, with the Chechessee preserve extending to the island's northern tip.

Community buildings are designed to have a rustic and welcoming appearance. Wood is the primary building material and colors are taken from a woodland and agricultural palette. Almost every building includes a porch, providing space for socializing and the enjoyment of the outdoors.

Marketing

Spring Island faced a marketing challenge, which is that the kind of buyer it sought was a rare person. The development needed to target well-heeled buyers, but no coastal Lowcountry project without a beachfront had ever tried to capture that market. For Caffin/Light, the million-dollar question was: Who are Spring Island's buyers?—quickly followed by: How do we reach them? and How do we convince them that our dream is worthy of their investment?

The developer knew of no market research that indicated that an inland, second-home community would appeal to the kind of buyers Spring Island needed to attract. Many potential buyers were from out of state, and they tended to gravitate to the oceanfront communities of Hilton Head and Charleston.

Chaffin/Light's market research led the developer to the following marketing strategies:

■ Because retirees are not generally residential pioneers, Spring Island's best prospects would be people looking for second homes, people planning ahead of time for retirement, and wealthy people.

■ The hook for the first wave of buyers would be their love of nature and the opportunity that Spring Island offered them to actively participate in the protection and preservation of a unique environment.

■ The first buyers could be counted on to spread Spring Island's message quickly and efficiently, which would likely attract the second wave of buyers.

The developer profiled potential buyers using the values alternatives system (VAL), which seeks to understand the psychology of consumers (what motivates them to buy) rather than the demographics of consumers (what they buy). This research revealed buyers motivated by principle and drawn by Spring Island's underlying concepts.

When marketing for Spring Island began, the Internet was not widely used, so a Web site was not a promising option and the market was too broad to make print ads cost-effective. Chaffin and Light felt that finding buyers for Spring Island would require a much more personal touch. To them, Spring Island was more a value system and a way of life than it was a residential community—and its gospel needed to be spread the old-fashioned way, by word of mouth.

Thus there came into existence the real estate equivalent of Tupperware parties: small get-togethers organized for the purpose of hearing Chaffin/Light's presentation about Spring Island. Many of these get-togethers took place in the Lowcountry, but marketing efforts extended up the East Coast into New England.

Serious prospects were invited to Spring Island, where they stayed in the old Walker house and enjoyed Chaffin/Light's hospitality for a day or two, falling into the rhythm of the island. Buyers in the first wave were sold on the strength of Chaffin/Light's vision—and especially Chaffin's ability to communicate it—rather than on the presence of amenities, since none were in place.

The peak age range for buying second homes is typically 48 to 52, but the early buyers at Spring Island were older. That trend has changed. In the last few years, the buyers have been mostly baby boomers, perhaps because the concepts that govern the island's development, environmental protection, and habitat conservation resonate more strongly with that particular demographic.

An unexpected number of people have elected to make Spring Island their year-round residence: 30 percent of island homeowners live there full-time; 40 percent say that their house on Spring Island is their primary residence and occupy it nine months a year; and the remaining 30 percent are still actively working and maintain a primary residence elsewhere.

Top: Walker Landing provides a venue other than the golf clubhouse that promotes a sense of community. It includes a equestrian center (left) and River House (right), a restaurant and events hall.

Bottom left: A community dock and pier on the island's northern tip.

Bottom right: Most houses on the island take advantage of the setting by embracing the land and maximizing spectacular vistas.

Examples of Spring Island houses. Most lots, which range from one-half to five acres, are located on the island's perimeter or around the nature preserves in the interior. Subject to approval by the Habitat Review Board, buyers design and build their own homes. Because McMansions are not permitted under the design guidelines, homeowners wanting to accommodate multigenerational families frequently develop a family compound—like that shown (bottom right)—composed of a number of relatively small structures.

Management

Spring Island's complex management structure was conceived to accomplish a number of tasks:

■ preserve and protect the island's ecosystems and wildlife habitats in perpetuity;

■ serve as a resource for context-sensitive residential development;

■ provide residents with recreation, leisure, and governance opportunities; and

■ oversee community finances.

A number of bodies, boards, and committees have been established to carry out these management tasks:

Spring Island Trust—responsible for maintaining the environmental and cultural integrity of Spring Island. The trust also educates residents so they can become good stewards of their own properties as viable habitats. It owns 90 percent of the two nature preserves and is supported by real estate assessment fees.

The Equity Club—through a board of directors, oversees all facilities and properties that make up the recreational portion of Spring Island, with the exception of the nature preserves. Residents are required to join the club, which imposes a one-time membership contribution for the golf and social components and annual dues for both.

Property Owners Association—governs the area comprising private properties, the golf course, open space, roadsides, and ponds; not responsible for the nature preserves or other recreational facilities. Like a homeowners association, the POA has a board of directors.

Stewardship Committee—tasked with overseeing a unified management philosophy. The committee interacts with both the trust and the POA.

Habitat Review Board—functions as a typical architectural review board, making sure that new residential projects abide by community covenants and design guidelines; also ensures that a consistent vision for Spring Island is maintained. A senior naturalist sits on the board.

Membership Committee—interviews and educates serious prospects. Buying a lot or property on Spring Island is viewed as a serious financial and philosophical commitment to a chosen lifestyle that is admittedly not for everyone. The membership committee functions as a reality check at the end of the sales process. The objective is to ensure that future residents understand the culture of the Spring Island community, and the responsibilities and benefits that come with membership in it. If the fit is not a good one, the committee can—like any coop board—turn the prospect down.

Experience Gained

■ A personalized, word-of-mouth marketing approach works very well in the beginning when enthusiasm is high and the first purchasers are pitching the project to everyone they know with an almost apostolic fervor. After the first or second wave, however, the referral base shrinks a bit. Experience has proven that residential projects typically get the most referrals in the first six to 12 months. Thus, a more well-rounded approach using traditional marketing methods would probably have shortened the sales cycle for Spring Island.

■ Making hospitality the linchpin of the marketing program can cause significant annual operating losses.

■ It would have been advisable to generate a marketing reserve fund derived from a small percentage of each lot sale—providing money for POA and developer use at the point when the personalized marketing approach lost momentum.

■ A property management professional should be brought in at least six months prior to the transition of ownership to residents; this allows the homeowners association to start operating from a base of knowledge when the transition takes place.

■ Providing a venue other than a golf clubhouse that would promote a sense of community was important. Taking a cue from their own experience in Colorado indicating that people living on 1,000-acre ranches need a place to congregate, Chaffin and Light saw the need for the Walker Landing complex, Spring Island's answer to the grange hall.

■ Being true to the Spring Island vision has served everyone's purpose—developer and residents. Putting a management structure in place that will keep the vision intact and create a legacy for future generations was essential for this project.

CONTACT INFORMATION

PROJECT WEB SITE

www.springisland.com

DEVELOPER

Chaffin/Light Associates
42 Mobley Oaks Lane
Okatie, South Carolina 29909
843-987-2001
www.chaffinlight.com

PLANNERS

Robert Marvin/Howell Beach & Associates (Master Planning/Site Planning)
601 Beach Road
Walterboro, South Carolina 29488
843-538-5471
www.marvinbeach.com

Edward Pinckney/Associates (Master Planning)
14 Westbury Park Way, Suite 200
Bluffton, South Carolina 29910
www.pinckneyassociates.com

GOLF COURSE ARCHITECT

Palmer Course Design Company
572 Ponte Vedra Boulevard
Ponte Vedra Beach, Florida 32082
904-285-3960
www.palmerdesign.com

COMMUNITY BUILDING ARCHITECTS

Thomas & Denzinger Architects
920 Bay Street
Beaufort, South Carolina 29902
843-524-6361
www.thomasanddenzinger.com

Historical Concepts LLC
430 Prime Point, Suite 103
Peachtree City, Georgia 30269
770-487-8041
www.historicalconcepts.com

DEVELOPMENT SCHEDULE

Site Purchased:	1990
Lot Sales Began:	1990
Construction Started:	1991
First Residences Built:	1991
Buildout:[1]	2000

1. Developer buildout; private home buildout not estimated.

LAND USE INFORMATION

Site Area:	3,000 acres
Dwelling Units:	
Planned	407
Completed (2004)	156
Residential Density:	
Gross	1 unit per 19 acres
Average Net of Amenities	1 unit per 18 acres

LAND USE PLAN

	ACRES	PERCENT OF SITE
Residential	1,600	53 %
Streets/Surface Parking	30	1
Golf Course	120	4
Open Space	1,200	40
Other	50	2

DEMOGRAPHIC PROFILE

	PERCENT OF ALL HOUSEHOLDS
AGE RANGE	
Under 44	2 %
45–54	4
55–64	64
65+	30
HOUSEHOLD TYPE	
Singles	3
Couples with Children	4
Couples without Children	93
GENDER (SINGLE-PERSON HOUSEHOLDS)	
Male	40
Female	60
USE OF SPRING ISLAND UNIT	
As Primary Residence	70
As Second Home	30

DEVELOPMENT COST INFORMATION

SITE ACQUISITION COST	$15,000,000
GENERAL COSTS	
Master Planning/Engineering/Landscaping	4,324,582
Road Paving	624,904
Bridge	1,873,823
On-Island Main Roads	1,196,201
Wastewater Facility (Bulk Plant)	1,802,349
Water Facilities (Bridge and Access Road)	636,503
Bulkhead/Promenade	1,490,679
Causeway	623,859
TOTAL	12,572,900
AMENITY COSTS	
Golf Club Facilities:	
Planning and Design	5,857,769
Maintenance Facility/Pump House	589,997
Golf House	3,577,994
Walker Landing Facilities:	7,231,545
TOTAL	17,257,305
LOT DEVELOPMENT COST	8,262,777
SOFT COSTS	
Project Management	11,769,000
Marketing	17,417,000
Construction Interest and Fees	8,760,000
Operating Losses during Sellout	10,638,000
TOTAL	48,584,000
TOTAL DEVELOPMENT COST	$101,676,982

Vickery

SIGNIFICANT FEATURES

- Mixed-use, higher-density residential neighborhood
- Broadly defined multigenerational market
- Pioneering development in its suburban setting
- Environmentally sustainable development practices
- Certified-green houses

Vickery is a 214-acre, mixed-use neighborhood under development in Cumming, Georgia, 30 miles north of Atlanta. A high-density village center containing a mix of civic and commercial uses as well as townhouses and live/work units is surrounded by small-lot, single-family housing. Planned as an alternative to the low-density development that is occurring elsewhere in this suburban area, Vickery is designed to provide a diversity of housing choices and community amenities—and thus create a multigenerational and demographically diverse neighborhood.

This is a greenfield project that emphasizes principles of new urbanist and traditional neighborhood design, especially a mix of uses and walkability; the conservation of the site's natural resources; energy conservation and other principles of sustainable development; high-quality building; and traditional style architecture.

Site and Surroundings

The project is located in southern Forsyth County, six miles west of the town of Cumming, the county seat. Economic growth, especially in the information technology sector, has made Forsyth County one of the fastest-growing counties in the United States in terms of per capita income. Its farmland, woods, and pastures are being developed at a rapid pace and generally in a sprawl development pattern.

The hilly Vickery site runs north to south between Bentley Creek to the west and Post Road to the east, with the creek and road converging at its southern tip. The terrain runs generally downhill from Post Road toward Bentley Creek and its surrounding wetland. Two small ponds on the property flow into Bentley Creek.

Low-density residential development lies to the north and west of the site. A working stable is located across Post Road to the east, beyond which lies Polo Fields, a well-known golf course community. Vickery Creek Elementary and the county middle school are located just across the creek to the southwest.

Development Process and Financing

The developer is Hedgewood Properties, owned by Pam Sessions and Don Donnelly, a husband-and-wife, privately held homebuilding company that has developed a number of smart growth and green housing projects in the greater Atlanta region—including more than 1,000 housing units in Forsyth County. Sessions and Donnelly acquired a 20-acre parcel in the heart of the Vickery site in the early 1980s.

By the mid-1990s, low-density suburban sprawl was beginning to define the area

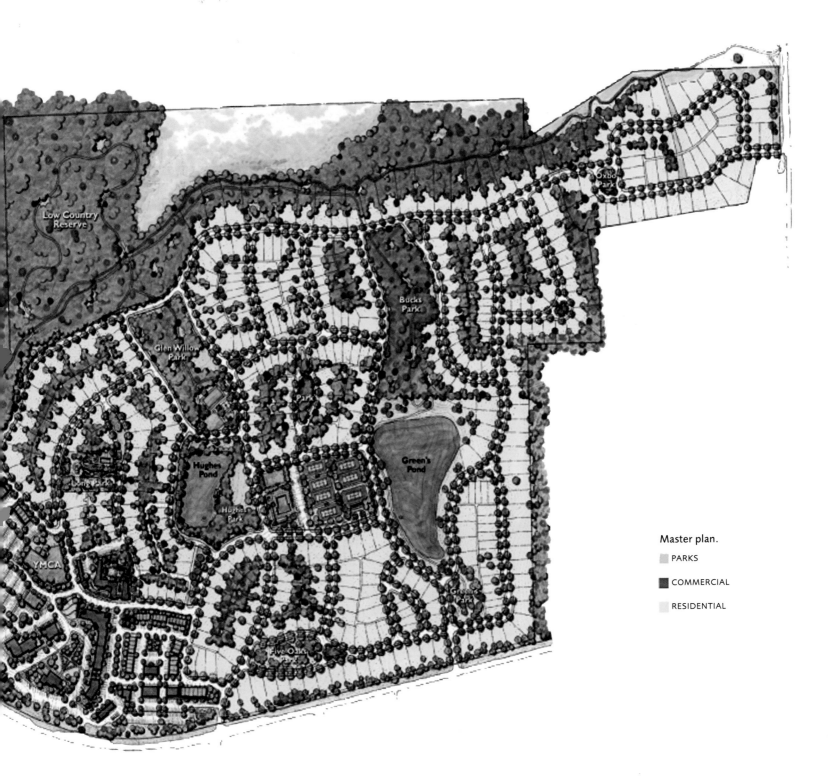

Master plan.

■ PARKS

■ COMMERCIAL

■ RESIDENTIAL

The new urbanist community of Vickery is an alternative to the sprawl development found elsewhere in this suburban Atlanta neighborhood. Small lots, narrow streets, and wide sidewalks help maintain a pedestrian-friendly environment.

around this site. At the same time, the Sessions-Donnelly family was itself unhappy with the lack of community in its own life, the lack of opportunities for its two young children to socialize and venture out on their own, the need to drive here and there on a daily basis. The concept of a child-friendly, walkable, mixed-use neighborhood style development grew out of this dissatisfaction—and the recognition that other young families were in the same boat.

Between 1998 and 2000, Sessions and Donnelly assembled land surrounding the 20-acre parcel. They purchased 154 acres from two adjoining landowners and entered into a codevelopment agreement on 40 acres with a third owner. The models and inspiration for the development concept that was emerging included their own smart growth, neighborhood-based development projects; European cities and villages; older, walkable neighborhoods in U.S. towns and cities (such

as Charleston, South Carolina; Savannah and Madison, Georgia, and the Virginia Highlands neighborhood of Atlanta; and towns on Martha's Vineyard island in Massachusetts); and the new urbanist Seaside community in Florida.

Andrés Duany of Duany Plater-Zyberk & Company in Miami, the Seaside planner, was brought in to initiate the planning process with a public charrette, which was held in May 2000. The weeklong charrette, which attracted more than 450 participants, introduced county officials, the project's neighbors, local environmental and civic groups, and the media to the idea of a traditional, higher-density, mixed-use neighborhood in this suburban context—and succeeded in drawing positive attention to the neighborhood conceptual plan.

The county's regulatory framework did not accommodate a mixed-use neighborhood development. Tal Harber, the project manager for Hedgewood Properties,

worked with county planners and a local planning consultant to draft a planning and zoning document that is compatible with local regulatory requirements. Vickery was approved as a planned unit development (PUD) enabled by variance within what was an agricultural zone. New urbanist zoning and design guidelines were developed to regulate building design and uses, streetscapes, roads, and landscaping in Vickery's three density zones.

The Vickery project sparked a lively public debate in the county about livability and density. The greatest opposition came from neighbors who had not attended the charrette workshops. The developer was able to allay some of their fears about traffic and the potential burden on schools by reference to the traffic-mitigating effects of the neighborhood's design and use mix and by the argument that the housing mix would attract many households without school-age children.

Construction began in October 2002. Vickery is be-

ing developed in seven phases; approximately 90 of the planned 564 housing units were completed by the end of 2004. Most of the infrastructure and four of eight planned parks were completed in Phases 1 and 2. Vickery Village, the commercial and civic center of the community, is being developed as part of Phases 2 and 3 and will be largely complete by the end of 2005. Buildout is expected to occur by 2011.

Hedgewood financed predevelopment for Phases 1 and 2 and formed Vickery Land Company (VLC) to develop the project. The partner who is owner/codeveloper of the 40-acre parcel that was not directly acquired shares amenity costs and sells prepared individual parcels directly to Hedgewood Properties. Wachovia Bank provided acquisition, development, and construction loans. Future phases will be financed through a combination of sales proceeds from Phases 1 and 2 and loans from Wachovia.

Houses are designed to meet high-performance environmental standards.

Many project costs were front-loaded. Key predevelopment activities—the charrette, the development of new zoning codes, design and engineering work, and the establishment of infrastructure and town planning standards—required up-front staff time and expertise. The project's land conservation efforts, park development, and extensive landscaping required early funding and, in some cases, entailed additional costs.

Community Planning and Design

Residential neighborhoods of descending density radiate from a mixed-use, high-density village center in Vickery's traditional neighborhood plan. The village center, which will be located at the southeast corner of the site along Post Road, incorporates a village green with outdoor seating areas; a commercial core that will have restaurants, specialty retail stores, a YMCA, and office condominiums; and 133 housing units, including townhouses and live/work units. The placement of the mixed-use area along Post Road has already helped attract other commerce to the area, including a neighborhood-oriented Kroger grocery store that is being built across the street.

North and west of the village center is the project's mid-density residential zone, which accommodates single-family houses on small lots of one-eighth to one-quarter acre. A clubhouse and events center and a swimming pool and tennis courts are located in the mid-density zone.

On the north and eastern edges of the site—the edge zone—housing is accommodated on lots of one-sixth to one-half acre.

Narrow streets and generous sidewalks that follow topographic contours create a pedestrian-friendly environment. A network of sidewalks and paths allows children to walk or bike to local schools. Shallow building setbacks—ranging from zero to 12 feet from the sidewalk—create intimate, human-scale streetscapes. Front porches are permitted to extend into setback zones. Pocket parks, including ponds and greenways, and mature trees weave through the neighborhood.

To minimize the presence of cars, 70 percent of the residential lots are served by back-loading alleys that access garages. The plan specifies a hierarchy of street configurations, sidewalks, and parking according to the zone's land uses and density. The street plan creates vistas for pedestrians and gives drivers reasons to proceed slowly. Streets are generally four feet narrower than typical suburban streets.

Unit Design

To encourage diversity in the community, Vickery's developer has designed 12 single-family house plans and six types of housing for the village core. Single-family units range in size from an 1,800-square-foot cottage to a 4,800-square-foot estate home. The units designed for the village core—lofts, live/work spaces, and townhouses—range in size from 1,600 to 3,000 square feet. The guiding concept is an interpretation of traditional architecture—including Greek revival, Craftsman, vernacular, Italianate, French eclectic, and early-20th-century Builder style—that can be integrated into a coherent neighborhood landscape.

Careful placement of the houses in relation to each other and to the sidewalk helps integrate a broad range of housing types into the neighborhood design. Front porches are used to extend household space and create spaces for neighborly interaction.

Block-by-block generational and household diversity is encouraged by including six to ten housing plans within a block. An 1,800-square-foot bungalow or a 2,000-square-foot cottage targeted to single homebuyers who work at home or childless couples may be next to a 3,400-square-foot house targeted to a growing family and a few doors down from a 4,800-square-foot, move-up estate home. Around the block, a 2,500-square-foot, high-end house may attract retired couples or newly empty nesters. Three blocks away in the village center, a 2,000-square-foot townhouse may attract single parents with children or single professionals without children.

On the interior, the housing units are designed to meet a range of contemporary homebuyer needs. They offer large kitchens—which are today's family and entertaining room—and generous closet space. One or two rooms are designed as flexible space that can be adapted to the homebuyer's need—a home office, a second bedroom, a playroom, or a guest room. Buyers,

Four examples of sustainable development practices at Vickery. Use of water-conserving pampas grass in a pocket park (top left). Small lots mitigated by private gardens (top right). Preservation of trees by various means, including transplanting those that must be moved (bottom left). The set-aside of land—totaling more than one-third of the site—for parks and open spaces (bottom right).

Hedgewood's research has shown, are willing to trade off size for good design and construction and to trade off one bedroom for a flexible space.

Foreseeing the possibility that the needs of aging residents of single-family houses may change, the developer aligned large closets on two or three floors and designed them with removable floors so that an elevator could be installed.

Homebuyers are provided with a broad range of customization options. Many choose to finish out basements, customize kitchens, and add special features. A number of buyers of single-family houses have elected to build studios or accessory living units on top of their garages. The initial buyers of the live/work units have opted to finish the "work" basements as semi-autonomous living spaces for their grown children or teenagers. Several buyers of townhouses have decided to install a terrace garden on the roof.

A growing number of homebuyers are concerned about the environmental impact of their buying choice, and are attracted to environmentally respectful approaches to land development and building. The houses at Vickery are designed and built to meet high-performance environmental standards and are certified through the EarthCraft House green building program, a voluntary environmentally friendly building program sponsored by the Greater Atlanta Home Builders Association. The siting of houses to maximize natural daylight; the use of energy-efficient building systems, including tight building envelopes with double-glazed, low-e windows; and the use of efficient fixtures and appliances save energy. Positive ventilation enhances indoor air quality. Wherever possible, low-impact materials and integrated water-efficient appliances are specified. Hedgewood's builders train their construction crews and subcontractors to properly design and install framing, insulation, and HVAC systems.

The developer takes a best practices approach to environmentally sustainable development and construction. Buildings are sited to conserve environmentally sensitive areas. Mature trees are saved wherever possible. Wood chips made from construction waste and removed trees are used for erosion control. A waste management plan that includes the recycling of construction material is prepared for each phase of construction. Leftover gypsum, for example, is ground and returned to the soil to improve its quality.

Target Market and Resident Profile

Envisioning a diverse, multigenerational neighborhood that would attract households in a broad range of life stages, sizes, and incomes, the developer identified at least four target groups whose needs are not being well met by conventional suburban development:

- families with children—seeking a safe environment in which children can be creative and independent without being driven everywhere;
- empty nesters and retirees—seeking to downsize but not downgrade the quality of their homes and potentially welcoming an opportunity to reduce their reliance on driving;
- nontraditional families and single-parent households—seeking housing products not available in suburban Atlanta; and
- singles—seeking a more urban lifestyle and liking the idea of a multigenerational community.

Sessions and Donnelly based their market assessment on their own experience and that of their peers, and on two decades of working with homebuyers. They bet the success of Vickery on the attraction of homebuyers who recognize quality and who are willing to trade large lots for lots of community amenities.

In the project's predevelopment phase, the developer convened focus meetings with two demographic groups: empty nesters over 55 and young people between the ages of eight and 18. Their feedback influenced town planning land use decisions.

A very broad range of housing types was initially envisioned, from affordable rental units and small apartments priced at just under $100,000 in the village center to $1 million estates in the edge zone. However, developing for the lower end of the market was made difficult by the county's insistence on less density and public resistance to "affordable" housing. The developer eventually decided to focus on quality execution rather than pricing as the best method of demonstrating the appeal of the region's first suburban new urbanist neighborhood to the broader market.

Rendering of live/work units in the village center.

Designing front porches to extend into house setback areas creates opportunities for neighborly interaction.

Robust sales suggest that Hedgewood has tapped into a broad market of households wanting to live in the suburbs but ready for a less car-oriented lifestyle.

At 37 percent, households aged 35 to 45 represent the largest share of Phase 1 homebuyers. The other age groups represented are 25 to 34, 45 to 54, and 55 to 64 (each constituting 18 percent of homebuyers); and over 65 (9 percent). Eighty-six percent of these homebuyers are couples—53 percent with children, 33 percent without—and 15 percent are singles. Vickery is attracting middle- and upper-middle-income households in a broad range of life stages.

Pam Sessions tends to characterize Vickery home-buyers in broader social terms—seeing them as people with a neighborhood spirit and a respect for the qualities of place, as inventive and pioneering people who prefer to live out their values in their lifestyle choices, as cultural creatives.

Many moderate- and middle-income households that are not in an income bracket to purchase Vickery homes are drawn to the neighborhood's quality, mix of uses, and walkability. Unfortunately, according to Sessions, the development cannot accommodate many prospects who strongly desire to live in Vickery but lack the economic wherewithal. If the regulatory process had allowed it, Vickery would have included smaller houses and rental units, says Sessions

Marketing and Sales

Interest in the project developed early. By the time the project's marketing campaign commenced in December 2002, 700 people had signed up on the Vickery Web site. The marketing materials are simple and effective. They emphasize Vickery's people-friendly neighborhood and simpler lifestyle.

At point-of-sale meetings, the sales staff emphasizes the wide range of community amenities, housing design and customization, building performance, and service. At this point, they also introduce prospects to the benefits of Vickery's certified green building program, which include lower energy costs, healthier indoor air, and reduced maintenance.

The base price for a house at Vickery ranges from $245,000 to $800,000, which represents a premium of about 30 percent over median county house prices in Forsyth County. Comparable houses in walkable neighborhoods in Atlanta sell for about $100,000 more. All homebuyers have chosen to customize their houses, adding 15 to 20 percent to the base price.

Among the plans that have proven very popular are a small "Emerson English" cottage and a mid-sized "Fox Glen" unit featuring an open floor plan and flex space. Buyers choose customization options on even the most modestly priced small house, which suggests an unmet demand for personalized, well-designed small residences. A second surprise has been the popularity of live/work units, all four of which have been bought by families—including two single parents with children—that have customized the basement "work" floor to meet their needs.

Experience Gained

■ A sizeable, segment of suburban residents are drawn to higher-density, walkable mixed-use neighborhoods. They are willing to trade square footage for well-designed housing and community amenities. And they welcome the opportunity to live in a multigenerational community that affords them an opportunity to interact with neighbors in a less structured way than is possible in conventional suburban projects.

■ Forsyth County's zoning codes did not readily accommodate Vickery's development. The practical application of new urbanist zoning and design codes required inventiveness and negotiation.

■ The public planning charrette proved valuable in building understanding of and support for the concept of a mixed-use, relatively dense suburban neighborhood development. Nevertheless, neighborhood resistance based on fears about density and traffic effectively reduced the density and affordability of the housing that could be developed.

■ Hedgewood's environmental stewardship and green building approach to development have received very positive responses from homebuyers.

■ The opportunity to adapt flex spaces has proved popular. All homebuyers have chosen to customize their homes—for an additional 15 to 20 percent cost—to meet their preferences and needs.

Townhouses will account for about one-quarter of the housing units at Vickery. The project's diverse mix of housing attracts a wide range of residents in terms of life stage, household size, and income.

CONTACT INFORMATION

PROJECT WEB SITES

www.vickeryvillage.com

DEVELOPER

Hedgewood Properties
5920 Odell Street
Cumming, Georgia 30040
770-889-3667
www.hedgewoodhomes.com

ARCHITECTS

Lew Oliver Inc. (Lead Architect, Town Architect)
100 Founder's Mill Court
Roswell, Georgia 30075

Hale Architects (Commercial Architect)
146 New Street
Decatur, Georgia 30030
404-373-3173

LAND PLANNERS

Duany Plater-Zyberk & Company
1023 Southwest 25th Avenue
Miami, Florida 33135
305-644-1023
www.dpz.com

Tunnell, Spangler, Walsh & Associates
881 Piedmont Road
Atlanta, Georgia 30309
404-873-6730
www.tunspan.com

LANDSCAPE ARCHITECTS

Scapes LLC
2030 Powers Ferry Road, Suite 121
Atlanta, Georgia 30339

Cornerstone Gardens
35 Old Canton Street
Alpharetta, Georgia 30004

DEVELOPMENT SCHEDULE

Site Purchased:	June 1998–June 2000
Planning Started:[1]	May 2000
Construction Started:	October 2002
Sales/Leasing Started:	December 2002
Project Completion:	
Phase 1	February 2003
Phase 2	January 2004
Phase 3	April 2004 and April 2005
Phase 4	October 2004
Phase 5	October 2005[2]
Phase 6	October 2006[2]
Phase 7	October 2007[2]
Buildout	December 2011[2]

1. *Charrette.*
2. *Expected.*

LAND USE INFORMATION

Site Area:	214 acres
Dwelling Units:	564
Residential Density:	2.6 units per gross acre

LAND USE PLAN

	ACRES	PERCENT OF SITE
Residential	108.2	51%
Mixed Use[1]	4.6	2
Roads/Parking	22.0	10
Open Space	75.4	35
Swim/Tennis Amenity	3.8	2

1. *Retail, office, and attached residential uses.*

RESIDENTIAL UNIT INFORMATION[1]

| UNIT TYPE | SIZE RANGE (SQUARE FEET). | NUMBER OF UNITS | | INITIAL SALE PRICE RANGE |
		PLANNED	SOLD[1]	
Single-Family Detached	1,950–4,400	431	73	$245,000–$1,200,000
Townhouses	1,900–2,775	125	14	250,000– 387,000
Live/Work Units	2,400	8	4	336,500– 437,000

1. *Units built and under contract as of December 31, 2004.*

DEMOGRAPHIC PROFILE

	PERCENT OF ALL HOUSEHOLDS
AGE RANGE	
25–34	18 %
35–44	37
45–54	18
55–64	18
65+	9
HOUSEHOLD TYPE	
Singles with Children	5
Singles without Children	10
Couples with Children	53
Couples without Children	33
GENDER (SINGLE-PERSON HOUSEHOLDS)	
Male	17
Female	83

DEVELOPMENT COST INFORMATION[1]

SITE ACQUISITION	$13,100,000
SITE IMPROVEMENT	15,000,000
CONSTRUCTION COSTS	
Direct Costs	127,000,000
Fees and General Conditions	18,000,000
TOTAL	145,000,000
SOFT COSTS	
Project Management	1,000,000
Marketing/Sales Commissions	12,000,000
Construction Interest and Fees	11,000,000
Other[2]	1,000,000
TOTAL	25,000,000
TOTAL DEVELOPMENT COST	$198,100,000

1. *Residential portions of development.*
2. *Includes general and administrative costs, taxes, and homeowners association funding.*

ILLUSTRATION CREDITS

FRONTIS © David Sundberg/Esto (top); Ross Chapin Architects (center); Jay Graham (bottom)

OVERVIEW 8, John Durant; 11 Doug Scott Photography (top), James F. Wilson/ Duany Plater-Zyberk & Company (bottom); 15, Jan Ingve & Associates (top left), Gregg Galbraith (top right), CSD PeopleArchitecture (bottom); 16: © David Engel/ Mezzaluna Studio Inc.; 19, © Tim Buchman; 20, Doug Scott Photography (top), RTKL Associates Inc (bottom); 22, RainbowVision; 24, Patrick Schneider (left), Stewart D. Halperin/ McCormack Baron Salazar (right); 25, New Town Builders (left), Arai Jackson Ellison Murakami (right); 27, C. Bruce Forster Photography; 28, Doug Scott Photography; 29, Albert Lewis; 30, King County Housing Authority (top), Randall J. Corcoran (bottom); 32, Rancho Mission Viejo; 35, The Albanese Development Corporation

AMELIA PARK 38, Duany Plater-Zyberk & Company; 40, 43, 45, Stan Cottle; 47, Brylen Homes

CAMPUS AT ALBUQUERQUE HIGH 48, Paul Kohlman; 50, Paul Kohlman (top left and right), Robert Reck (bottom left and right); 51 Dekker/Perich/Sabatini; 53, Carla Breeze (left), Paul Kohlman (right); 54, Carla Breeze

THE EDGE LOFTS 58, 69, GBD Architects; 58, 63–64, 65, ©David Sundberg/Esto

FALL CREEK PLACE 70, 73, 75–76, 78 Mansur Real Estate Services; 72 Schneider Corporation; 81, Rottmann Architects

FRONT STREET AT LADERA RANCH 82, Lance Gordon; 84, Standard Pacific Homes; 85–86, 89, Lance Gordon; 91, Bassenian/Lagoni Architects

FRUITVALE VILLAGE 92, 101, McLarand Vasquez Emsiek & Partners Inc.; 94, 97– 98, Keith Baker Photography

GREENWOOD AVENUE COTTAGES 102, 105–107, 109, 111, Ross Chapin Architects

HEARTHSTONE 113, Scott Dressel-Martin (top), Aero Arts (bottom); 115, Wonderland Hill Development Company; 116, Ron Pollard (top left), Wonderland Hill Development Company (top and bottom right), Perry Rose, LLC (bottom left); 118, 120, Wonderland Hill Development Company

JEFFERSON COMMONS AT MINNESOTA 122, 124–127, 129, 131 JPI; 126, Dorothy Verdon

LASELL VILLAGE 132, 134, Seffian Bradley Architects; 137, Seffian Bradley Architects (left), Stewart Woodward/Visual Talent Group (right top, center and bottom); 138–139, Stewart Woodward/Visual Talent Group; 140, 143, Seffian Bradley Architects

SANTANA ROW 144, 151, Jay Graham; 147–148, Federal Investment Realty Trust; 152, Federal Investment Realty Trust (top), Doug Dun (bottom); 153, Dorothy Verdon; 154, Doug Dun; 155, SB Architects; 157, BAR Architects

SOLIVITA 158, Canin Associates, Inc.; 160, Canin Associates (left and center top), Ken Sussman (center bottom); 161, 163, Canin Associates; 164, Dorothy Verdon

SPRING ISLAND 168, 170, 172, Chaffin/Light Associates; 173, Robert Marvin/ Howell Beach & Associates (top), Chaffin/ Light Associates (bottom); 175, Chaffin/Light Associates (top left and right, bottom left), © William Struhs (bottom right); 176, © William Struhs (left), Chaffin/Light Associates (right top and bottom)

VICKERY 180, Duany Plater-Zyberk & Company and Tunnell, Spangler, Walsh & Associates; 182–183, 185, 187–188, Hedgewood Properties

JACKET COVER Front, from left to right, top to bottom: Mansur Real Estate Services; Urban Design Associates; © David Sundberg/Esto; Prairie Holdings Corporation; Jay Graham; Lance Gordon; Ross Chapin Architects; Canin Associates; RainbowVision. Back cover, from left to right, top to bottom: Jan Ingve & Associates; Elton & Associates; © David Engel/Messaluna Studio Inc.; Patrick Schneider; Hedgewood Properties; Chaffin/Light Associates; Doug Scott Photography; Chaffin/ Light Associates; RainbowVision